Genetics, Crime and Justice

Genetics, Crime and Justice

Debra Wilson

Senior Lecturer in Law, School of Law, University of Canterbury, New Zealand

Edward Elgar
PUBLISHING

Cheltenham, UK • Northampton, MA, USA

Published by
Edward Elgar Publishing Limited
The Lypiatts
15 Lansdown Road
Cheltenham
Glos GL50 2JA
UK

Edward Elgar Publishing, Inc.
William Pratt House
9 Dewey Court
Northampton
Massachusetts 01060
USA

A catalogue record for this book
is available from the British Library

Library of Congress Control Number: 2015935867

This book is available electronically in the **Elgar**online
Law subject collection
DOI 10.4337/9781783478828

MIX
Paper from responsible sources
FSC® C013056

ISBN 978 1 78347 881 1 (cased)
ISBN 978 1 78347 882 8 (eBook)

Typeset by Columns Design XML Ltd, Reading
Printed and bound in Great Britain by T.J. International Ltd, Padstow

Contents

Preface

In the course of researching this book, I came across the story of James Fallon, a neuroscientist who underwent personal genetic testing as part of his research. His test results showed that he had the Low MAOA gene, which is the subject of much of the discussion in this book. His story made me wonder how I would feel knowing this and it made me realize that for me, at least, the less known the better. When it comes to genetics, I don't want to know and I don't want anyone else to know, either. I completely understood when James Watson, the co-discoverer of DNA, allowed his genome to be sequenced as part of the Human Genome Project – all but the area that coded for hereditary Alzheimer's Disease. Sometimes, ignorance is bliss.

Fallon commented that the results of his own genetic test had made his research personal to him. I had my own moment of personal connection in the course of this research. I was re-reading a longitudinal study of MAOA and childhood maltreatment in Christchurch, New Zealand (also known as my birthplace) when the sample data leapt off the page at me: 'a birth cohort of 1265 children born … in mid-1977.' Now, being born in mid-late 1977, this raised an important question: Had I been reading about myself? Had other people? I would have remembered being interviewed growing up, but my family had moved away from Christchurch for several years, so I could have been one of the dropouts. A quick email to my mother ('do you remember when I was born? Could you possibly have …') suggested that I wasn't part of the birth cohort, and a subsequent article based on the study showed that I had, in fact, been born a month outside the cohort dates. But, many of my childhood friends clearly were part of it. This data suddenly became very real to me, and the statistics very frightening. Reading the statistics began to change the way I thought about my childhood friends and the various events of our youth.

I am beyond grateful to so many people who have contributed in some way to this project. Much of this book was written while on sabbatical at Georgetown University, where I was based at the Centre for Australian, New Zealand and Pacific Studies in the Edmund A Walsh School of Foreign Service. The Head of the Centre, Alan Tidwell, was the perfect host and was always willing to act as an intelligent sounding board, despite the increasingly bizarre nature of the conversations and my frequent requests for meetings over lunch at a specific restaurant. Claire Sullivan, a fellow visiting academic at the Centre, was just as willing to accommodate my lunch meeting requests, and to debate genetics with me. Both made this book better than it would otherwise have been.

I was very fortunate to be at Georgetown as a Fulbright New Zealand Visiting Scholar, and so I must thank Fulbright New Zealand from the bottom of my heart for selecting me as a reward recipient. The experience was, without a doubt, life-changing on so many levels.

My friends and colleagues at the University of Canterbury Law School were also supportive and willing to engage in debates on the issues raised in this book, or just to encourage me in the final proofreading stages. Whether it is fair or not, I've come to expect no less from them. The School of Law also provided financial support, allowing me the use of my excellent research assistant, Aileen Odgers. I should probably apologise to my students (both at Canterbury and at Georgetown) for being guinea pigs in lectures when I threw ideas from this book at them. But I won't. I'll just thank them for letting me learn from them during those lectures, as much as they learnt from me in other lectures.

Finally, to my parents. It doesn't matter that I don't know (and will hopefully never know) which form of the MAOA gene they passed on to me, because, either way, the positive childhood environment in which they raised me, places me squarely in the 'low risk of antisocial behavior' end of Caspi's graph.

Debra Wilson
Christchurch
New Zealand

1. Introduction

1.1 THE CASE OF CHILD A AND CHILD B

A seven-year-old boy, Andy Scott, has been found murdered. He has been stabbed approximately 20 times with a sharp object, and also exhibits bruising consistent with trauma from a blunt instrument, likely a baseball bat or stick. His body is found in a small park near the school he attends. He appears to have fought his attacker, and police find hair, skin and blood samples under his fingernails. DNA analysis suggests there were at least two attackers.

The DNA is run through the National DNA Database, but no matches are found. The police decide to conduct a DNA dragnet in the area (asking that everyone who lives or works within a 1 km radius of the crime scene provide DNA samples to the police). Mr A, a 40-year-old teacher, refuses. He tells the police he has done nothing wrong, was out of town on the day in question, and therefore wishes to retain his privacy. The police advise him that if he does not comply, they will seek a court order for a sample, and the newspapers will find out. Scared that he will be branded a child murderer by the media, he unhappily complies.

At the same time, the police run a second search of the DNA database, this time looking for a familial match (searching the database for someone whose DNA is close enough to the samples to be a close relative of one of the attackers). This produces a result. Mr B is not the source of the DNA, but is a close familial match to the person who is. Mr B's DNA is in the database because he was arrested several years before, for being present at a sports event when a major fight broke out. Mr B was released without charge, but his DNA was taken and retained in the database. The DNA tells the police to look for a close family member of Mr B, who is likely to have blonde hair and blue eyes.

When the dragnet results are processed, it is revealed that Mr A is also a familial match.

The police begin to investigate the close relatives of Mr A and Mr B, and the community is stunned when it is revealed that the DNA at the crime scene belongs to Mr A's 10-year-old son, and Mr B's 10-year-old nephew. The police had identified the nephew through surveillance, which included collection of DNA from a Coke can he had drunk from and then abandoned. When questioned, the boys admit that they had attacked the victim, explaining that he had been teasing them and they had just lost their tempers and attacked him.

At trial, Child A argues that he has the MAOA gene, also known as the criminal gene. He claims that the presence of the gene meant that he was not able to form the requisite mens rea for murder. To phrase it another way, he did not intend to kill, he simply had no choice in the situation but to act as he had. His genes had made him do it. For this reason, he claims that he cannot be guilty of murder. His lawyer presents scientific evidence in defence that the presence of the MAOA gene, coupled with childhood maltreatment, would make a person more likely to react aggressively than a person without these factors. While the judge accepted the scientific evidence, there was not sufficient evidence that Child A had suffered childhood maltreatment, and so this argument was rejected.

Hearing this argument, the police seek a court order that Child B submit to testing for the MAOA gene. Child B's family is known to be violent, and the police are aware of several hospital admissions for Child B as a result of maltreatment. Child B's lawyer protests, but the DNA test is ordered. Child B also has the MAOA gene. The police argue that Child B is a 'remorseless violent killer, genetically predisposed to murder' and that for the safety of the community, he should receive a longer sentence.

Despite evidence that the two boys had been involved in the murder to roughly the same extent, the sentences given following conviction are very different. Child B receives a substantially longer sentence than Child A. Child B is also told that even when he has served his sentence, he will be required to take specified medication for the rest of his life, or be returned to jail. The medication is intended to compensate for the low MAOA, but its long term side effects are not known. The judge comments at sentencing that he has given the strongest sentence he can to Child B because 'he's genetically programmed to be a killer, and there's no doubt he will kill again when released'.

The lawyers for Child B have announced their intentions to appeal the conviction and sentence. One of the grounds for appeal is that it was not appropriate for Child A and Child B to be treated equally for the purpose of determining criminal responsibility for their actions. They claim that Child B's MAOA status affected his ability to be morally responsible for his actions and that this should have been taken into account during the trial phase. In a media interview they commented:

> If B is found to be legally responsible for the killing he should of course be sentenced. We are not denying this. But first he must be found to be legally responsible. B's genetic makeup must be a major factor in determining this legal responsibility in the same way that scientists tell us that it is a major factor in determining how he responds to situations. Think of it this way: the criminal justice system does not treat adults and children the same way, because scientists tell us that their brains don't reason in the same way. The system doesn't treat mentally competent and mentally incompetent people in the same way, because again scientists tell us that their brains don't process information in the same way. If scientists also tell us that the brains of High MAOA and Low MAOA don't respond in the same way in given situations, why are we treating them the same? It is inconsistent to ignore what scientists are clearly telling us, and it is unfair to B.

Things have not been easy for Child B's family since the trial. Newspapers began asking the question of whether Child B's parents should also be considered legally responsible, whether criminally or in tort, for the killing. They argue that if the parents had not mistreated Child B, he would not have acted in the way that he had, and therefore they ought to bear some responsibility for the events.

His younger brother was excluded from school as a result of being in a fight. The other child, whom some witnesses claimed provoked the fight by teasing the brother about Child B, received only a one hour detention. The school has demanded that the brother supply them with the results of an MAOA test before permitting him to return, and claims that this is 'in the interests of the safety of the other students'.

Child B's older brother, who had previously been a model student and athlete has now joined a gang. He has been arrested and charged with property damage and assault and reportedly told the police 'its genetic, right? I'm going to be a criminal, so why not just get on with it.'

Child B's uncle was recently convicted of assault. He was given the maximum penalty available, and the judge commented that 'there's just too much of this [violent behavior] in the family. That's three, the child, his parents [maltreating B] and now his uncle. That's enough.' The Uncle has appealed the sentence for being disproportionate and unfair.

Child B's mother is reportedly pregnant with her fourth child, thought to be a boy. One newspaper has published an editorial, which has gained significant public support, arguing that she should not be allowed to have any more children.

The above story is not true. It is not unrealistic, in fact it is a combination of several true stories, but it has been written to demonstrate some of the issues that will be discussed throughout this book.

1.2 THE CASE OF ANTHONY YEPEZ

This story is true:

Anthony Yepez has been charged with murder. The facts are unpleasant. The victim was George Ortiz, the 75-year-old step-Grandfather of Yepez's girlfriend, Jeannie Sandoval. Yepez attacked Ortiz, choking and beating him, then soaking his body in cooking oil and setting fire to him. It is unclear whether Ortiz was still alive at the time. Sandoval, who took a plea deal and pleaded guilty to second degree murder for helping pour the cooking oil, has told the police that Ortiz had attacked her, striking her in the throat. Yepez had then 'attempted to intervene on her behalf' and shoved Ortiz. Ten minutes later, Yepez attacked Ortiz again, and this attack resulted in his death. Sandoval must testify at Yepez's trial as part of her plea deal.

Yepez's lawyer plans to argue that Yepez has Low MAOA, and suffered childhood maltreatment. His lawyer has explained that this argument might help convince the jury that 'this wasn't premeditated, and open up the possibility of conviction on a lesser offence, such as second degree murder'. On 29 January 2015 a hearing took place to determine whether this information could be introduced through three expert witnesses. The Prosecutors argued that the science was 'too young'. It had only been used 'in one or two cases' and 'would only confuse the jury'. The judge agreed and excluded the information, commenting that she felt 'iffy' as to whether 'the science was reliable enough to prove what it proposes to prove'.

At the time of writing (February 2015), Yepez's lawyer plans to appeal. He feels that the exclusion of this evidence prevents Yepez's 'main defence if not his only defence'. The ground of appeal, should it go ahead, will be that the judge 'held the defendant to a burden of proof not required by any law or statute'. One of the planned expert witnesses commented 'We're as certain that MAOA is related to violence as we are that cholesterol is related to heart disease … this is good science, done the way science is supposed to be done. I don't know any serious behavioral scientist that disputes it.'[1]

The case has not, as of yet, attracted much media attention, apart from the attention grabbing headlines like '*Judge Rejects "Warrior Gene" Testimony In Murder Trial*'. My prediction is that if the appeal is filed, by

---

[1] This summary was taken from newspaper reports. See, for example, Phaedra Haywood, 'Judge Rejects "Warrior Gene" Testimony In Murder Trial' *The New Mexican*, 29 January 2015.

the time you read this book this will have changed and newspaper headlines surrounding this case will be easy to find. They may read something like:

Murdering: it's not my fault, it's genetic

From murder bumps to brain scans: new ways to excuse crime

Violence genes may be responsible for one-in-10 serious crimes

Pity the poor murderer, his genes made him do it

Lighter sentence for murderer with 'bad genes'

Scientists find that Nazis were correct about heredity and criminality

1.3 AIM OF THIS BOOK

Since the mid-1990s there has been an increasing amount of scientific research investigating the link between genes, the environment and crime. Much of this research has focussed on the MAOA gene, although more recently genes related to serotonin and dopamine are also being studied for their effects on behavior. Within months of the publication of the first scientific study on MAOA and its possible link to 'abnormal behavior', the study and its findings were introduced into court as part of a capital murder trial in the United States. While the genetic argument did not succeed in this case, the scientific research continued and several recent cases have accepted genetic arguments as relevant in determining liability or appropriate sentence.

This book aims to provide the basis for a much-needed discussion on the increasing use of genetic information during police investigations and criminal proceedings. It will achieve this through a consideration of the relevant science and law, focussing on relevant cases in order to consider how judges and juries have responded to legal arguments based on this emerging scientific understanding. It will also take a broader-picture approach, considering the potential impact these genetic arguments might have on the criminal justice system as a whole, including its theoretical concepts of punishment theory and sentencing and how genetics arguments might affect these. Finally, it will look to the future, and identify some potentially problematic or challenging consequences of accepting genetics arguments. Throughout this book reference will be made back to the hypothetical case of Child A and Child B, and consideration given as to how the issues raised in each chapter might impact on the scenario.

A more detailed description of chapter content follows.

1.4 STRUCTURE OF THIS BOOK

Chapter 2

Chapter 2 will attempt to place the current genetics arguments into a historical context. This is not society's first use of genetics in relation to criminal justice, and an understanding of why such an argument can be found throughout history is useful in understanding the role it can play with today's increasing scientific knowledge.

Chapter 3

Chapter 3 introduces some of the uses for genetic evidence during a criminal investigation. It discusses the increasing use of DNA databases and dragnets to link DNA samples found at a crime scene to potential suspects. It comments on the ever increasing phenomenon of 'function creep', and discusses two examples of this, familial testing and phenotype testing. Finally, the chapter considers calls for a universal database.

Chapter 4

This chapter provides an introduction to the science. Using XYY Syndrome, an earlier potential 'crime gene' as an example and a lesson, the chapter then considers the genes currently thought to have a link to criminal or antisocial behavior. This chapter explains the science, and the various studies that have been carried out on these genes, in an attempt to go beyond the label of 'crime gene' to consider what in fact the science is telling us about these genes.

Chapter 5

Chapter 5 considers how genetic evidence may be used in a trial or in a sentencing hearing. It discusses rules relating to admissibility of evidence, before considering relevant cases and the particular issues they raise.

Chapter 6

Chapter 6 asks some important theoretical questions. What gives society the right to punish people? How do we determine appropriate punishment? And most importantly, can these established justifications survive the genetics cases discussed in Chapter Five? Are these cases leading society away from the concept of 'free will', which is arguably the basis for criminal responsibility, and (again) towards an idea of genetic determinism? Do we need to reconsider the operation of the criminal justice system as a result of the emerging scientific understanding of behavioral genetics, and in light of the way in which genetic arguments have been applied in court to date?

Chapter 7

Chapter 7 looks to the future. If the scientific studies convince us that particular genes, coupled with particular childhood maltreatment, result in a greater chance of antisocial behavior, how should society respond to this? Should it proactively test people to identify those with the particular gene? If so, then what? This chapter raises ethical issues that might be considered unrealistic, futuristic, or even science fiction. With the speed that science can move, however, it is best that some of these potential issues are considered now, rather than reacted to later.

1.5 CONCLUDING REMARKS

While this book discusses the issue of a so-called 'crime gene' from a range of perspectives: criminal law, behavioral genetics, neuroscience, philosophy, sociology and history, it is far from a complete debate on the area. The human rights and privacy implications of the material discussed in this book, (to name just two areas of study) are formidable, and deserve much fuller analysis than it will be possible to provide here. A MAOA-type argument in a courtroom has implications far beyond the particular defendant and his (genetically, it is almost always a male defendant) specific case and requires a much larger discussion as to what acceptance of the argument might mean for society in terms of paths taken and paths better left alone. This book aims simply to contribute to that debate.

2. History of genetics and criminal justice

2.1 INTRODUCTION

The idea that a person's genetic make-up is the sole determinant of his or her physical and behavioural characteristics is difficult to understand and accept. As a society, we pride ourselves on the idea that free will and self-awareness distinguish us from other forms of life. As individuals, we value concepts like freedom of expression or freedom of choice. Individual freedoms to make our own decisions, to control our own fate, to learn, and to grow are seen as fundamental rights that must be protected. A genetic determination argument, at its most extreme, is incompatible with these ideas. It suggests that none of those freedoms which we value so highly actually exist. Although as individuals we prefer to believe that we make decisions and choose to act in certain ways, genetic determinism considers that every part of our personality is in fact pre-determined by our genetic make-up. If as a society we favour the idea of free will and regard it as a beneficial, and perhaps necessary, element of our society, what is the appeal of a genetic determinism argument? Why does it frequently reoccur in discussions of criminal conduct, and in arguments in the criminal justice system?

This chapter will provide a brief overview of the history of genetic-type arguments. It will begin by looking at early discussions amongst classical writers about the heritability of characteristics, and how this developed into early genetic-based thought and policy. It will then consider how this early theoretical thought was strengthened by developing scientific understanding in the 19th century, resulting in what became known as the eugenics movement. Some relevant legal cases from the early 20th century considering eugenics in general and genetics in the criminal justice field specifically will then be referred to in order to provide some insight into contemporary thought. The decline of eugenics in the 1940s and its subsequent re-emergence utilizing less controversial language will suggest that even following the events of World War II, eugenic thought never really disappeared, but simply changed language.

The chapter will conclude by considering why the appeal of genetic arguments, particularly in criminal cases, remains present in a society which professes to value free will.

2.2 GENETICS AND HERITABILITY OF CHARACTERISTICS IN ANCIENT HISTORY: PLINY, ARISTOTLE, CICERO

Ancient societies took a practical, unemotional approach to life. If a child was born with a physical deformity which meant that he or she was unlikely to be able to contribute to society, he or she would be exposed to the elements and left to die. In the *Life of Lycurgus*, Plutarch described 8th century BCE practice:[1]

> Offspring was not reared at the will of the father, but was taken and carried by him to a place called Lesche, where the elders of the tribes officially examined the infant and if it was well-built and sturdy, they ordered the father to rear it, and assigned it one of the nine thousand lots of land; but if it was ill-born and deformed, they sent it to the so-called Apothetae, a chasm-like place at the foot of Mount Taygetus, in the conviction that the life of that which nature had not well equipped at the very beginning for health and strength, was of no advantage either to itself or the state.

In Roman times this examination was generally carried out by the father, in his role as paterfamilias. While exposure of infants as described by Plutarch was common (indeed Romulus, the legendary founder of Rome, had himself been exposed but rescued and raised by wolves) the Laws of the Twelve Tables written in 449BCE stated more specifically that 'a father shall immediately put to death a son recently born, who is a monster, or has a form different from that of members of the human race'. Seneca concurred, writing that 'we put down mad dogs; we kill the wild, untamed ox; we use the knife on sick sheep to stop their infecting the flock; we destroy abnormal offspring at birth; children, too, if they are born weak or deformed, we drown. Yet this is not the work of anger, but of reason – to separate the sound from the worthless.'[2]

The idea of moving beyond exposing undesirable children and towards a planned eugenics programme was first introduced by Plato, in *The*

---

[1] Plutarch, *Life of Lycurgus* (trans. B. Perrin) (Cambridge: Harvard University Press 1914) at 16.

[2] Seneca, *Moral and Political Essays*, Book 1, XV. (trans. J. Cooper) (Cambridge: Cambridge University Press 1995).

Republic. In this book, Socrates comments that 'the best of either sex should be united with the best as often, and the inferior with the inferior, as seldom as possible; and that they should rear the offspring of one sort of union, but not of the other.'[3] He continues to describe how this programme must necessarily be carried out in secret, to prevent rebellion. Weddings, and therefore children, would be left to the discretion of the rulers, through an 'ingenious system of lots', rigged to favour the more desirable marriages. The undesirables would 'accuse their own ill-luck and not the rulers' of their lack of success in the lottery. Deformed or otherwise undesirable children would be 'put away in some mysterious, unknown place, as they should be', which appears to be a euphemism for being exposed.

While most discussion on exposure focussed on physical characteristics, Aristotle and Plato appear to hint that behavioural characteristics could also be seen as hereditary. Aristotle commented that 'man is generated from man; and thus it is the possession of certain characters by the parent that determines the development of like characters in the child.'[4] While he is mostly talking about physical characteristics, the next few sentences reference 'arts', which suggests a wider scope to his commentary.

Plato writes 'let there be a general rule, that the disgrace and punishment of the father is not to be visited on the children, except in the case of someone whose father, grandfather, and great-grandfather have successively undergone the penalty of death. Such persons the city shall send away with all their possessions to the city and country of their ancestors.'[5] The idea of a father, grandfather and great-grandfather (in other words of three repetitions of conduct forming a trend) is an important one, which will be adopted in the 20th century developments of eugenic ideals.

2.3 19TH–20TH-CENTURY DEVELOPMENTS

In the 19th century the idea of traits and characteristics being heritable was revived. Certain scientific discoveries in this time gave credence to

[3] Plato, *The Republic* (trans. B. Jowett) (Oxford: Clarendon Press 1894) Chapter 459.

[4] Aristotle, *On the Parts of Animals*, Part 1 (trans. W. Ogle) (Oxford: Oxford University Press 1912).

[5] Plato, *Dialogues*, Book 9 (trans. B. Jowett) (New York: Prometheus Books 2000) at 856.

what had previously been an unsubstantiated belief, or a belief based on science that might not be valid. The first key event occurred in 1865 when Gregor Mendel published the results of experiments with pea plants which demonstrated that certain characteristics could be passed down from generation to generation in a predictable manner. In the same year, Charles Darwin published his seminal work, *On The Origin Of The Species*. The book, while focussed on plants and animals, advanced the theory that there was a process of natural selection in nature, which resulted in favourable variations tending to be preserved and injurious ones being destroyed. While Darwin did not directly apply his ideas on natural selection to humans, this link was made by Francis Galton, Darwin's cousin, in 1869.[6] Darwin admitted privately shortly thereafter in a letter to Galton that 'you have made a convert of an opponent'[7] and in his 1871 book, *Descent of Man*, that 'we now know, through the admirable labours of Mr Galton, that genius … tends to be inherited'[8] in humans.

In 1883 Galton coined the term 'eugenics', an anglicized version of 'eugenes' from the greek eu (well) and genes (born). Eugenics was 'the science of improving stock – not only by judicious mating, but whatever tends to give the more suitable races or strains of blood a better chance of prevailing over the less suitable than they otherwise would have had.'[9] Eugenics consisted of two branches. The first was referred to as positive eugenics, and focused on encouraging the most desirable people to reproduce, resulting in the highest quality offspring. The second form was negative eugenics, which had the aim of preventing the least desirable people from reproducing and therefore passing their defective traits and characteristics on to the next generation. According to Galton and Darwin, positive eugenics was the more important of the two branches.

Popular interest in eugenics in the United States was triggered by a period of intense societal change at the turn of the 20th century. This societal change consisted of three factors. First, there was an increasing

---

6 Francis Galton, *Hereditary Genius* (1869) (reprint) (UK: MacMillan & Co 1925).

7 Charles Darwin, letter to Francis Galton December 23 1859, reproduced online at http://www.galton.org/letters/darwin/correspondence.htm (accessed March 2015).

8 Charles Darwin, *The Descent of Man* (1871) (reprint) (USA: Empire Books 2012) p. 28.

9 Francis Galton, *Inquiries Into Human Faculty And Development* (1883) (reprint) (London: Elibron Classics Series 2000) p. 17.

amount of both external (from different countries) and internal (from rural areas) migration to the cities. Second, the role of women in society was beginning to change, evidenced by a trend of young women moving to cities to take up retail positions and living alone. Third, the life expectancies of the lower classes began to increase due to social reforms and advances in medicine. The combined result of these factors was a perceived increase in crime and other forms of vice in the cities, when in reality, these had merely become more noticeable to the upper classes due to the increase in numbers of the lower classes. This perception was enhanced by the publication of genealogical studies, often fictitious or biased, which demonstrated clear examples of the hereditary nature of these social defects. In 1911, Cesare Lombroso published two books. The first, *Crime, Its Causes And Remedies*, considered potential causes of crime including heredity, physical and moral make-up, emotional temperament and environmental factors. The chapter on heredity began by reporting statistics on criminals. In one study of 104 criminals, for example, Lombroso found that 71 criminals had 'some hereditary influence'. This influence included familial criminality, alcoholism, insanity or prostitution. He additionally quoted other studies with similar results, before moving on to discuss some genealogical studies.

In the second book, *Criminal Man*, Lombroso commented more strongly that 'heredity is the principal organic cause of criminal tendencies'. This heredity could be 'indirect' (from a 'genetically degenerate' family with a history of insanity, deafness, syphilis, epilepsy or alcoholism) or 'direct' (from criminal parentage).[10] He continued that 'official statistics show that 20% of juvenile offenders belong to families of doubtful reputation and 26% to those whose reputation is thoroughly bad'.

This so-called 'scientific evidence', often taken from limited studies of less than 100 criminals and using a flexible definition of criminality, was generally supported by genealogical studies. Lombroso referred in both books to the Jukes family, described in a book published by Richard Dugdale in 1877. Dugdale claimed to have traced 709 members of a family (although he admits that only 540 were blood related), a number of which displayed anti-social behaviour.[11] Dugdale's thesis was that both environment and heredity were to blame for this behaviour, however, Lombroso and subsequent authors used the study to focus on the

[10] Cesare Lombroso, *Criminal Man* (1911) (trans. M. Gibson) (North Carolina: Duke University Press 2006) p. 137.

[11] This number included 76 criminals (of which seven were murderers), 120 prostitutes, and 200 welfare recipients.

heredity aspect. A similar genealogical study was published by Henry H. Goddard in 1912, based on the Kallikak family. Martin Kallikak was a revolutionary war hero who had conceived an illegitimate son with a feeble-minded barmaid before marrying a more morally upstanding Quaker woman. Of the 480 traced descendants of the illegitimate child, 75% were classified by Goddard as degenerates of some description.[12] The 496 legitimate descendants, on the other hand, were prosperous, intelligent, morally-upstanding citizens.

The combined effect of the increasing numbers in lower classes, the decreasing numbers of the upper class, and the changing role of women resulted in a society that was not pleasing to the upper classes. Faced with the prospect of becoming heavily outnumbered, the upper classes turned to the eugenics movement in an attempt to try to maintain their position in society. More specifically, the focus of eugenics began to shift from the positive form advocated by Darwin and Galton to the negative form of preventing 'undesirable' people from having children. Alexander Graham Bell, who commented that improvement of the race 'depends on increasing the number and proportion of desirables born in successive generations of the population hence this should be the chief object of eugenics' continued that 'it is to be regretted that the efforts of eugenists have been mainly directed to the diminution of the undesirable class'.[13] By 1917, 16 US states had enacted legislation allowing sterilization of feebleminded individuals. Sterilization of criminals began later, but by 1942, 13 states had legislation permitting this.

2.3.1 The Testing of the Legality of Eugenics Policies: *Buck v Bell*

In 1916 Dr Albert Priddy of the Virginia Colony For Epileptics And Feeble-Minded was sued by a mother and daughter, both of whom had been sterilized following admission to the Virginia Colony for 'disreputable habits'. Priddy testified that as Colony Physician it was his prerogative and duty to provide whatever medical care was required, and that in his belief their sterilizations were a therapeutic necessity. The jury accepted this argument, but included in their decision a warning that this practice ought not to continue without specific legal authority.[14] Priddy responded by advocating for such a law, and when it was enacted he used

---

[12] 143 were classified as 'degenerates' due to mental retardation.

[13] A.G. Bell, 'How to improve the race' (1914) 5 *Journal of Heredity* 5, 5.

[14] Paul Lombardo, 'Medicine, eugenics and the Supreme Court: From coercive sterilization to reproductive freedom' (1996) 13 *Journal of Contemporary Health Law And Policy* 1, 9.

a test case to test the statute's validity. The subject he chose was an 18-year-old, Carrie Buck.

Carrie had been committed to the Virginia Colony as a result of being considered 'epileptic, feebleminded and morally delinquent' by her foster mother, the latter charge being evidenced by the fact that Carrie had become pregnant while unmarried.[15] At trial, Dr Priddy's main argument was that there was evidence of three generations of mental defectives in the family.[16] In Carrie's case, her mother Emma had been a resident of the Virginia Colony since Carrie was three[17] and was described as being indigent and as having given birth to illegitimate children, including Carrie.[18] Carrie herself was described as 'having a record during life of immorality, prostitution and untruthfulness; had never been self-sustaining and has had one illegitimate child' and also as having a mental age of nine.[19] The third generation was Carrie's daughter, Vivian, deemed

---

15 Stephen Gould, 'Carrie Buck's Daughter' (1984) 93 *Natural History* 14, 18. It would appear that Carrie was in fact pregnant as the result of being raped by the nephew of her foster mother, and Carrie's admittance to the Colony was an attempt by the foster mother to hide this from the general public. By the time of the trial, the child Vivian was born and was living with the same foster mother.

16 The reference to 'three generations' recalls Plato's mention of the banishment of a man due to three generations in his family having been condemned to death. It is perhaps arguable that in society we see something happening once as an incident, twice as coincidence, but three times as demonstrating a pattern.

17 Emma was described as having 'a record during life of immorality, prostitution, and untruthfulness; … never been self-sustaining; … maritally unworthy, having been divorced from her husband on account of infidelity; … a record of prostitution and syphilis; … one illegitimate child and probably two others inclusive of Carrie': Paul Lombardo, 'Medicine, eugenics and The Supreme Court: From coercive sterilization to reproductive freedom' (1996) 13 *Journal of Contemporary Health Law and Policy* 1, 10.

18 David Smith and Ray Nelson, *The Sterilization of Carrie Buck (Aubrey Strodes Recollections*) (1989) 15. It has since been argued that neither claim was true. Matthew Martin, 'The dysfunctional progeny of eugenics: Autonomy gone AWOL' (2007) 15 *Cardozo Journal of International and Comparative Law* 371, 382, claims she had inherited money in the bank. Paul Lombardo states that her parents were married: 'Three generations, no imbeciles: New light on *Buck v Bell*' (1985) 60 New York University Law Review 30, 52.

19 Carrie had in fact passed 6th grade with the comment 'very good deportment and lessons' when she was removed from school by her foster mother to be her housekeeper. She was a consistent church attender and member of two church choirs. Seven of the witnesses against her had never in fact met her, and were working solely from information provided by Dr Priddy: Paul Lombardo, 'Three generations, no imbeciles: New light on Buck v Bell' (1985) 60 New York University Law Review 30, 52.

to be mentally defective on the vague testimony of a Red Cross social worker: 'there is a look about it that is not quite normal, but just what it is, I can't tell'.[20]

The Virginia Supreme Court considered Carrie Buck to be the 'probable parent of socially inadequate offspring, likewise affected as she is' and stated that 'her welfare and that of society would be promoted by such sterilization'.[21] In 1927 an appeal was heard by the Supreme Court of the United States of America and was rejected by a majority of seven Justices to one.[22] The only written judgment was by Justice Oliver Wendell Holmes, who was known to be a eugenicist. Chief Justice Howard Taft assigned the majority opinion to Holmes, commenting in a written memo that:[23]

> Some of the brethren … are troubled about the case, especially Butler [Justice Pierce Butler, who dissented]. May I suggest that you make a little full the care Virginia has taken in guarding against hasty action, the proven absence of danger to the patient and other circumstances tending to lessen the shock many may feel over such a remedy? The strength of the facts in three generations [of imbeciles] is of course the strongest argument for such state action.

Holmes' judgment considered whether an order for sterilization could ever be justified, and concluded that:

> We have seen more than once that the public welfare may call upon the best citizens for their lives. It would be strange if it could not call upon those who already sap the strength of the state for these lesser sacrifices, often not felt to be such by those concerned, in order to prevent our being swamped with incompetence. It is better for all the world, if instead of waiting to execute degenerate offspring for crime, or to let them starve for their imbecility, society can prevent those who are manifestly unfit from continuing their kind. The principle that sustains compulsory vaccination is broad enough to cover cutting the Fallopian tubes. *Jacobson v Massachusetts*, 197 US 11. Three generations of imbeciles are enough.

---

[20] Vivian was in fact intelligent, receiving A's and B's in school for deportment and B's and C's for classwork, making the honour roll in April 1931. She died age eight from infectious disease. Stephen Gould, 'Carrie Buck's Daughter' (1984) 93 *Natural History* 14, 18.

[21] Mary Dudziak, 'Oliver Wendell Holmes as a eugenic reformer: Rhetoric in the writing of Constitutional Law' (1986) 71 *Iowa Law Review* 833, 853.

[22] *Buck v Bell* 274 US 200 (1927).

[23] G. Edward White, *Justice Oliver Wendell Holmes: Law and the Inner Self* (Oxford University Press 1993) 404–5.

2.4 GENETICS IN EARLY CRIMINAL TRIALS

2.4.1 Introduction

There are two early cases in the 1920s–40s involving issues of genetics and crime. In the first, *Illinois v Leopold and Loeb*, genetics was argued as a defence, and in the second, *Skinner v State of Oklahoma,* genetics was relevant to punishment.

2.4.2 *Illinois v Leopold and Loeb*

The first notable case in which a genetics argument was raised was in 1924 in *Illinois v Leopold and Loeb*. In this case two teenage boys, aged 18 and 19, were convicted of the murder of 14-year-old Bobby Franks. Leopold and Loeb had wanted to commit the perfect crime. They had spent seven months planning the logistics of a murder, but the choice of victim had been random. Franks had been merely walking home from school when they were ready to commit the crime; he was beckoned by them and approached their car. Both Leopold and Loeb confessed to the crime when it became clear that a pair of glasses found near the body could be traced back to Leopold.

Clarence Darrow was hired as their defence lawyer. In arguing for a sentence of life imprisonment rather than the death penalty, he chose to focus on the fact that both boys were 'diseased of the mind' at the time. This had been rejected by psychiatric evidence in the trial, yet Darrow had no other mitigating factors to rely on.[24] Darrow argued that the medical evidence should be disregarded. His argument developed into one of genetics, rather than psychiatry:

> Why did they kill little Bobby Franks? Not for money, not for spite; not for hate. They killed him as they might kill a spider or a fly, for the experience. They killed him because they were made that way. Because somewhere in the infinite processes that go to the making up of the boy or the man something slipped, and those unfortunate lads sit here hated, despised, outcasts, with the community shouting for their blood.

In his opinion, all actions are caused by genetics:

---

[24] Both were wealthy and intelligent, having already completed undergraduate university degrees. Leopold attended Chicago Law School, and Loeb had been accepted to Harvard Law.

> Is Dickey Loeb to blame because out of the infinite forces that conspired to form him, the infinite forces that were at work producing him ages before he was born, that because out of these infinite combinations he was born without it? If he is, then there should be a new definition for justice. Is he to blame for what he did not have and never had? Is he to blame that his machine is imperfect? Who is to blame? I do not know … . I know that somewhere in the past that entered into him something missed … I know it is something. I know that nothing happens in this world without a cause.

The prosecutor rejected this argument:

> Hereditary influence. Well, let's see what their doctors say, on page 139: 'there is nothing about the patient's condition to show any evidence of a hereditary nature, and there is not the slightest reason to suppose that a condition of this kind will be transmitted to future generations by any of his siblings or relatives. This condition is acquired within the life history of the individual, and dies out when he dies.' It is something of his own construction, and his ancestors are in no degree responsible for it.

The court disregarded Darrow's argument, commenting that there were no mitigating factors. Leopold and Loeb were, however, spared the death penalty due to their ages, and were both sentenced to life plus 99 years.

2.4.3 *Skinner v State of Oklahoma*

In 1942, the US Supreme Court considered the sterilization of a criminal in *Skinner v State of Oklahoma.*[25] The Oklahoma Habitual Criminal Sterilization Act 1935 permitted sterilization of an 'habitual criminal', defined as someone twice convicted of crimes involving 'moral turpitude', with the exception of offences resulting from the violation of prohibitory laws, revenue acts, embezzlement or political offences. Jack Skinner had two prior convictions for theft and armed robbery when he was convicted for a second armed robbery. The Oklahoma Supreme Court in a 5:4 decision ordered a vasectomy to be carried out. The US Supreme Court overruled this, with the leading judgment of Justice William O. Douglas arguing that this was due to a lack of equal protection. The legislation in *Buck v Bell* was noted to apply to all people, whether residing within or without the Colony. Conversely, the legislation in *Skinner* exempted white collar crimes:

---

[25] 316 US 535 (1942).

> Sterilization of those who have thrice committed grand larceny with immunity for those who are embezzlers is a clear, pointed, unmistakeable discrimination. Oklahoma makes no attempt to say that he who commits larceny by trespass or trick or fraud has biologically inheritable traits which he who commits embezzlement lacks. … we have not the slightest basis for inferring that that line [between fraud and embezzlement] has any significance in eugenics, nor that the inheritability of criminal traits follows the neat legal distinctions which the law has marked between those two offences.

In his private notes, Justice Douglas appeared less than certain about whether criminality could be heritable, 'whether there are any scientific authorities in support [of sterilization] is not clear. Moronic minds are different. No statistics as to criminals, if criminals do not produce their own kind, then we have serious question.'[26]

The concurring decision of Chief Justice Stone focussed on the lack of due process in the legislation. Those classified as habitual offenders had no ability to prove that they did not have a genetic criminal tendency:[27]

> Moreover, if we must presume that the legislature knows, what science has been unable to ascertain, that the criminal tendencies of any class of habitual offenders are transmissible regardless of the varying mental characteristics of its individuals, I should support that we must likewise presume that the legislature, in its wisdom, knows that the criminal tendencies of some classes of offenders are more likely to be transmitted than those of others. And so I think the real question we have to consider is not one of equal protection, but whether the wholesale condemnation of a class to such an invasion of personal liberty, without opportunity to any individual to show that his is not the type of case which would justify resort to it, satisfies the demands of due process.

2.5 THE DECLINE AND RE-EMERGENCE OF EUGENICS

2.5.1 The Decline of Eugenics

The 1930s marked the beginning of a decline of eugenic policies worldwide. Three main reasons can be identified as contributing to this. First was the fact that emerging scientific knowledge began to cast doubt on the validity of eugenic beliefs. Second, the eugenics movement was

---

[26] Justice William O. Douglas, SC Conference Notes (11 April 1942) on file with Manuscript Division, Library of Congress.

[27] 316 US 535, 545.

thirty years old. The leaders and original advocates were no longer actively involved, and new leaders were not coming forward to take their place. Third, and most significant, was the impact of World War II. Doctors, who as a group had previously been amongst the strongest supporters of eugenics, were being sent to war and were therefore removed from the debates. With the rise of Adolf Hitler and his eugenics policies, the upper classes saw clearly for possibly the first time what the extreme effects of eugenics could be, and rejected it as a policy.

Eugenic practices therefore declined, but it would be an oversimplification to suggest that they died out completely. The language has changed and policies have modernized, particularly with the increase in scientific knowledge, but eugenic motivations and laws are still notable today.[28] Two examples can be used to demonstrate this: chemical castration for sex offenders, and three strikes laws.

2.5.2 Example of New Eugenics: Chemical Castration

In the 1960s, surgical castration for sex offenders, as seen in *Skinner*, began to be slowly replaced by chemical castration due to concerns that surgical castration was 'cruel and unusual' and an irreversible form of punishment. Chemical castration involves the injection of a drug that reduces testosterone, the theory being that this will diminish the sex drive of the individual, and therefore lower his chances of recidivism. Many countries today have some form of chemical castration programme, although the form it takes can vary. In the United Kingdom, Sweden and Denmark it is a voluntary programme, which does not affect the duration of the prisoner's sentence. In other countries like Poland, Moldova, South Korea, Estonia and Russia, it is a mandatory programme. In several states of the United States, it can be imposed as a condition of parole.

The reason why some commentators have considered it to be a eugenic policy is due to its arguably low potential success rate. Psychiatrists comment that sex offenders can be classified as belonging to one of four categories: those who use unacceptable stimuli such as children (paraphiliacs); those who confess to committing a sex offence but transfer blame to non-sexual or non-personal forces like alcohol, drugs or stress; violent offenders; and those who deny either the criminal nature of their actions, or that they have committed the crime. It is only the first category that is likely to benefit from chemical treatment to reduce

---

[28] Mary Ziegler, 'Reinventing eugenics, reproductive choice and law reform after World War II' (2008) 14 *Cardozo Journal Of Law And Gender* 319, 322.

fantasies, and a United Kingdom study suggests that this category contains less than 5% of sex offenders.[29] It has been suggested that not only will the treatment be ineffective for offenders in the other categories, but that it might actually be detrimental. Even amongst the 5% of sex offenders that it could help, psychiatrists agree that chemical castration is most effective when combined with therapy, which the US states do not provide. If chemical castration is not an effective form of treatment, as these statistics suggest, there must be some other reason for its use.

Hints of a possibly eugenic nature to the policy in the United States arise from two features of the laws. First is the nature of the drugs used. The initial drug used, Medroxyprogesterone Acetate (MPA), is a female birth control pill, given in significantly higher doses.[30] Given to males, it can have a similar effect – the prevention of reproduction. Second, is the criterion for the application of this drug. In many states, it will be required as a parole condition following the third sexual offence. This calls to mind the wording in *Buck v Bell* about three generations, and the three offence requirement in *Skinner.* It is arguable that this is an updated version of the law challenged in *Skinner*. The drug itself is unlikely to have a serious impact on recidivism rates,[31] but it will prevent the offender from having children, and therefore passing on any heritable criminal tendencies.

2.5.3 Examples of New Eugenics: Three Strikes Laws

The second example is of three strikes laws. In the United States, approximately 28 states have some form of a three strikes law, which results in a person who is convicted of a felony, who has two or more previous convictions for violent crimes or felonies, being awarded a harsher than normal sentence. This sentence generally ranges from 25 years without parole to life imprisonment. While the increase in sentence might appear to be justified on the basis of deterrence it does not appear

---

[29] Owen Dyer, 'Drug treatment is proposed to manage child sex offenders' (2007) 334 *British Medical Journal* 1343.

[30] These doses can amount to 400–500mg per week, as opposed to 150mg per month for females.

[31] This cannot be determined accurately, due to the impossibility of performing studies using placebos to test effectiveness. Studies which rely on self-reporting show some reduction of sexual fantasies amongst users (between 0–50% of offenders), but self-reporting of unacceptable sexual fantasies which will result in a recall of parole is unlikely to be accurate.

to have had this effect. A US study in 2004, showed that the law had no significant deterrent effect, suggesting that these individuals do not logically consider penalties before choosing to engage in violent criminal conduct. If anything, being on the 'third strike' made the individual more reckless and more likely to behave violently, on the basis of having nothing to lose.[32] Despite these findings, another four states subsequently enacted three strikes laws.

If the 2004 study is correct, and there is no real deterrent value in such a law, the justification for the law must be considered. Incapacitation is one option, the person cannot commit further crimes while being locked up. Oswald, however, makes an interesting point. He argues that the cost of incarceration, approximately $US45,000 per person per year, is too substantial to be sustainable and that one benefit of chemical castration is to allow the individual back out into the community.[33] If his estimation of the cost of incarceration is accurate, this raises the question of why three strikes laws for violent offenders are so popular, when the effect is to incarcerate for at least 25 years? The answer might be found in a combination of the *Buck* and *Skinner* cases. In *Buck*, women like Carrie were to remain in the colonies until they reached the age of natural infertility. In *Skinner*, the punishment of castration for a third offence was unrelated to the crimes he had committed, but would have the effect of preventing him from having children and passing his criminal genes on to them. If a three-strikes law does not increase deterrence, and is financially unsustainable, there must be some justification for its enactment. A eugenics style policy might be one explanation. A prison sentence of 25 years to life would generally mean that if the person is released, he would no longer be biologically able to have children.

While it is probably going too far to suggest that a eugenics rationale was a conscious motivation behind these laws, the lack of justification from a deterrence perspective suggests that another motive, even a subconscious one like a eugenics motive, might be present.

---

32 John Worrall, 'The effect of Three-Strikes legislation on serious crime in California' (2004) 32 *Journal of Criminal Justice* 283.

33 Zachary Oswald, '"Off with His __": Analyzing the sex disparity in chemical castration sentences' (2013) 19(4) *Michigan Journal of Gender and Law* 472.

2.6 CONCLUSION: THE APPEAL OF GENETIC ARGUMENTS

This chapter started by asking why as a society we keep returning to the idea of genetics controlling behaviour. One answer might be that it is simply a narrative that works for us. As a people we like the idea that we have free will and therefore the ability to decide our own destinies. We also, however, like the idea of control. As parents, we want our children to inherit what we consider to be the best of our qualities and even to surpass us in these qualities, a factor which is evident through the increased interest in trait selection in embryos. We also want to believe that we are doing our best for our children, so therefore when they do something wrong it is useful to look for an explanation that does not suggest that we failed as parents. This point also applies to society in general. A genetics explanation prevents us, as individuals or as society as a whole, from having to question whether our own personal acts or omissions played some role in the wrongdoing, even a minimal role. Could we have done more to help this person before he or she felt the need to turn to crime? If conduct is a result of environment, then the answer is yes. Society can almost always do more to help individuals financially or through the provision of social services or better educational or employment opportunities. If conduct is the result of genetics, then the answer is no. Even if we had done more to help the poorer, troubled or less educated members of society, the outcome would not have changed. A genetics argument absolves us as a society from responsibility. Finally, often we simply need answers when violence occurs. Absent any other rational explanation, genetics provides an answer.

Clarence Darrow in the *Leopold and Loeb* case commented:

> I know that any mother might be the mother of Richard Loeb and Nathan Leopold … the trouble is this, that if she is the mother of a Nathan Leopold or of a Richard Loeb, she has to ask herself the question: 'How come my children came to be what they are? From what ancestry did they get this strain? How far removed was the poison that destroyed their lives? Was I the bearer of the seed that brings them to death?' Any mother might be the mother of any of them.

His aim in this speech was to have the jury put themselves in the position of the parents of the two boys, and to find an explanation for the events that minimizes their feeling that they failed their children somehow.

As a more recent example, in December 2012, Adam Lanza killed 20 children and six adults at Sandy Hook Elementary school before killing himself. Within days, it was being reported that the medical examiner had ordered DNA testing on Lanza, to see if he had an 'evil' gene that would explain his aggressive nature. The parents of one victim, Avielle Richman, set up the Avielle Foundation, which has the objective of 'understand[ing] the underpinnings in the brain that lead to malevolent behaviors'. The website comments that '[t]oo little is known in the field of brain health in regard to what drives violent behaviors. Clearly something is wrong with a person capable of such atrocities, and there must be a better understanding of the biological and environmental factors associated with these pathologies.'[34]

It seems likely that even though we cling to a notion of free will, we also return to a genetic determinism explanation for conduct when it is in our best interests to do so. While we might understand that a belief in both free will and genetic determinism may be illogical and inconsistent, we overlook this when it is in our interests to do so. This therefore explains the reoccurrence of arguments of genetic determinism in criminal cases. It also indicates that these arguments will not vanish as scientific understanding of the link between behavioural traits and genetics increases. Unless the scientific understanding reaches a point of certainty, we will likely continue to cling to answers that provide useful explanations for us.

---

[34] www. aviellefoundation.org (accessed 20 March 2015).

3. Use of genetics in criminal investigations

3.1 INTRODUCTION

In 1986, Richard Buckland confessed to the rape and murder of 15-year-old Dawn Ashworth, providing police with specific details of the crime scene that had not been released to the public. An issue with the confession arose, however, when it was discovered that Buckland's blood type differed from that of blood found at the crime scene. British scientist Alec Jeffreys (who two years before had discovered DNA profiling) ran a DNA test on Buckland and confirmed the lack of a match with the crime scene blood sample. After he had informed the police of this result, a senior police officer commented 'Jeffreys does a test that we've never heard of and comes back and says "you've got the wrong guy". You can't challenge it. How can you challenge brand new science? Nobody else in the bloody world knows anything about it.' While this first use of DNA profiling was to exonerate Buckland, it was also subsequently used in this case to catch the killer, Colin Pitchfork, via a technique called a dragnet, or sweep.[1]

This chapter will consider the use of genetic material during the investigation of a crime. It will begin by examining the laws in relation to DNA profiling and databases, using several jurisdictions to compare approaches. From there it will consider some of the ethical issues associated with databases, including the use of samples or profiles in dragnets, familial testing and phenotyping. It will conclude by considering the implications of calls for a universal (compulsory) DNA database.

[1] As Pitchfork confessed, the new DNA techniques were never tested at trial. The first trial was that of Robert Melias for rape in October 1987.

3.2 DNA, DNA SAMPLING AND PROFILING

Deoxyribonucleic acid (DNA), is found in each human cell. It consists of two sets of 23 chromosomes each containing various genes. A person inherits one set of chromosomes from each parent, which are then combined in a way unique to the individual. Each chromosome contains both coding and non-coding regions. Coding regions contain the individual's complete genetic make-up, which thus includes information about medical predispositions, physical characteristics and ancestral or racial indicators. Non-coding (also known as junk) regions are generally considered to not contain any of this genetic or personal information, however some debate exists about this.

The human genome is 99.9 per cent identical for all individuals, with the 0.1 per cent difference coming from a variance in the Short Tandem Repeats (STRs) between genes. These variants in genes are known as alleles and can be specifically identified with a DNA test through examining markers (the number of STRs) at certain locations (loci) in a gene.

DNA testing involves the taking of a DNA sample (containing both coding and non-coding regions) by means of a buccal swab on the inside of the individual's cheek. This sample is then sent to a laboratory, where a DNA profile is derived through examining the markers at between 10 and 13 STR loci of the junk, or non-coding, DNA regions. The profile is then uploaded to a DNA database, along with an Agency Identifier (indicating which agency submitted the profile). To address privacy concerns, no names or personal details are uploaded. Instead, a Specimen Identification Number is assigned to the profile. Once in the database, the profile can be compared to DNA collected at crime scenes to search for a match. An example of a DNA profile is:

14,18; 30,31.2; 16,17; 13,14; 28,11; 12,14; 19,23; 6,7; 12,14; 21,23; X,Y.

This string of 20 numbers represents the markers from each chromosome at 10 loci.[2] The X,Y at the end is a gender identifier.

3.3 CURRENT POSITION: DNA DATABASE LAWS

In order to understand, compare and evaluate DNA database laws from various countries it is useful to focus on two stages of the use of DNA:

---

[2] NDNAD Annual Report, 2012–13, p. 5.

first, the criteria for collection of the sample, and second, the rules relating to its use and retention once collected. These tend to differ between countries, and in some cases, between states.

3.3.1 The United Kingdom

3.3.1.1 Introduction

It is unsurprising, based on the fact that it was a British scientist who first developed DNA profiling, that the UK has the oldest DNA database, known as the National DNA Database (NDNAD). It can also claim to have the largest per capita database, containing over 6.7 million people, or 10.5 per cent of the country. It has been suggested that these statistics might be explained by the fact that there is a tradition of police adopting new technologies, and also due to a lack of constitutional protection for privacy in the United Kingdom. Despite this long tradition of acceptance, there is no one piece of legislation governing the collection, use and retention of DNA. The various Acts contributing to the UK DNA database regulation will be discussed below.

3.3.1.2 Collection

Although the National DNA Database was officially launched on 10 April 1995, the earliest relevant legislation is the Police and Criminal Evidence Act 1984 (PACE). As enacted, this required the suspect to give consent for the collection of intimate bodily samples. At this time, an intimate bodily sample was defined as including 'saliva … or swab taken from a bodily orifice', therefore including a DNA buccal swab. In 1993, however, the Royal Commission on Criminal Justice suggested a re-categorisation as non-intimate:[3]

> DNA profiling is now so powerful a diagnostic technique and so helpful in establishing guilt or innocence, we believe that it is proper and desirable to allow the police to take non-intimate samples (eg saliva, plucked hair etc) without consent from all those arrested for serious criminal offences, whether or not DNA is relevant to the particular offence.

These recommendations were adopted the following year in the Criminal Justice and Public Order Act. Since consent was no longer required, it became necessary to clearly identify from whom a sample could be taken. The new Act addressed this by permitting collection from anyone charged (not necessarily convicted) of any recordable offence.

---

[3] Report of the Royal Commission on Criminal Justice (1993), p. 16.

Two subsequent pieces of legislation further expanded the categories of individuals subject to collection. In 1996, the Criminal Procedure and Investigations Act permitted collection from anyone arrested, charged, or informed that they would be reported for a recordable offence. In 1997, the Criminal Evidence Amendment Act further expanded the criteria to include prisoners convicted of certain offences (sex, violence, burglary) before 1995.

3.3.1.3 Use and retention

Under PACE, the original purpose of taking the DNA was stated in the requirements for collection. Under s62 (as enacted), a police officer could authorise collection if he had reasonable grounds to suspect that firstly, the individual was involved in a serious arrestable offence, and secondly, that the sample would tend to confirm or disprove this involvement. This suggests that DNA was to be used as an investigative tool for one specific crime only. This is also clear from the requirement in s64 (as enacted) that if the individual was cleared of the offence, was not prosecuted, or was not suspected of involvement, the sample 'must be destroyed as soon as it is practicable after that decision is taken'.

In 1993, the Royal Commission report, as quoted above, suggested a change in approach. It recommended the taking of samples without consent 'from all those arrested for serious criminal offences, whether or not DNA is relevant to the particular offence'. For the first time, this indicated that the anticipated use of the database was shifting from investigation of a particular offence to the collection of DNA for the investigation of future offences. The Criminal Justice and Public Order Act did not, however, adopt this recommendation. The new s64 stated that information derived from the sample of a person entitled to its destruction due to a lack of conviction for the offence it was collected in relation to 'shall not be used … for the purposes of any investigation of an offence'.

One of the first challenges to retention of a profile from an individual who was not convicted came in *R v B*. B was arrested, but subsequently acquitted, of a burglary. A DNA sample was taken in 1998, and therefore under PACE (as amended by the Criminal Justice and Public Order Act) the sample was required to be destroyed following acquittal. This did not happen, and B's DNA profile remained in the database. It was subsequently used to link him to a case of rape and assault. B argued that evidence of this link was inadmissible. The trial judge agreed, based on the wording of the legislation. In 2000, in a subsequent Attorney General's reference case, the Court of Appeal upheld the trial judge's ruling, stating that 'it would have been perfectly possible for Parliament to conclude that the fight against crime was so important that there should be no restriction on the use of DNA samples so that where such samples were lawfully obtained by the Police the information derived from them could be retained on a database for all purposes.'[4] The legislation had, however, expressly required destruction in certain cases and therefore prevented further use of the sample for criminal investigation.

Later in 2000 the House of Lords considered the Court of Appeal's approach and found that it was was 'contrary to good sense' and an 'austere'[5] interpretation that unnecessarily limited the powers of both the police to investigate, and the Crown Prosecution Service to prosecute. DNA evidence should, their Lordships considered, be treated in the same manner as other improperly obtained evidence. This would mean that it would not be automatically inadmissible, but admissibility would be at the judge's discretion.

One month after the House of Lords decision the Home Secretary introduced amendments to the relevant sections of PACE through the Criminal Justice and Police Act 2001. This permitted DNA and fingerprints to be retained indefinitely, even where the individual had been subsequently acquitted, or where proceedings against him had been dropped. As a result of this amendment, DNA profiles collected in relation to an investigation for one crime could now be used in investigations of other crimes. The 2003–4 UK National Database Annual Report referenced the positive implications of this, reporting that of the 128,517 profiles that would have previously been required to be destroyed, 5922 had matched with crime scene profiles. Of these, 53 had been murder cases.

In 2003, the Criminal Justice Act extended the powers of collection further, allowing samples to be taken from those arrested regardless of whether they had been charged. It is interesting to note a change in language in the legislation: the phrase 'one time suspects' replaced the previously used 'innocents'. Further minor amendments occurred in 2005, with the Serious Organised Crime and Police Act allowing samples to be taken from any deceased individual, and in the 2008 Counter-Terrorism Act, which permitted samples to be taken from anyone subject to a control order.

The next significant reconsideration of the law relating to retention occurred following the European Court of Human Rights decision in

---

4 [2000] EWCA Crim 42.

5 *Attorney General's Reference (No 3 of 1999)* [2001] 2 AC 91.

S and Marper. In 2001 S, a 12-year-old boy, had a DNA sample taken following his arrest for attempted robbery. He was subsequently acquitted. Since the Criminal Justice and Police Act 2001 had been enacted, allowing for retention even following acquittal, he was advised that his profile would be retained in the database. Marper was also arrested in 2001, and charged with harassment of his partner. A DNA sample was taken, but the charge was subsequently dropped. As in the case of S, Marper's solicitors were informed that his profile would be retained due to the new Act. The Chief Constable informed Marper's solicitors that, unless exceptional circumstances existed, profiles would now be retained in all cases.

Both S and Marper challenged this decision in court, claiming a breach of Article 8 European Convention on Human Rights.[6] The Divisional Court found that there was no breach. The Court of Appeal and the House of Lords found that retention in these circumstances did breach Article 8(1), but that the breach was justified and proportionate under Article 8(2). The House of Lords considered that retention was justified on grounds of the prevention and detection of crime.[7] Lord Steyn, for example, thought that any interference with privacy would be minimal compared to the benefits of retention to society. Interestingly, his Lordship thought there would be no adverse impact on the individual as a result of his profile being retained, unless he was implicated in a future crime. In other words, the mere presence of his profile in the database was not considered to adversely impact the individual. Further, the Chief Constable did not necessarily need to review every case where no conviction had resulted to determine whether the profile should remain in the database. Such individual consideration 'would involve the examination of many thousands of cases and involve large numbers of decision-makers' and furthermore 'would not confer the benefits of a greatly extended database'.[8]

---

6 Article 8 states: – Right to respect for private and family life:

1. Everyone has the right to respect for his private and family life, his home and his correspondence.
2. There shall be no interference by a public authority with the exercise of this right except such as is in accordance with the law and is necessary in a democratic society in the interests of national security, public safety or the economic well-being of the country, for the prevention of disorder or crime, for the protection of health or morals, or for the protection of the rights and freedoms of others.

7 [2004] UKHL 39.

8 Ibid, [59].

In 2008 the European Court of Human Rights heard the case, and disagreed with the House of Lords, finding that:[9]

> The blanket and indiscriminate nature of the powers of retention … fails to strike a fair balance between the competing public and private interests and … the respondent state has overstepped any acceptable margin of appreciation in this regard. Accordingly, the retention at issue constitutes a disproportionate interference with the applicant's right to respect for private life and cannot be regarded as necessary in a democratic society.

Unlike the approach taken by Lord Steyn, the ECHR considered that mere retention impacted on an individual's rights under Article 8. An individual could legitimately be concerned about possible future use of the information by the police. Further, the court drew a distinction between fingerprints and DNA on the basis that DNA contained more personal information, and therefore the retention of DNA had a 'more important impact' on private life.

The decision in *Marper* resulted in a reconsideration of the law. The New Labour Government published a consultation paper, Keeping the Right People on the DNA Database: Science and Public Protection, and subsequently introduced the Crime and Security Bill. This contained a provision requiring the destruction of profiles after six years (or three years for children) if the individual was not convicted.[10] The Parliamentary Joint Committee criticised the Bill, calling it 'unacceptable' considering that it took a 'very narrow approach' to the *Marper* decision. The blanket retention period of six years for adults or three years for children meant that the policy remained 'disproportionate and potentially arbitrary.' The Bill was enacted, but the provisions were not brought into force, due to a change in government. The new Coalition Government instead enacted the Protection of Freedoms Act 2012. This amended PACE by repealing s64 and inserting new sections 63D-U. Under these sections, 's63D material' (which includes fingerprints and DNA profiles, but not DNA samples) must be destroyed unless retained under powers conferred by ss63E-0 PACE. There is no time limit for destruction, but the explanatory notes suggest that this should occur as soon as reasonably practicable. If an individual is convicted, the DNA profile may be

---

[9] [2008] ECHR 1581, [119].

[10] The consultation paper had proposed six years for non-serious and 12 years for serious, but this was not followed.

retained indefinitely.[11] DNA samples are addressed separately under s63R, which requires destruction either as soon as a DNA profile has been derived, or at the latest within six months of the sample being taken. The Chief of Police can apply to a District Judge to extend this time period, but the profile can then only be used in relation to proceedings for that particular offence.

3.3.1.4 Relevant statistics

As of 31 March 2013, there were 6,737,973 profiles from individuals in the NDNAD, an increase in 362,319 profiles in the last year. It is estimated that 11.6 per cent of these are duplicates (explained as being the result of the same individual being sampled twice under different names), giving a total of 5,953,810 individuals.[12] In 2012–13, 592,777 DNA profiles were deleted from innocent people, in preparation for the Protection of Freedoms Act coming into force.

In terms of demographics, 78 per cent of individuals profiled are male, with 21 per cent female and 1 per cent unknown. Approximately 75 per cent of profiles are of white ethnicity, with 7 per cent black, and 6 per cent Asian.[13] Over 98 per cent are adults. Of the children's profiles included in the database the youngest group (of 47,172 individuals) are between the ages of 10–15 years.

In 2012–13, there were 211 matches from urgent searches (including 55 homicides and 60 rapes) and 24,894 matches from routine loading searches (of these, the most common is burglary, with 10,976 matches, followed by vehicle crime, with 3772). The 2012–13 Annual Report claims that 19,147 crimes were solved in that year following a DNA match, and that there is a 61 per cent chance that the database will provide a match to crime scene DNA.

3.3.1.5 How useful or accurate is the information?

When considering the Protection of Freedoms Act, the Human Rights Joint Committee commented that 'we are disappointed that accurate statistical information about the operation of the National DNA Database does not appear to have been routinely gathered …'. While the Annual

---

[11] 'Convicted' was defined as being given a caution, warning or reprimand, being found not guilty by reason of insanity, or being found to be under a disability and to have done the act charged (s.65B).

[12] Interestingly, it also includes 6847 sets of identical twins and 10 sets of identical triplets, who have the same DNA profile.

[13] The 2008–9 report has very similar figures, suggesting a consistency to these numbers.

Report referenced above has provided some statistics, these can be misleading. The report mentions a 61 per cent chance of a match with crime scene DNA, but does not mention that DNA is obtained in less than 1 per cent of reported crimes. If DNA is obtained, it must still be a useful sample before it can provide a match. In many cases, DNA from crime scenes is partial, degraded, or mixed with other DNA, with obvious implications for results. Where there is a match, it has been commented that only about half of these result in an arrest or other resolution, and only about half of those result in a custodial sentence (meaning, one in eight matches result in imprisonment).[14] One estimate, reported by the House of Commons Home Affairs Committee, had the conviction rate from crime scene DNA being as low as 0.3 per cent.[15]

One potential issue is the possibility of false or fortuitous matches, where an individual's profile matches the crime scene profile even though they did not commit the crime. The original method of generating a profile in the United Kingdom considered markers at six loci, and it was thought that a claimed match probability (the odds of two individuals sharing the same profile) was one in millions. This was forcibly revisited in 1999 when Raymond Easton was arrested for a burglary due to a database match. Easton had an alibi, and in addition, common sense suggested that he could not have travelled 200 miles from his home and committed the burglary as he suffered from Parkinson's Disease and could not drive, or barely dress himself. This was clearly a fortuitous match, and a further DNA test, testing at 10 points rather than six, exonerated him. The following year, the six loci standard test was replaced with a 10 loci test. The 2012–13 Annual Report considers the chance of two unrelated people having the same DNA profile with the 10 loci test was a 'billion to one'.[16]

3.3.1.6 Commentary

In tracing the development of the DNA database in the United Kingdom, several interesting developments can be identified. The initial legislation was designed to aid in the identification of those committing a very limited number of serious crimes, specifically homicides and violent sex offences. Subsequent legislation incrementally broadened this to include

---

[14] Sheldon Krimsky and Tania Simoncelli, *Genetic Justice* (New York: Columbia University Press 2010) p. 181.

[15] The National DNA Database, Eighth Report, (2009–10) p. 5.

[16] Alec Jeffreys (the founder of DNA Profiling) has called for an increase to 15 or 16 test points to further increase accuracy.

all crimes. The next development was the shift in focus from identification and investigation of a specific crime, to databasing for future crimes, to identifying potentially criminal individuals. While there has been some narrowing of the use, in terms of the recent removal of profiles following the Protection of Freedoms Act 2012, it appears that the focus is now on collecting profiles for use in future crimes. Rose describes this as 'a shift from a disciplinary society in which individual behaviour is regulated by institutions that mould dispositions and orientate self-surveillance, to a control society'.[17] Williams and Johnson agree, noting that regulation of crime has shifted from 'the development of new ways to diagnose, intervene and change the moral conduct of an individual' to 'the deployment of methods designed to intervene and delimit corporeal activities'[18] or, the management of individual actions rather than individuals per se.

3.3.2 The United States

3.3.2.1 Introduction

The first state DNA database in the United States was established in Virginia, in 1989. The following year the Federal Combined DNA Index System (CODIS) was initiated as a pilot project. It consists of four separate indexes: the Convicted Offender Index, the Forensic Index, the Unidentified Human Remains Index, and the Relatives of Missing Persons Index. To complicate matters, CODIS has three tiers: National, State and Local. Each US State can individually determine criteria for uploading to their own database, while Federal laws create requirements to upload to the National Database. DNA Database laws in the US are therefore a mixture of Federal and State laws. This section will first consider the Federal law before looking briefly at some of the state laws.

3.3.2.2 Federal law: collection

In 1994 Congress passed the DNA Identification Act which established a forensic laboratory to analyse DNA under the authority of the FBI. The official launch of CODIS occurred in 1998, with uploading to the database limited to those convicted of serious violent crimes (murder and felony sex offences). Broadening of the inclusion criteria occurred in 2000, with the DNA Analysis Backlog Elimination Act allowing profiles

---

[17] Nikolas Rose, *Powers of Freedom: Reframing Political Thought* (Cambridge University Press 2012) p. 234.

[18] Robin Williams and Paul Johnson, *Genetic Policing: The Use of DNA in Police Investigations* (London: Taylor and Francis 2008) p. 9.

to be uploaded for those in custody or on probation, parole or supervised release after being convicted of a 'qualifying federal offense'. These qualifying offences included homicide, sexual abuse or exploitation, kidnapping, robbery and burglary. In 2001, the USA Patriot Act extended the qualifying offences to include terrorism. In 2004, which was also notable as the year that all 50 states were connected to the database, the Justice for All Act broadened the criterion for collection from conviction to merely requiring that an individual be charged with an offence. By 2006, the DNA Fingerprint Act allowed collection from arrestees, and in 2008 the Department of Justice Final Rule[19] not only allowed, but in fact mandated, collection from those fingerprinted following arrest or detention.

3.3.2.3 Federal law: use and retention

None of the Acts discussed above included any restrictions on use, but focussed solely on collection. The DNA Analysis and Backlog Act, for example, simply states:

> (b) ANALYSIS AND USE OF SAMPLES. – The Director of the Bureau of Prisons or the probation office responsible (as applicable) shall furnish each DNA sample collected under subsection (a) to the Director of the Federal Bureau of Investigation, who shall carry out a DNA analysis on each such DNA sample and include the results in CODIS.

The DOJ Final Rule considered requirements for use in more detail. It referred to solving crimes through fingerprints of DNA that has (past tense, possibly meaning collection before the crime) been collected. It then commented that collecting DNA at the time of arrest 'can prevent and deter subsequent criminal conduct' and that 'the added value of early DNA-sample collection in solving and preventing murders, rapes and other crimes, was a specific motivation for the enactment of the legislation that this rule implements.'

The focus on collection in the US Federal laws further means that the legislation failed to consider the removal or destruction of DNA profiles. There are no provisions relating to the automatic removal of a profile from a database, even where there has not been a conviction. An individual seeking removal must obtain a court order showing that he was acquitted or that the charges against him were dismissed.

---

[19] Also known as 'DNA-Sample Collection and Biological Evidence Preservation in the Federal Jurisdiction'.

In 2013 the US Supreme Court considered the effect of the Federal legislation in *Maryland v King*.[20] In 2009 King had been arrested for assault, and a DNA sample was subsequently taken. His DNA profile later matched to DNA found at the scene of a rape, and was the sole evidence used to convict him of this crime. King challenged this conviction on the ground that the collection of his DNA was an unconstitutional search 'not authorised by a warrant or based on some level of individualised suspicion', and therefore a breach of his Fourth Amendment rights.[21]

The Maryland Court of Appeals[22] applied a balancing test to the analysis of the Fourth Amendment, considering the degree of intrusion on King's privacy and then comparing this to 'the degree to which [the intrusion] is needed for the promotion of legitimate government interests'. In performing this balancing exercise the Court made several interesting points. First, it considered that an arrestee has a higher expectation of privacy than a convicted criminal, but a slightly lower expectation of privacy than a member of the general public. Second, DNA sampling should not be considered analogous to fingerprinting. Unlike fingerprinting, obtaining a DNA sample involves a physical intrusion, albeit a 'minimal' one, and the sample itself contains more personal information than a fingerprint. Third, the court considered that the relevant government interest was in solving cold cases, not in identifying the arrestee. If it was the latter, DNA sampling would be redundant as fingerprinting could achieve the same result much faster. The Court considered that a government interest in solving cold cases was a legitimate one, but that this did not justify the 'warrantless' taking of DNA. On balance, therefore, King's Fourth Amendment rights had been violated.

The state of Maryland sought leave to appeal to the US Supreme Court and requested a stay of the Court of Appeal's judgment. Chief Justice Roberts granted both. In relation to the decision to allow the appeal,

---

20 567 U. S. ____ (2012).

21 The Fourth Amendment states: '[t]he right of the people to be secure in their persons, houses, papers, and effects, against unreasonable searches and seizures, shall not be violated, and no Warrants shall issue, but upon probable cause, supported by Oath or affirmation, and particularly describing the place to be searched, and the persons or things to be seized.'

22 425 Md. 550, 42 A. 3d 549.

Kaye[23] put this in context by commenting that '[o]ver and over, the Court had denied requests from convicted offenders and, more recently, from arrestees to address the legality of state and federal laws mandating routine collection of their DNA'[24] but that this case was different, since the lower court had deemed the relevant law unconstitutional. In relation to the stay, the Chief Justice commented that there was a 'fair prospect' that the court would reverse the Court of Appeals decision as it 'subjects Maryland to ongoing irreparable harm'.

The subsequent decision of the Supreme Court reversed the Maryland Court of Appeals decision as anticipated, but it was a five to four majority decision. The likelihood of a divided court was clear from the beginning of the oral argument, with Justice Scalia suggesting that the Chief Justice's reference to a 'fair prospect' of overruling might not be unanimous:

> MS. WINFREE: Mr. Chief Justice, and may it please the Court: Since 2009, when Maryland began to collect DNA samples from arrestees charged with violent crimes and burglary, there have been 225 matches, 75 prosecutions, and 42 convictions, including that of Respondent King.
>
> JUSTICE SCALIA: Well, that's really good. I'll bet you, if you conducted a lot of unreasonable searches and seizures, you'd get more convictions, too. (Laughter.)
>
> JUSTICE SCALIA: That proves absolutely nothing.

The majority accepted that DNA testing was a search for the purposes of the Fourth Amendment, and that in King's case it had been performed without a warrant. The issue was whether this was a reasonable search, and like the Maryland Court of Appeals, the majority addressed this by applying a test balancing the government interest with the degree of intrusion on King's expectation of privacy. The majority agreed with the Court of Appeals that an arrestee has a diminished expectation of privacy, however they disagreed with the conclusion that fingerprinting and DNA testing were not analogous. There was, in their opinion, no meaningful

---

[23] David Kaye, 'Why so contrived? Fourth Amendment balancing, per se rules, and DNA databases after *Maryland v King*' 104 J Crim L and Criminology 535, 537–8.

[24] Indeed, during oral arguments, Justice Samuel Alito had flagged the case during the oral argument as '[B]y the way, I think this is perhaps the most important criminal procedure case that this Court has heard in decades.'

difference between the two.[25] In the majority's opinion, the relevant government interest was in identifying the person arrested. 'Identification' here appeared to cover numerous factors, including the individual's name, whether he was a potential danger to others or himself, whether he was a flight risk if granted bail, and whether his identification might free someone 'wrongfully imprisoned for the same offence'. The conclusion reached was that the government interest in identification outweighed the arrestee's diminished expectation of privacy, and the collection of DNA in King's case was therefore a reasonable warrantless search under the Fourth Amendment.

The dissenting opinion was notable for two reasons, first, the rare fact that it was read aloud, and second the language used by Justice Scalia. Kaye[26] commented that '[f]or eleven minutes, he mocked the majority's defense of Maryland's law as a means of identifying arrestees'. The dissent begins: 'the Court's assertion that DNA is being taken, not to solve crimes, but to identify those in the State's custody, taxes the credulity of the credulous'. Identification in this case, Justice Scalia argues, simply means 'searching for evidence that [the arrestee] has committed crimes unrelated to the crime of his arrest.' If taking the DNA was truly for identification purposes, it would have been carried out earlier than three days after the arrest, and would have been compared with samples in the 'convict and arrestee collection' rather than the 'unsolved crimes collection.' His Honour's conclusion was that 'if the Court's identification theory is not wrong, there is no such thing as error.' The majority decision was a precedent-shattering and 'scary' foundation for the 'construction of … a genetic panopticon'.

3.3.2.4 State laws

Individual US state laws vary significantly. Almost all states permit collection from those convicted of felonies, and at least 37 states for misdemeanors, with New York in 2012 becoming the first 'all crimes state'. In 28 states collection is permitted following arrest, with 15 of these specifically referring to the time of booking as the relevant time and seven requiring probable cause first. All states except Hawaii allow collection from juveniles. Twelve states allow for the use of reasonable

---

[25] Both were discussed in depth, leaving confusion as to which was the dominant point. Either there is no privacy interest in DNA, or there is a privacy interest but King had a diminished right of privacy due to his status as arrestee.

[26] David Kaye, 'Why so contrived? Fourth Amendment balancing, per se rules, and DNA databases after *Maryland V King*' 104 J Crim L and Criminology 535, 538.

force in collection, and interestingly, several states require the arrestee to pay for the privilege of collection. Utah, for example, requires a payment of $150, unless the court considers the arrestee indigent. Several other states 'loan' the arrestee the money, and then collect the payment if the arrestee is convicted.

3.3.2.5 Relevant statistics

As of November 2014, there are 11,261,417 offender profiles and 2,095,147 arrestee profiles in CODIS. With the decision in *Maryland v King*, the number of arrestee profiles is likely to grow. In 2011 alone there were almost 12.5 million arrests, and Justice Scalia in *King* commented that nearly one third of Americans are arrested for some offence by the age of 23.

3.3.2.6 How useful or accurate is the information?

As was the case with the UK NDNAD, the effectiveness of the database is difficult to determine. The FBI collects statistics based on 'where CODIS has added value to the investigative process', which is a vague, undefinable, measure of utility. According to these statistics, CODIS has produced over 266,897 hits as of November 2014, which have assisted in more than 255,153 investigations.

3.3.3 Australia

The Australian National Criminal Investigation DNA Database (NCIDD) was established in June 2001. It became fully functional in 2007, when all states had legislated in relation to it. It analyses markers at 9 loci. Similarly to the United States, there is a mixture of Federal (Commonwealth) and State/Territory laws.

3.3.3.1 Commonwealth law: collection

The relevant Commonwealth law is found in Part 1D of the Crimes Act 1914. Under this Act, a sample of saliva or sample by buccal swab is classified as a non-intimate forensic procedure. The effect of this is that a DNA sample can be taken from an adult, whether or not in custody, following either informed consent of the adult or Order of a Magistrate. In addition, a DNA sample can be taken by order of a Senior Police Officer if the adult is in custody. For such an order to be made by a Senior Police Officer the suspect must first be asked for, and refuse to give, informed consent. Additionally, the senior police officer must be satisfied on the balance of probabilities that: the suspect is in lawful custody, there are reasonable grounds to believe that the suspect committed a relevant offence, there are reasonable grounds to believe that taking the DNA sample is 'likely to produce evidence tending to confirm or disprove that the suspect committed a relevant offence', and that taking the sample without consent is justified under all the circumstances. A 'relevant offence' is generally defined as an indictable offence.

In 2003 the Australian Law Reform Commission and Australian Health Ethics Committee published a report entitled 'Essentially Yours: The Protection of Human Genetic Information in Australia'. It recommended removing the consent procedure, therefore requiring a court order for collection of every sample in order to address privacy concerns. At the present time, this recommendation has not been adopted.

3.3.3.2 Commonwealth law: use and retention

Forensic material taken must be destroyed after 12 months if no proceedings have been instituted, or if instituted proceedings have been discontinued. It must also be destroyed if the suspect is acquitted, or if a conviction is subsequently quashed. A Magistrate has the discretion to extend the retention period for 12 months at a time if there are special reasons to do so. Any evidence introduced in court that ought to have been destroyed is deemed inadmissible.

Use of the information appears to be restricted to use in relation to a specific investigation only. In the provisions of the Act permitting the Senior Police Officer or a Magistrate to order the procedure to be carried out without consent, there must be reasonable grounds to believe both that a relevant offence had been carried out, and also that the forensic procedure is likely to produce evidence confirming or disproving that a relevant offence was committed.

The 2003 Australian Law Reform Commission report and a 2004 Victorian Parliament Law Reform Committee report entitled 'Forensic Sampling and DNA Databases in Criminal Investigations' both rejected proposals to broaden these powers to align with the UK PACE Act. The Victorian Committee commented that:

> The current system of court orders … affirm[s] a connection between the taking of the sample and its forensic utility in a specific investigation. This serves to ensure that the primary purpose of DNA sampling of suspects remains the detection of offences for which [individuals] have already been identified as suspects.

3.3.3.3 State laws

As with the US, individual Australian states and territories have their own laws, and again, these vary significantly. In Tasmania, the Northern Territory, and the Australian Capital Territory, buccal swabs are classified as non-intimate, therefore not requiring consent for collection. In Victoria, they are classified as intimate, and in South Australia they are intimate and intrusive. New South Wales declined the traditional classifications, and placed it in a separate category.

3.3.3.4 Relevant statistics

The most recent report on the NCIDD from January 2013 records 718,462 profiles recorded on the database. In the 2012–13 financial year there were reportedly 135,992 matches between crime scenes and individuals, and 51,600 matches between crime scenes.

3.3.4 New Zealand

3.3.4.1 Introduction

New Zealand has the distinction of being second in the world (after the United Kingdom) to create a DNA database. Established in August 1996, it consists of two databases, the DNA Profile Databank (or DNAPD) (containing profiles of individuals) and the Crime Sample Database (containing profiles from unsolved crimes).

3.3.4.2 Collection

The initial Act to address DNA collection was the Criminal Investigations (Blood Samples) Act 1995. This Act required consent for the collection of blood samples to be included in the database. Buccal swabs were not permitted to be taken due to concerns about reliability. In 2003, an Amendment Act changed the name of the legislation to the Criminal Investigations (Bodily Samples) Act 1995, and allowed the collection and use of buccal swabs. Collection could be actioned by consent, or by a court order following conviction for a relevant offence. A further amendment in 2009 substantially broadened the law. Samples can now be taken from those detained for an imprisonable offence, or from a convicted person following a compulsion order issued by a police officer. The Amendment Act does create some protection for those individuals merely detained for an offence. It creates a stand-alone Temporary Database into which profiles of detainees are entered. These profiles are only transferred to the DNAPD if conviction follows. If there is no charge or conviction, the profile is destroyed.

3.3.4.3 Use and retention

Based on the requirements for collection, use of the DNA profile appears to be restricted to investigation of the particular offence charged. Like the Australian legislation, the language of the section referring to authorised taking of the bodily sample requires good cause to suspect that the individual has committed an imprisonable offence, and that the sample will confirm or disprove the individual's involvement in that offence. This suggests that the use of the sample is to relate to that offence. In addition, the New Zealand Police Operational Guidelines restrict the taking of a sample to situations where the DNA would be relevant to investigating that particular offence. A further point is that the Guidelines permit the taking of a sample if the suspect has given the officer reasonable grounds to believe that other offending has taken place and that the DNA would be relevant to investigating that crime. The fact that this is specified as a permissible use suggests that use for other situations (for example, for investigation of an unknown future crime) are not permissible.

It could be noted that it was recently announced that the four of the five 'Five Eyes' countries (USA, UK, Canada and Australia) had signed a memorandum of understanding to allow each other to search their DNA databases. New Zealand, the fifth country, had asked to be left out of this memorandum, as it did not consider that its laws allowed for data sharing. This again suggests a more restricted scope to permissible use than the other countries.

The 2003 Amendment Act specifically provides for the removal of DNA in certain specific circumstances, notably 'no later than 10 years after the date on which the person ceases to be subject to a sentence of imprisonment in respect of the offence.'

3.3.4.4 Statistics

As of 2014, the NZ DNAPD contains 152,691 samples. New Zealand claims to lead the world in DNA matching, with nearly 70 per cent of crime sample DNA matching an individual profile, and 30 per cent matching another crime scene.[27] New Zealand is, however, a proportionately smaller country both in terms of population and crime rates.

---

[27] These can be found at www.esri.cri.nz (accessed 20 March 2015).

3.4 CURRENT POSITION: DNA DRAGNETS OR SWEEPS

3.4.1 Introduction

The first use of DNA profiling to exonerate Richard Buckland of the rape and murder of Dawn Ashworth was discussed above. Following this, and with no other suspects, the police announced that they would take the 'revolutionary step' of using DNA dragnetting to assist in their investigation. All males between the ages of 17–34 living in the village where Ashworth disappeared, and in two nearby villages, would be asked to voluntarily submit blood and saliva samples to eliminate them as suspects. Approximately 4000 men gave samples between January and April 1987, but no matches were found with the crime scene DNA. Several months later it was discovered that a man named Ian Kelly had presented himself as another man, Colin Pitchfork, and submitted a sample under his name during this time. When he and Pitchfork were subsequently overheard discussing this deception in a pub, they were both arrested and Pitchfork confessed to the murder.

3.4.2 Definition

A DNA dragnet can be described simply as being when a certain subset of society is identified based on physical characteristics, and members of that subset are asked to give voluntary DNA samples as a means of reducing potential suspects. These physical characteristics can be very vague. In the Pitchfork case the subset consisted of males aged 17–35 in a specific geographic area. Race or skin colour is also a logical characteristic for a subset. The key feature of a dragnet is that samples are voluntarily given, avoiding issues of collection without consent, although the validity of this will be considered below.

3.4.3 Statistics

Some dragnets have been extensive in size. The largest in the United Kingdom, for example, included 4500 men from the Chipping Sodbury area. In the United States, the largest was in Miami, including 2300 men. The largest German case involved 12,000 samples, which was two thirds of the men aged 18–30 in Cloppenberg and 35 surrounding towns.

Dragnets are commonly used in the United Kingdom, with 292 occurring in the years 1995–2005. They are not as common in the United

States, with one study suggesting approximately 20 between 1990–2008. Whether they are effective or not is unclear. As the Pitchfork case demonstrated, they can be manipulated by the relevant individuals, or even avoided altogether due to their voluntary nature. Walker,[28] in 2004, considered that the use of dragnets to that point in time had been 'entirely ineffective'. Of the 20 dragnets carried out in the US, he found that only one resulted in a resolution, and this barely met the definition of a dragnet.[29] The others were resolved through other means, or left unsolved.[30] Krimsky and Simoncelli[31] report that of 7000 people tested as part of dragnets between 1995–2005, only one match resulted. The sheer number of samples collected suggests the time and cost involved in performing a dragnet are greater than the potential payoff.

3.4.4 Voluntariness and Consent

Although dragnets are described as involving a voluntary submission of a sample, this may not be the case. If people are coerced into providing, or are required to provide, a DNA sample, this negates the voluntariness of the act and can lead to issues of unwarranted search and seizure, privacy and the right against self incrimination.

In 1994, 600 African Americans were asked for samples in Ann Arbor, Michigan. Over 400 refused and 160 subsequently began a class action, claiming that the police had told them that they would become suspects if they refused. One claimed to have lost his job after the police informed co-workers that they wanted to interview him in relation to the case.

Following the 2002 Baton Rouge dragnet, Shannon Kohler filed a suit claiming that coercive methods had been used to convince him to provide a sample. These methods reportedly included threats to obtain a court warrant and to give his name to the press. He continued to refuse to provide a sample, and a court order was therefore sought and obtained. The evidence cleared Kohler of involvement. The 5th circuit court found that the coercive actions of the police affected his ability to consent, and that the physical characteristics used to form the subset of the population for the dragnet 'are so generalised in nature that hundreds if not

---

[28] Samuel Walker, quoted in Sheldon Krimsky and Tania Simoncelli, *Genetic Justice* (New York: Columbia University Press 2010) p. 59.

[29] In this case, a female comatose patient had become pregnant and the police took DNA samples from the 25 employees of her care facility.

[30] Sheldon Krimsky and Tania Simoncelli, *Genetic Justice* (New York: Columbia University Press 2010) p. 62.

[31] Ibid, 62.

thousands of men in the Baton Rouge area could have possessed them.'[32] The court order therefore lacked probable cause.

In another example, in 2008, 800 male residents of Cape Cod were asked to provide samples to eliminate them as suspects in the 2002 murder of Christa Worthington. A class action by 100 males argued successfully that there had been coercion on the part of the police and District Attorney who both stated that anyone refusing to volunteer a sample would be treated as a suspect, even in the absence of other evidence linking them to the murder.[33]

These consent issues also appear to exist in the United Kingdom. In Operation Minstead in March 2004, consent was sought from 1000 black men to provide samples. Approximately 125 refused, based on discrimination and human rights concerns. The police then applied pressure to obtain consent through indicating that their refusal to volunteer samples was suspicious, and through sending intimidating letters.[34]

Overall, reasons for refusal to provide a sample tend to be based around the fact that it is a suspicionless search (often based on vague racial and age descriptions), and concerns over errors being made in processing or analysing the samples, leading to false positive results.

A final point to mention is that even if there is no coercion present, the consent must still be informed consent in order to be valid. This would require the individual to be told of all potential uses of the sample (in other words, whether the sample will be used for just the current case, or for all future cases), the likely duration of retention (whether it will be retained indefinitely or not) and the steps required to have the profile removed from the database.

3.4.5 Conclusion

It is likely that the ability to carry out dragnets has contributed to the trend identified above of changing the approach to investigation, from comparing a suspect's DNA to confirm an already held suspicion, to relying on DNA as the primary investigative tool. While phrased as voluntary, it is clear that the circumstances surrounding the agreement to provide a sample must be carefully considered in order to determine

---

[32] *Kohler v Englade* 470 F3d 1104.

[33] In this case, the murderer was not a resident of Cape Cod, but only worked there as a garbage collector, so was not caught by the dragnet.

[34] Of the 125 that refused, five were subsequently arrested, and cleared following DNA testing.

whether it was truly voluntary and whether enough information was provided to result in informed consent being given.

3.5 ETHICAL AND HUMAN RIGHTS CONCERNS

The increasingly broadening criteria for collection and use discussed above raise some important ethical and human rights concerns. These include privacy, implications for the presumption of innocence, stigmatisation of profilees and racial profiling.

3.5.1 Privacy

The most common ethical or human rights concern raised in relation to DNA databases is the interference with privacy. As has been seen above, this was considered in both *Marper* and *King*. There are several different interests in privacy that might be infringed by taking a DNA sample.[35] The first is physical or bodily privacy, which may be infringed by the taking of the sample via a cheek swab. The second is informational privacy. The information contained in a DNA sample might reveal predispositions related to medical conditions, or behavioural traits. Maclean[36] argues that the fact that these might be probabilistic rather than deterministic predispositions makes the protection of this information from third parties even more important. The third is geographic (or spatial or locational) privacy, related to where a person was at a particular time, which would be impacted during a dragnet. The final interest is in familial or relational privacy, where information obtained in relation to one family member reveals information about other family members, due to its genetic nature. This creates additional concerns and is therefore better discussed below in a separate section on familial testing.

One issue that arises with a consideration of privacy rights is the limited nature of its protection under the law. In those jurisdictions with a recognised privacy right[37] it is generally not regarded as absolute, but

---

[35] Andrew Roberts and Nick Taylor, 'Privacy and the DNA databases' (2005) EHRLR 373, 377.

[36] Charles Maclean, 'Creating a wanted poster from a drop of blood' (2013) 38 Hamline L Rev 357, 374.

[37] The UK is a notable exception, although the Human Rights Act 1998 might have incorporated into domestic law the privacy right in Article 8 European Convention on Human Rights.

can be subject to reasonable limitations. In both *Marper* and *King* a reasonable proportionality test was applied, in which the public interest in solving crime was balanced with the personal interest in privacy. In *King*, the government or public interest prevailed, but in *Marper* the opposite result was reached. This lack of consistency is a likely consequence of engaging in a reasonable proportionality balancing exercise.

The idea of privacy rights in genetic material is one that we, as a society, are not entirely convinced of. When it comes to insurance companies or (potential) employers wanting access to genetic material, many feel that there is a privacy right that requires protection and outweighs the interests of the other parties. When it comes to health, however, we are not as convinced. Arguments that more diseases or illnesses could be treated or cured by using large scale biobanks to investigate diseases tend to attract a significant amount of academic, scientific and public support. However, there are also significant numbers of these same groups expressing valid concerns about discrimination. When considering the prevention of crime, society appears even less sure of a privacy right. This can perhaps be explained by the suggestion in the previous chapter about the need to understand why people commit crime, or perhaps due to the fact that criminal conduct directly affects other people and therefore we feel that any tool to investigate crimes and apprehend criminals is valid. Whatever the reason, the issue of whether there is a privacy right in genes, and if so the extent and importance of this right, is the subject of ongoing debate.

In the majority of examples of legislation discussed above, there is an obvious trend of a limited initial interference with 'genetic privacy' which slowly becomes a greater interference, and further examples of this will be discussed below. This incremental shift also makes it more difficult to identify the point where the balance tips from being a reasonable and proportionate interference to being unreasonable and in breach of a privacy right. In other words, the opportunity to really debate the issue of genetic privacy is simply being lost through lack of identification of when things have gone too far. The UK Information Commissioner picked up on this point when noting that the UK's proposed national identity card scheme and expansion of CCTV coverage was leading to the possibility that the UK was 'sleepwalking' into a 'surveillance' society.

If we accept that there is a right to genetic privacy, the issue of where to draw the line between a reasonable and a non-reasonable interference is difficult. US Supreme Court Justices have warned of the 'catastrophic potential' of allowing an administration to choose to 'exalt order at the cost of liberty',[38] or more subtly that 'the government's unrestrained power to assemble data that reveals private aspects of identity is susceptible to abuse',[39] but recognise that the point at which we should draw the line is not easily discernable. In *Marper*, the prevention of crime and protection of society justified the retention of DNA in the eyes of the House of Lords, but not in the European Court of Human Rights due to the 'blanket and indiscriminate nature' of the retention policy. Roberts and Taylor would consider the likelihood of the individual committing a serious offence as one test, whereas others like Krimsky and Simoncelli would look at the classification of the individual, considering that as soon as nonconvicted individuals can have samples taken, it has crossed the line from an 'investigative' tool to a 'surveillance' tool.

Some of these privacy concerns can be addressed by regulation and database design. The obvious example of this is the storage in the database of profiles (which contain no identifiable information), rather than samples (which do contain this information). If the samples are destroyed once the profile is generated, this addresses concerns about other people accessing medical or behavioural information. The distinction between privacy issues in samples and profiles was recognised by the European Court of Human Rights in *Marper*, although the court still concluded that this did not prevent the invasion of privacy resulting from the inclusion of the profile in the database as being unreasonable. If the samples are not destroyed, however, the potential breach of privacy is clearly greater. In the United Kingdom, it was revealed in 2006 that some of the DNA database work had been subcontracted out to private companies. One such company had retained the sample information of hundreds of thousands of individuals. Similarly, in New Zealand in 2009, it was revealed that an Environmental Science and Research worker had illegally disclosed information from the database. It is likely that the same contracting out occurs in the United States, particularly in light of the sheer number of arrestee samples being entered. The funding allocated by President Obama in the DNA Analysis Backlog Elimination Act was likely used to subcontract work rather than train new workers.

3.5.2 The Presumption of Innocence

A foundational principle of criminal law is that a person has the right to be presumed innocent. While the collection of DNA from an individual

---

[38] *US v Kincade* 379 F3d 813 (9th Cir) 2004, per Justice Reinhardt in dissent.

[39] *US v Jones* 565 US (2012) per Justice Sotomayor.

who is already a suspect for the purpose of investigating a particular offence does not interfere with this, retaining the DNA for future investigations does challenge this presumption. This is especially true where the individual was not charged or convicted of an offence. Campbell[40] argues that it 'speaks to the State's suspicion of [the individual's] likelihood to (re-)offend,' and thus distinguishes them from 'truly' innocent people who have not come to the attention of the police. She continues that '[i]t entrenches an interim categorisation of suspicion which adheres to individuals once they have come to be charged or arrested, evident in the differential treatment accorded in the storage of their cellular material'. This point was made by the applicants in *Marper*, who claimed that their inclusion in the database implied that they were 'not wholly innocent'. The European Court of Human Rights appeared to agree, expressing concern that persons entitled to the presumption of innocence were treated in the same manner as those convicted.[41] In *Van Der Velden*,[42] on the other hand, it was suggested by the court that inclusion in the database actually assisted the individual, as it would exclude him from the list of suspects rather than cast doubt on his innocence.

Whether the presumption of innocence is even relevant to inclusion on a database is unclear. In the United States, the presumption is more a 'rule of evidence which allows the defendant to stand mute at trial'.[43] Ashworth considers that the same may be true in the UK, pointing out that the scope of the presumption is 'eminently contestable'.[44]

3.5.3 Stigmatisation

Campbell[45] argues that what is actually being alluded to in cases is not privacy or the right against self-incrimination, but is in fact an interest in not being stigmatised. The potentially negative consequence of being

---

[40] Liz Campbell, 'Criminal labels, the European Convention on Human Rights and the presumption of innocence' (2012) University of Edinburgh Research Paper p. 33.

[41] The court saw this as a privacy breach, however, not a separate issue.

[42] *Van der Velden v The Netherlands* E Ct HR no 29514/057 (December 2006).

[43] John Mitchell, 'Bail reform and the constitutionality of pretrial detention' (1969) 55 Va L Rev 1223, 1242.

[44] Andrew Ashworth, 'Four threats to the presumption of innocence' (2006) 10 Int J of Evidence and Proof 241.

[45] Liz Campbell, 'A Rights-based analysis of DNA retention' (2010) 12 Crim LR 889, 890.

included in the database is that an individual is being treated as a criminal by the system, and may additionally be treated as such by society if this inclusion is discovered. This is more correctly described as a stigmatisation concern than one of privacy.

Whereas privacy issues can be at least partially addressed by regulation, stigmatisation issues are more difficult to address. One argument is that the associated stigma can be removed by simply including everyone on the database. The idea of a universal database will be discussed below.

3.5.4 Racial Profiling

There is a natural concern that since racial profiling is widely regarded as being prevalent in criminal investigations, minorities will be arrested or detained more frequently for offences, and will therefore be more likely to appear in databases. One US statistic suggested that one third of African Americans will be arrested by the age of 23. In the US, African Americans are approximately 14 per cent of the general population, but about 40 per cent of the prison population. As another example, in New Zealand, Maori are 14 per cent of the general population but 50 per cent of the prison population. There is a strong concern that databasing will make these racial disparities worse.

3.5.5 Conclusion

The above discussion has highlighted several different approaches to collection and use of DNA profiles and databases. It has demonstrated that policies and practices in the UK are the most permissive, likely due to the lack of recognition of a privacy right. In contrast, the United States at the Federal level and in many states has been more circumspect in extending DNA collection and retention to non-convicted persons. The *Maryland v King* decision, however, may be the beginning of a shift to a more permissive collection and use regime. Countries like Australia and New Zealand appear to remain restricted in their approach, due to the importance placed on privacy rights in these jurisdictions.

The United States and United Kingdom legislation both demonstrate a shift from use of DNA evidence for the investigation of a particular crime, to databasing for future crime and to identifying potential future offenders. Again, Australia and New Zealand have displayed a more conservative approach, as has the European Union (as evidenced through *Marper*).

This part of the chapter concluded by identifying some ethical concerns to be kept in mind when considering the use of DNA databases. The next part of this chapter considers some of the newer, perhaps more controversial, uses of DNA samples and some of the specific issues that these might raise. It will then consider calls for the final stage of DNA database development – the Universal Database.

3.6 FUNCTION CREEP

'Function Creep' is the term used to describe the process through which a new technology is introduced for one particular purpose or function and then its use is gradually widened to include use for other purposes or functions. The issue in relation to this process is that while legal and ethical concerns in relation to the initial function were likely debated before introduction, function creep occurs almost under the radar, and there is therefore limited opportunity for debate. Cynical commentators would describe function creep as a deliberate tactic, a way of introducing these new purposes through a backdoor, 'despite the initial promises of their creators'[46] that the technology would not be used for these reasons.

This chapter has already described some aspects of function creep in relation to DNA databases, through the initially intended function of identification of suspects in relation to a particular crime being widened to allow for the use of the profile in solving different crimes, and then potentially to identification of individuals likely to offend in the future. Function creep can also be seen occurring in the use of dragnets.

The collection of DNA samples carries an inherent risk of function creep, due to the amount of potentially identifying information about to be derived from the sample, unless the legislation specifically required destruction of the sample once the profile was created. Lazer and Mayer-Schonberger[47] argue that storing the DNA samples 'invites re-purposing at a later stage'.

One emerging, almost hidden, example of function creep is in the increased permitted uses of the profile and/or sample. It has been reported that the British Home Office has given permission for 20

---

[46] Barry Steinhardt, 'Privacy and forensic DNA databanks' in David Lazer (ed.), *DNA and the Criminal Justice System: The Technology of Justice* (Boston: MIT Press 2004) p. 173.

[47] Schonberger, 'Statutory frameworks for regulating information flows: drawing lessons for the DNA databanks from other governmental data systems' (2006) 34 J Law Med and Ethics 372.

research studies using databases focussing on, for example, whether ethnicity or skin colour be determined by genes. No consent has been sought for these. Some US states also explicitly permit use for this reason. Maryland permits use for 'research and administrative purposes', Massachusetts for 'advancing … humanitarian purposes' and Alabama 'to assist medical research'.

This section will discuss two increasingly debated examples of function creep, familial testing and phenotype testing, and the issues that arise from these.

3.6.1 Familial Testing

3.6.1.1 Introduction and science

Familial testing, more formally known as 'outer-directed database trawling' is an intentional search of the database for a partial match. CODIS, for example, has the ability to search using three different criteria: high-stringency (where all 26 alleles must be identical), moderate stringency (where all alleles must match, but the target and candidate profiles can contain different numbers of alleles) or low stringency (where one or more alleles match at a loci). CODIS uses moderate stringency for standard searches, as this allows matches to be identified but takes into account that the DNA at the scene may be degraded, or maybe mixed with DNA from another individual. A partial match is conducted at low stringency. As described above, an individual inherits one allele from each parent, so having a number of alleles matching at specific loci might suggest a familial relationship. First degree relatives (parents and siblings) would be expected to share 50 per cent of alleles, and second degree relatives (aunts/uncles, half siblings, grandparents) would likely share 25 per cent. People that are unrelated would obviously have a lower match rate. On average, siblings match at between 16–17 of the 26 alleles, whereas unrelated people might have eight of the 26.[48] For this reason, while some US states require 13 of the 26 alleles to match in a familial search (meeting the CODIS/FBI definition for a low stringency search) other states require a higher number. Florida, for example, requires 21 of the 26 alleles to match.

---

[48] Sheldon Krimsky and Tania Simoncelli, *Genetic Justice* (New York: Columbia University Press 2010) p. 66. Note that in the UK, where 10 loci are tested, it has been commented that unrelated people would be expected to match at 6–7 alleles out of 20.

3.6.1.2 Accuracy of familial testing

The accuracy and efficiency of familial testing is unclear. Greeley[49] has commented that the chance of an unrelated person matching 13 of the 26 alleles (known as a 'false positive' result) is around three per cent, and the chance of an unrelated person having 13 of the 26 alleles matching with every marker having at least one match, is one in 2000. However, in a database of millions, this can still result in a significant number of false positives. Carmody[50] suggests that a partial match search might result in 8000 false positive results for every 'genuine positive' sibling. It has been suggested that in the UK 1500–3000 partial matches are identified on average.[51] These are then narrowed by geography and by Y-STR sampling, which looks for genetic markers along the Y chromosome, to trace family relationships among males. While it might seem like narrowing these numbers by eliminating false matches would be costly, the UK Forensic Science Service has claimed that the reduction of investigation time due to familial searching saves between UKP 0.5 and 2 million per murder investigation.

However, if the issue in relation to accuracy is phrased not as whether there will be false positives, but as whether a sibling who is in the database will actually be identified by the low stringency search, the answer becomes problematic. In a memo sent to the Attorney General of California by the head of the state DNA unit, it was commented that the FBI definition of partial match will preclude detection of 99.9 per cent of brothers, as many will not have alleles in common at enough genetic loci. Siblings could in fact potentially match at 0 alleles. Barca[52] concludes that 'familial searching remains an inexact science governed by probability and luck and does not yet have the same accuracy or finality as a well-executed direct DNA identification'.

In terms of statistics, the success rates of familial searching are unclear. One website which collects familial DNA reports lists 50 cases where it has been used successfully in an investigation of a cold case.[53]

---

[49] Henry Greeley, 'Family ties, the use of DNA offender databases to catch offender's kin' (2006) 34 J Law Med and Ethics 248, 252.

[50] Quoted in Sheldon Krimsky and Tania Simoncelli, *Genetic Justice* (New York: Columbia University Press 2010) p. 72.

[51] Ibid, p. 80.

[52] Dane Barca, 'Familian DNA testing, House Bill 3361 and the need for federal oversight' (2013) 64 Hastings LJ 499, 510.

[53] Denverda.org/DNA/Familial_DNA_Database-searches.htm. The most recent case listed is September 2014. The site is run by Denver District Attorney Mitchell Morrissey.

Of these, the vast majority, 37, occurred in the United Kingdom. Ten were US cases, two from New Zealand and one from Australia.[54]

3.6.1.3 Examples

The first reported use of familial testing occurred in 2001. In 1973, three girls were raped and murdered in South Wales. While DNA was found at the crime scene, the killer was never caught. In 2000 a forensic scientist searched the NDNAD for a match, but was unsuccessful. The following year he tried again, looking for a partial match. This revealed a 50 per cent match with Paul Kappen, a car thief. A subsequent investigation led to his father, Joseph Kappen, who had died 10 years previously. An exhumation and DNA test confirmed that Joseph Kappen was the killer.

The first conviction occurred in the United Kingdom in 2003. Michael Little died when a brick smashed through the windscreen of a car he was driving and struck him in the chest, causing a heart attack. The brick had clearly been thrown at the car from a footbridge. On examining the brick, some blood was revealed and was DNA tested. No match was found, nor was a subsequent dragnet of 300 people successful. Finally, the police searched for a familial match. This revealed 3525 potential siblings (on the basis of matching 11 out of 20 alleles). This number was then reduced to 25 by excluding all who were not white males living in the area. One of these matched 16 out of 20 alleles. Investigating this man led to his brother, Craig Harman, who was subsequently convicted of manslaughter.

One of the most famous US examples is that of the Grim Sleeper, an individual who had committed 10 murders in total between 1985 and 2007.[55] Familial searching identified Christopher Franklin as a relative of the offender. When the police interviewed him, he suggested that they should look at his father, Lonnie. The police followed Lonnie Franklin until they obtained his DNA, surreptitiously taken from an abandoned pizza crust, and used this to identify him as the killer.

3.6.1.4 Law

3.6.1.4.1 United States Familial searching is not regulated under Federal legislation. Initial FBI CODIS policy disallowed it, permitting states to share information only if an exact match was found. In 2006 this was

[54] The Australian example was not solved, but matched another crime scene sample.

[55] The nickname came from the fact that there was a hiatus in killing between 1988 and 2002.

amended to allow for sharing of partial matches, but the FBI CODIS unit director the following year was firm that 'the FBI does not do familial searching.' States, however, can set their own policy, and some states do permit familial searching, including California, Colorado, Texas, Nebraska and Virginia. Others, like Maryland, expressly prohibit partial matching.

3.6.1.4.2 United Kingdom Familial searching in the UK has been described as 'routine', although each search requires approval from the NDNAD Strategy Board. Between 2002 and 2011 familial searching was used in over 200 cases,[56] and in 2012–13, an additional 33 searches were performed. There have been 54 cases in which a relative has been identified where police have had no other lead, resulting in 38 convictions.

3.6.1.4.3 Australia There is nothing in the Australian Federal or State legislation that would prevent familial searching, suggesting that it is impliedly permitted. Indeed, there has been one example of use.[57]

In 2010 an independent review of the Crimes Act for the Minister for Home Affairs[58] concluded that while familial testing might be 'legally possible', the national database 'would need substantial modification in order to accommodate it'. It noted that some of this work was already under way.

3.6.1.4.4 New Zealand The New Zealand legislation discusses collection, but does not extend to use. As a result, the New Zealand Police have drafted a 2012 Protocol for Familial Testing. This requires that there be a serious offence, for which there has been no match with a database search. The District Crime Manager must approve any proposed familial search. The Protocol concludes that while a familial search is not considered to be in breach of the Act, the ethical issues involved in this kind of search necessitate consideration on a case by case basis, and that this would be accomplished through the requirement of the District Crime Manager's approval.

---

[56] Maguire, 'Familial Searching' (2014) 8(1) Forensic Sci Int Genet, 1.

[57] Denverda.org/DNA/Familial_DNA_Database-searches.htm.

[58] DNA forensic procedures: Further independent review of Part 1D of the Crimes Act 1914 (2010).

The first familial search occurred in 2004, and there have been at least 38 subsequent searches resulting in two convictions.[59] The legality of familial searching was challenged in *Police v Reekers*, where it was argued that the Act permitted only the use of a profile to determine whether it matched another sample. This argument was rejected, with Woodhouse J concluding that the Act permitted access to any information stored on the database 'for the purpose of forensic comparison' under s27, and that this therefore allowed for familial testing.

In January 2013 familial testing was openly criticised by a District Court judge, who commented 'it's a debate we haven't had, and should have. It shouldn't be something that comes in by default'.[60] The Justice Minister, Judith Collins, indicated satisfaction with the Police Guidelines in response, and did not see the issue as requiring legislative intervention.[61]

3.7 ETHICAL ISSUES WITH FAMILIAL TESTING

Some jurisdictions that do not permit familial testing have expressly taken this approach due to the ethical concerns involved. Some of these will be discussed below.

3.7.1 Familial Testing Effectively Expands the Database to Include Numerous Innocent People

One of the most serious concerns about familial testing is that it identifies people to the police for investigation, not due to any actions of their own, but due to a genetic link to another person. This effectively expands the database to include millions of innocent people who may be treated as suspects without any reasonable grounds for this. As has been discussed above, most States have some legislative restriction on when a person can be required to provide DNA for inclusion in the database. In addition, many States require the removal of the profile from the database if there are no charges filed, or no resulting conviction, or after a period of time. It is inconsistent to include these provisions but to allow familial testing,

---

59 *Police v Reekers* HC Auckland CRI-*2008*-404-0221, 8 October 2008 and *R v Jarden* [2009] NZCA 367.

60 Quoted in Tony Wall, 'Privacy Fear for DNA Dragnet', 20 January 2013, www.stuff.co.nz.

61 Ibid.

which effectively includes individuals in the database who would possibly not otherwise have come to the attention of the police in the relevant investigation. In both *King* and *Marper* it was thought that individuals arrested for an offence have a lower expectation of privacy than completely innocent people. Familial testing reverses this thinking, as current laws at least provide an arrested or detained person some protections in terms of requirements for collection and retention. There are no protections in the current laws for a family member, who may not even know that a close relative has provided a sample, but who is effectively included in this database due to their familial relationship with someone who has been required, or who has volunteered, to provide a sample.

3.7.1.1 Familial testing has a disproportionate effect on certain racial groups

While numerous innocent people will potentially be brought to police attention through familial testing, it is important to recognise that this will have a disproportionate effect on some racial groups. This will occur for two reasons. First, it is widely recognised that certain racial groups are overrepresented in the prison system. In New Zealand, for example, Maori comprise approximately 14 per cent of the general population, but 50 per cent of the prison population.[62] In the United States, African Americans are again approximately 14 per cent of the population, but make up about 40 per cent of the prison population. Indeed, one in three African American males are expected to go to prison in their lifetime.[63] A 2014 Prison Policy report showed that in the United States the national incarceration rate of African Americans was 2306 per 100,000, compared to the Hispanic rate of 831 per 100,000 and the White rate of 450 per 100,000. Nakashima[64] argues that if each person in the database has five first degree relatives, this may place approximately 33 per cent of African Americans under surveillance due to familial testing, compared to only approximately 7.5 per cent of Europeans.

In addition, these racial groups tend to have larger families, which also increases the likelihood that a close family member will be arrested. In New Zealand, demographic statistics from 2012 indicate that the average woman has 2.2 children. Among Maori women, however, the rate is 2.8. In the United States, census data from 2012 showed that people of

---

62 Department of Corrections Statistics, March 2013.

63 Sentencing Report on Racial Disparities in the US Criminal Justice System, submitted to the UN August 2013.

64 Nakashima, 'From DNA of family, a tool to make arrests' *Washington Post*, April 21, 2008.

central/south American descent have a birth rate of 96 per thousand, compared to 73 per thousand among Mexicans, 65 per thousand among African Americans, and only 63 per thousand among non-Hispanic Whites.

3.7.1.2 Familial testing raises privacy concerns

The obvious effect of familial searching is to bring to the attention of the police a person who would otherwise not be on their radar. There are clear issues involved with this. First, it amounts to holding people responsible for who they are, rather than what they have done. A person will be investigated purely because he is related to someone who has been previously arrested. Second, identifying individuals as relatives of someone in the database may in fact reveal personal facts about these individuals that they did not know, and perhaps did not wish to know. In some cases, it might reveal, for example, a genetic link to a particular person. In other cases, it might reveal the opposite – the lack of a genetic link where one had previously been assumed.

As an example of a family member's privacy being infringed, in the investigation of the BTK killer, police obtained a DNA sample and possible indication as to the killer's identity from a letter sent to the media.[65] Instead of investigating their suspect, and therefore revealing the evidence to him, the police investigated his daughter. They obtained his daughter's DNA from a pap smear and used this to ascertain that the killer was her father.

A familial search also potentially impacts on the privacy of the arrested person. If the police identify one person as a relative of the offender, this reveals to the family that this person has been arrested or has otherwise come into contact with the police (depending on the collection criteria). This might be a fact he had chosen not to share with the family, particularly if the reason for his inclusion in the database was a 'wrong place, wrong time' type situation where no charges resulted. Family members might reasonably assume that his presence on the database meant that he had been convicted of a serious offence, thereby affecting his standing or reputation within the family.

---

[65] The letter was sent on a floppy disk, which contained meta-data with the name Dennis, and a reference to a Lutheran church. A Google search of both of these revealed that Dennis Rader was a deacon of that church.

3.7.1.3 Familial testing may affect the functioning of the family

The fact that family members are being investigated because one member appears in the database may affect the functioning of that family. The databased member becomes in effect a genetic informant, who may be ostracised as a result. Erica Haimes,[66] an anthropologist, makes an interesting observational point:

> Realising that one is part of such a large pool of potential relatives could change individuals or family's self perception. Individuals might gain or lose social capital through that membership and the collectivity might experience an enhanced self-consciousness of themselves as a group. They might also for the first time, define themselves as being 'related' to each other.

3.7.1.4 Conclusion

While there have been some successes with using familial testing in criminal investigations, there are clearly issues with this type of testing. These issues, which relate to accuracy of the testing and ethical issues associated with the testing, explain why countries like the United States do not permit it, and countries like Australia and New Zealand have been hesitant in using it. These are matters that require careful consideration before accepting familial testing as a routine investigative tool.

3.7.2 Phenotyping

3.7.2.1 Introduction and science

Phenotyping, or Forensic DNA Phenotyping, involves genetic testing to identify an individual's phenotype, or their observable physical characteristics or traits.[67] It first appears to have been used in a criminal investigation in 2006, however, research into its use in criminal investigations has been carried out for far longer. Until recently, phenotyping has had a reputation for being problematic in terms of accuracy, but there are now hints that the science is developing to the extent that this could be an important investigative tool in the future.

The biggest challenge for using genes to determine phenotype is that most physical traits do not stem from one specific gene, but from a combination of genes (many of which we have yet to identify) and environmental influence. For this reason, testing for some traits may suffer from a low degree of accuracy. In other cases, the results may be

---

[66] 'Social and ethical issues in the use of familial searching in forensic investigations' (2006) 34 J Law, Med and Ethics, 263, 271.

[67] The word comes from the Greek: phainen – to show, and tupos – type.

difficult to translate into useful information. Imagine that a test reveals that a person has 45 per cent African, 30 per cent European and 25 per cent Native American ancestry. What would such a person look like in terms of skin colour? Unless the results can be translated into accurate visible traits, they will be of limited use in the investigative process.

In 2002 a company called DNA Print created a product called DNAWitness which was able to examine 176 genetic markers related to eye colour and racial ancestry. DNAWitness was used to help catch killers in two investigations in 2003 and 2007, but there was a feeling of discomfort about the technology and the company went out of business in 2009.

In 2013,[68] a study in the *International Journal of Legal Medicine* suggested that the issue with multiple genes determining phenotype might have been addressed, at least in relation to some traits. The study related to a tool called the 'Identitas Version 1 (v1) Forensic Chip' which enables 'parallel interrogation' of genetic material from numerous sites 'for inference of biogeographic ancestry, appearance, relatedness, and sex'. The study utilised 3034 blinded DNA samples, testing its accuracy for predicting various phenotypes. The results will be discussed below in relation to individual traits.

3.7.2.2 Testing for race/ancestry

Population-specific alleles can be used for ancestral genotyping, to distinguish between genotypes of Europeans, Africans, Native Americans and Asians. The difference in genetic markers between racial groups stems from the fact that as humans spread across the globe they developed different variations in appearance. Those variations that conferred an evolutionary advantage remained.

This form of phenotype testing, through a product called DNAWitness, was first used in an investigation in the United Kingdom in 2003 related to the murder of three women. Early eyewitness reports suggested that the offender was a white male aged approximately 35 years of age, and a dragnet of 1000 men was carried out on this basis with no success. The creator of DNAWitness was given a blind test of 20 samples by the police, and when his product was correct in all cases, was given the killer's sample to test. The test concluded that the police should be looking for a man who was 85 per cent sub-Saharan African and 15 per

---

[68] Keating, 'First all in one diagnostic tool for DNA intelligence: Genome-wide inference of biogeographical ancestry, appearance, relatedness, and sex with the Identitas V1 forensic chip' (2013) 127(3) IJLM 559.

cent Native American. As a result the creator informed the police that 'your guy could be African-American or Afro-Caribbean, but there is no chance that this is a Caucasian'. Based on this, the police widened the search and obtained a DNA sample from Derrick Todd Lee, an African-American male, who was later convicted of the murders. Interestingly, the police had earlier identified Lee as a potential suspect, but had excluded him following the witness description of a Caucasian male.

In 2007 DNAWitness was again used in the United Kingdom in Operation Minstead, a hunt for a sex offender known as the Night Stalker who had attacked more than 200 women and men between the ages of 68–93. DNAWitness suggested that the ancestral markers pointed to a person of Afro-Caribbean origin. As a result of this, hundreds of men fitting this description were asked to take part in an ultimately unsuccessful dragnet. Delroy Grant was finally arrested in 2010. Born in Jamaica, he fitted the DNAWitness profile.

Although ancestral markers were useful in identifying racial phenotype in the two cases discussed above, there were doubts about its accuracy. A 2001 study by Lowe[69] found that testing for ancestral markers was only accurate in 56 per cent of cases identifying a Caucasian, 67 per cent an Afro-Caribbean and 43 per cent a South Asian. More recent studies, however, have suggested more accurate testing and results are emerging. In 2011 a study of 145 samples showed 71 per cent accuracy in identifying African, 88 per cent Asian and 90 per cent Caucasian.[70] The 2012 Identitas study, however, has provided the most promising results. By examining multiple markers simultaneously, it reported 94 per cent accuracy on biparental continental ancestry. The issue of translating the information provided in the test into what the person might actually look like remains.

3.7.2.3 Testing for eye colour

A second characteristic that might be identifiable through phenotype testing is eye colour. Twin studies have suggested that eye colour is 85 per cent genetic. While there is no one gene that codes for eye colour, the OCA2 gene seems to be a major determinant gene. As with race, however, the issue is with how much of this is expressed (or visible). A

---

[69] 'Inferring ethnic origin by means of an STR profile' (2001) 119 *Forensic Science International* 17.

[70] Nevin, 'A preliminary mitochondrial DNA SNP genotyping assay for inferring genealogy' (2011) 43 Aust J Forensic Sci 39.

2007 study[71] showed 62 per cent accuracy between those individuals who had the genetic sequence in the OCA2 gene for blue eyes, and those who actually had blue eyes. A 2011 study across seven European countries showed accuracy of between 76–99 per cent for blue and brown eye colour using a tool called IRISPLEX.[72] The 2012 Identitas study showed similar accuracy, with an accuracy rate of 85 per cent for brown eye colour and 70 per cent for blue.

3.7.2.4 Testing for hair colour

The first test to appear for hair colour was for red hair. One gene, MC1R, has 30 identified variants. Of these, three commonly coincide with red hair, fair skin and freckling. Testing for this gene is thought to have about a 90 per cent accuracy rating. However, since red hair occurs naturally in only about 1–2 per cent of the population, it will be of limited use in an investigation. The Identitas test has further developed testing for hair colour, and the study reported accuracy rates of 72 per cent for brown hair, 63 per cent for blond, 58 per cent for black, and 48 per cent for red.

3.7.2.5 Testing for age

Since telomeres (the ends of chromosomes) degrade with age, it may be possible to determine a person's approximate age through genetic testing. Articles published in 2010 and 2011 have discussed the ability to predict a person's age from their genes. This appears to be accurate to within about five years.[73]

3.7.2.6 Future possible tests for visible traits

The Identitas study concluded by providing indications of possible future developments in phenotyping. It commented that the current version of the tool contains SNPs associated with freckles, moles, curly hair, skin color, earlobe shape and body height, however the prediction values of the currently-known markers were not high enough at that time to be practically useful. In addition, the study referred to the fact that the first study on facial shape features had just been published.

---

[71] Dickinson, 'Eye Color Explained' *Discover*, March 13 2007, quoted in Sheldon Krimsky and Tania Simoncelli, *Genetic Justice* ((New York: Columbia University Press 2010) p. 103.

[72] Walsh, 'DNA-based eye colour prediction across Europe with Irisplex System' (2012) 6 Forensic Sci Int'l; Genetics 220.

[73] Sven Bocklandt, 'Epigenetic predictor of age' (2011) *PLOS ONE* 6(6) e14821, Zubakov et al, 'Estimating human age from T-cell re-arrangements', (2010) *Current Biology* 20 (22).

3.7.2.7 Medical conditions

Another form of phenotyping might include medical traits and characteristics. With genetic testing available for over 1000 diseases,[74] DNA could be examined for a medical condition, and people could then be tracked through relevant hospital or pharmacy records. Other, more minor medical conditions, like some forms of adult stuttering or being left handed are also thought to have a genetic basis, and could similarly be tested for.

3.7.2.8 The law

3.7.2.8.1 United States Phenotyping is currently not permitted through CODIS. This appears to be a deliberate decision. The ability to test for phenotype was known when CODIS was first developed, but Krimsky and Simoncelli[75] have commented that phenotyping was not included as an acceptable use due to political sensitivity. This position may change, however. Murphy refers to the National Institutes of Justice[76] funding of studies on Alternative Genetic Markers of 'ethnic origin, physical characteristics, and skin, hair or eye colour'.[77] She concludes that 'if money talks, then the government – including the law enforcement arm of the government – is telling us that it is very interested in genetic tests that go far beyond the "string of numbers"'.

The laws of individual states vary. As many have basically adopted the Federal law, this amounts to not permitting phenotyping, although this conclusion is implicit in the language used and may be subject to interpretation. Only Indiana, Rhode Island and Wyoming explicitly disallow the use of DNA to obtain phenotypic information.

3.7.2.8.2 Europe The Council of the European Union has urged member states to exchange only non-coding loci information, and not to exchange information 'not known to provide information about hereditary characteristics'.[78] In addition, under the Prum Convention of 2005,[79]

---

[74] Genetics Home Reference, ghr.nlm.nih.gov.

[75] Sheldon Krimsky and Tania Simoncelli, *Genetic Justice* (New York: Columbia University Press 2010) p. 95.

[76] This is the research arm of the Department of Justice.

[77] National Institutes of Justice, Forensic DNA: Alternative genetic markers research projects list, referred to in Erin Murphy, 'Legal and ethical issues in forensic DNA phenotyping'. NYU School of Law Working Paper (2013), p. 1.

[78] Council Resolution of 25 June 2001 on the exchange of DNA analysis results (2001/C 187/01). This provision is repeated in Council Resolution of 30 November 2009 on the exchange of DNA analysis results (2009/C 296/01).

party states are not permitted to make available to other states data from coding segments of the DNA.

Within individual countries, only Belgium and Germany specifically prohibit phenotyping (although Germany allows testing for gender which is technically a phenotype). In Belgium, it is in fact a criminal offence to test non-coding portions of DNA.

Holland is interesting as it specifically permits phenotype testing. A 2003 amendment to the Dutch Code of Criminal Procedures (the Wetboek van Strafvordering) permits the phenotyping of DNA found at a crime scene and belonging to an unknown suspect, but limits this to certain specific 'External Visible Characteristics' (EVCs) that are visible at birth.[80] At present this extends to only gender and race, but more traits can be included in the future by Order in Council.[81]

3.7.2.8.3 United Kingdom While phenotyping is carried out in the United Kingdom there does not appear to be any specific legislative policy regulating this. The Police, Science and Technology Strategy 2003–8 indicated a commitment to support development of research which will 'predict physical characteristics' from DNA, and it has been seen above that the DNA database profiles have been used to further studies in this area.

3.7.3 Ethical Concerns

There are three main ethical concerns with phenotyping. These are issues of privacy, the 'right not to know', and racial profiling.

3.7.3.1 Privacy

In *Maryland v King* the court's decision that collection of DNA was a reasonable, warrantless, search was influenced by the fact that the DNA profile used non-coding DNA only. When the government was pressed by the court about the more personal, sensitive material contained in the sample, it responded that it was 'probably correct that the individual will retain a reasonable expectation of privacy in the genomic material that

---

[79] Also known as Schengen III, its full title is the Convention on the stepping-up of cross-border cooperation, particularly in combating terrorism, cross-border crime and illegal migration.

[80] This would exclude, for example, testing for age and height.

[81] For more information, see Koops, 'Forensic DNA phenotyping: regulatory issues' (2008) Columbia Sci and Tech LT 158.

does not reveal identity'.[82] Phenotype testing requires use of the coding regions of DNA, suggesting that there might be more of an expectation of privacy, thus preventing this form of testing.

While this increased expectation of privacy might exist in relation to a sample collected from an individual, phenotyping would be carried out not on a sample provided by an individual, but on a DNA sample which has been abandoned at a crime scene. This abandoned DNA likely has no expectation of privacy.[83] Even if this is not a correct interpretation of the limits of an expectation of privacy, the broad definitions of 'identity' discussed in *Marper* and *King* would probably include physical characteristics, and therefore permitting phenotype testing as part of identifying the offender.

3.7.3.2 The right not to know

The Universal Declaration on the Human Genome and Human Rights of November 1997 in Article 5(c) states that 'the right of each individual to decide whether or not to be informed of the results of genetic examination and the resulting consequences should be respected'. The European Convention on Human Rights and Biomedicine Article 10.2 states that 'everyone is entitled to know any information collected about his or her health. However, the wishes of individuals not to be so informed shall be observed.'

These two Articles are generally considered to refer to a right not to know information about medical conditions. If the phenotype testing reveals medical conditions, then using this as a way of searching for an offender will likely result in the offender finding out about this condition during the trial. If he is unaware, this may be in breach of the right not to know.

An argument under this heading is clearly of limited scope, and would not apply to any characteristics that were readily observable. This might be the reason behind the Dutch law restricting phenotype searching to External Visible Characteristics only.

3.7.3.3 Racial profiling

There is some argument that phenotyping will exacerbate racial profiling, as it will focus investigations on particular racial groups. While there will

---

[82] 567 US_ (2012).

[83] See, for example, 'There is no subjective expectation of privacy in discarded genetic material, just as there is no subjective expectation of privacy in fingerprints or footprints left in a public place' per Justice Johnson, *Washington v Athan* 160 Wn 2d 354 (2007).

be a focus on race if ancestry markers are searched for, using the term 'racial profiling' to describe this is misleading. Racial Profiling uses race as the primary reason to suspect an individual. Phenotyping on the other hand leads the police to search for a person of a particular race because the DNA indicates that the person is part of a particular racial group. The use of the DNA in this case is no different to an eyewitness telling police about skin colour, and police restricting their search to a racial group as a result.

It is even possible that testing for ancestry will reduce racial tension. In 1999 a 16-year-old Dutch girl, Marianne Vaastra, was murdered. The police were unable to identify the offender, and the community became frustrated. Some began pointing to a local hostel, in which Kurdish, Iraqi and Afghani asylum seekers were staying, and tension mounted in the community. A forensic geneticist examined the semen found on the body and was able to show that the offender was from Western Europe. While the geneticist knew that his actions were 'completely illegal', he was able to diffuse tensions, and this case led to the Netherlands law permitting ancestral testing.[84] Murphy[85] provides another example of a Californian murder, thought to be Asian gang related until testing showed the offender was Native American/Hispanic.

3.7.4 Conclusion

While phenotyping sounds problematic, an analysis of the issues suggests it is possibly less so than familial testing. Provided the genetic material is taken from crime scene samples, and is restricted to information that an eyewitness could provide (in other words, not including medical information) it is probably closer to fingerprint evidence than private information.

The real concern should actually be with accuracy, and with understanding the results. Accuracy appears to be improving, at least for some eye and hair colours. Understanding the results will be more tricky. What does a person of mixed race actually look like? This may cause problems with the investigation, if the police are encouraged by their interpretation of the data to search for one external visible characteristic, when the offender does not externalise it.

---

84 Martin Enserink, 'Emerging forensic field may hit legal, ethical obstacles' (2011) 331 *Science* p. 840.

85 Erin Murphy, 'Legal and ethical issues in forensic DNA phenotyping' NYU School of Law Working Paper (2013).

3.8 THE FUTURE: A UNIVERSAL DATABASE?

The next likely stage in the development of DNA databases is a consideration of a universal database where every person is required to provide a sample. Calls for a universal database are emerging from both politicians and judges. As examples of the former, in 1999, New York Mayor Rudolph Guiliani proposed collecting DNA samples from all newborns as part of newborn screening for both medical and law enforcement purposes. In 2006, UK Prime Minister Tony Blair argued for universal collection, giving multiple options for the appropriate time (state newborn screening, as part of child vaccination, as a requirement for entering school, as a requirement for a driver's or marriage license, or as part of a national identification card). As examples of the latter, Lord Justice Stephen Sedley in 2007 stated that 'everybody, guilty or innocent, should expect their DNA to be on file for the absolutely rigorously restricted purpose of crime detection and prevention.'[86]

3.8.1 Arguments in Favour of a Universal Database

3.8.1.1 Crime prevention and investigation

Some academics have suggested that a universal database would act as a strong deterrent to crime. People contemplating committing crime would be aware that there would be a high likelihood of their being caught due to their DNA being in the universal database, and would therefore likely refrain from criminal conduct. In addition, Quarmby[87] notes that a universal database would prevent terrorists from assuming false identities.

It is not clear that this would be a sufficient deterrent. The prospect of being caught may logically sound like it would deter crime, but this is often not the reality. In 1999, the Scottish Office Central Research Unit carried out a survey which found that more than 70 per cent of respondents thought that CCTV cameras would deter crime, as offenders would be more easily identified. The UK Parliament, however, considered it 'difficult to quantify the benefits of CCTV'[88] in this regard. A

---

[86] Quoted in 'All UK "must be on DNA database"' *BBC News*, 5 September 2007, at 27.

[87] Ben Quarmby, 'The case for national DNA identification cards' (2003) Duke L and Tech Rev 2.

[88] Select Committee on Home Affairs, 5th Report.

study by Prainsack and Kitzberger[89] of 26 inmates revealed that they believed DNA forensics to be 'very effective and extremely difficult to avoid', and were knowledgeable enough to be able to explain how DNA could be found in blood, hair or saliva. Yet, their status as inmates suggests that this did not deter them from committing the crime.

In terms of the investigation of crime, while a universal database may appear like the ultimate investigative tool (under the theory that if everyone is on the database, there will be a hit) it may in fact impede investigation. A universal database will effectively bury the offender in a mound of innocent people who would never have come to police attention in connection with the particular crime (or even in their lives). While there will be a guaranteed needle in the haystack, the haystack will more closely resemble a hay field or hay farm, making the search perhaps unworkably large. Further, the more people in the database, the more likely it is that false positives will arise. The time and effort required to eliminate these additional people will deflect resources from the investigation. Finally, DNA is only collected in 1 per cent of crimes, so it will not assist in the other 99 per cent.

3.8.1.2 To reduce discrimination of some groups

Lord Justice Sedley pointed out in his proposal that if there was a universal database 'at least one aspect of the criminal justice system would not be weighed disproportionately with respect to any racial or ethnic group.'[90] Some statistics about demographics of the database, and the impact of familial searching on particular racial groups, were discussed above. Including everyone on the database would remove this disproportionality. Further, a universal database removes ethical considerations under the current system of having non-charged or non-convicted people on the database, and familial searching, and dragnets.

The problem with these arguments is that creating a system which potentially breaches the rights of a large number of people because the current system breaches the rights of a different, smaller, number of people is not a solution. It may address the concerns about stigmatisation, but an individual who feels that their inclusion in the database is a breach of privacy is unlikely to be suitably placated by the argument that everybody else's rights are being breached as well.

---

[89] Prainsack and Kitzberger, 'DNA behind bars: Other ways of knowing forensic DNA technologies' (2009) 39 Soc Stud of Sci 51, 54.

[90] Quoted in 'All UK "must be on DNA database"' *BBC News*, 5 September 2007, at 27.

3.8.1.3 It is inevitable

As Smith[91] puts it, 'if we do not design and build an inclusive database, the databases we have will expand anyway, without necessary protections and without realising the full public safety benefit of the technology'. The statistics on familial searching have suggested that 33 per cent of black people in the United Kingdom can come to the attention of the police through a familial search. If this is effectively a universal database anyway, perhaps it is better to design and create a universal database, and specifically debate and attempt to resolve the ethical reasons rather than allow function creep to ignore them. Better some protections, than none at all. This is probably the strongest argument in favour of a universal database.

3.8.2 Arguments Against a Universal Database

3.8.2.1 Overall concept of genetic privacy

Although Lord Justice Sedley would 'rigorously restrict' the use of DNA to use for crime prevention, this restriction is unlikely to be possible to enforce. The theme of function creep throughout this chapter is likely to continue. It would further be difficult to restrict unauthorised access. We have already seen above how lab technicians in the United Kingdom and in New Zealand have been shown to have retained DNA evidence instead of destroying it. In addition, there are valid concerns about hacking into the database, which would be difficult to prevent.

There are currently energetic debates about genetic privacy, particularly in terms of medical treatment, with some groups arguing that the individual claim to privacy in their DNA is outweighed by the benefit to society in curing diseases, or in treating illnesses early to maximise health and to minimise the financial burden on the state. If there was a universal database, and people were required to submit a sample for the public benefit of crime prevention (and also for the benefit of reduction in public expenditure in crime investigation and punishment) pressure would likely emerge to access these samples for the public benefit of health maximisation (and reduction in public health expenditure). It would be difficult to argue that the latter is not as worthy an objective as the former.

More broadly, it is difficult already to reconcile the differing approaches to genetic privacy in the strong protection in the employment

---

[91] Smith, 'Let's make the DNA identification database as inclusive as possible' 34 J Law Med and Ethics 385, 388.

and health contexts, and the weaker protection in the criminal justice context. A universal database would possibly reopen this debate.

3.8.2.2 Protection of democracy

Creating what allows for mass surveillance by database goes against western ideas of democracy. As Campbell and Lynch[92] state, 'such a crime control mechanism would run contrary to the prevailing political principles of limited state intervention and shift the ethos of the criminal justice system'. It is unclear what this would do to society, but there is likely to be a negative response to a government acting in such a way. While the current inclusion of those not convicted in the database has challenged this, a universal database would damage it, if not destroy it.

3.8.2.3 Resources

It currently costs approximately $US100 to process DNA for inclusion into the database. Some scholars have estimated that a universal database in the United States would cost $670 million per year, not including additional costs for increased personnel, training, equipment and lab space. To put this in perspective, the United Kingdom NDNAD currently contains over 6.7 million profiles, out of a population of 64 million. To add another 57 million at a cost of UKP 65 per person[93] is a substantial cost. On the other hand, it was suggested in the United Kingdom that familial searching saved between UKP 0.5 and 2 million per murder investigation and there appears to be an average of 550 murders in the United Kingdom per year. The initial costs in creating a universal database might be financially viable if a longer term view was taken.

In terms of resources (for example laboratory equipment, personnel) there are already reports of backlogs in US states in processing DNA samples. A 2013 newspaper article[94] reported that Houston had a backlog of 6663 rape kits dating back 10 years. Other states have also admitted to having substantial backlogs.[95] It has been estimated that several hundred thousand convicted offender samples nationwide are awaiting processing

---

92 Liz Campbell and Nessa Lynch, 'Competing paradigms? The use of DNA powers in youth justice' (2012) 12(1) *Youth Justice* 3, 17.

93 This is based on an estimate of US$100 per profile.

94 Cindy Horswell, 'Expanded DNA database becoming a crime solver' *Houston Chronicle* 2 January 2013.

95 In Arizona, for example, there appears to be a several year delay in receiving results, see 'Funding might help ease backlog of Arizona's DNA cases' *Eyewitness News* 3 August 2013.

due to resource issues. The current backlog has led to errors in submitting samples, leading to the samples not being accepted by CODIS. Increasing the workload of these laboratories by 300 million samples[96] does not seem feasible. In 2001 Dr Samuel Baechtel, of the FBI Laboratory, commented:[97]

> Personally, I cannot imagine doing DNA typing on every person who is arrested or even every person who is indicted. People that suggest these things have probably not been near their local crime laboratory in a long time. We have our hands full just handling cases going to trial and getting the evidence out there to either exclude or include someone.

By March 2003, it was reported that there was a backlog of 350,000 rape and murder samples to process. California's broadening of collection criteria from violent felons to all felons resulted in a 10-fold expansion of the database and quadrupled its backlog. For these reasons, Simoncelli concluded that a universal database was 'absurd'.[98]

3.8.3 Conclusion

While calls for a universal database are emotionally or intuitively appealing to society (and are likely intended to be so) this needs to be carefully considered before being implemented. It must be asked whether the calls for a universal database are because there is a genuine belief in such a database's ability to substantially reduce crime, or because this is an effective way to highlight a flawed system. The potential ethical, social and resource issues argue persuasively against universality, particularly when it is considered that the potential benefits may not be significant.

3.9 RECONSIDERING THE CASE OF CHILD B

The scenario described in Chapter 1 raised several issues in relation to this chapter. Some of these will be discussed below.

---

[96] This figure equates to the approximate number of people in the US not currently in the database.

[97] Tania Simoncelli, 'Dangerous excursions: The case against expanding forensic DNA databases to innocent persons' (2006) J Law, Med and Ethics 390, 393.

[98] Ibid, 394.

3.9.1 Mr B was Arrested and Released Without Charge but his DNA was Taken

The taking of a DNA sample when an individual has not been charged is permitted in the United Kingdom, although the sample and profile must be destroyed as soon as reasonably practicable (and the sample within six months of taking at the latest). In the United States it is also permitted from arrestees, but with no requirements for destruction, unless a court order is sought. In Australia, it can only be taken by consent, or by an order from a Senior Police Officer or Magistrate. Such an order requires, inter alia, a belief on reasonable grounds that the individual committed an imprisonable offence, and that the DNA sample will confirm or disprove his involvement. A fight at a sports event may not result in sufficient charges, and since Mr B was arrested at the scene, DNA evidence may not be required for identification purposes, unless it is used to show whether he was just ‘present’ or actually involved in the fight. In New Zealand, a sample can be taken from those detained for an imprisonable offence, but this is to be entered into a separate, temporary database, and is to be destroyed if no charge or conviction results.

The taking of samples from arrestees has been considered in two cases. In *Marper*, the European Court of Human Rights considered a blanket retention policy to be a breach of the individual’s rights under Article 8 European Convention on Human Rights. The United Kingdom law changed (as above) in response, but it has been questioned whether this is sufficient. In *King*, the majority of the Supreme Court considered that the governmental interest in identification outweighed any privacy right the individual in question might have.

In this case, Mr B might be able to challenge the retention of his profile in the DNA database, depending on jurisdiction. Child B might be able to challenge the inadmissibility of the DNA evidence on the grounds that (depending on jurisdiction), his uncle’s DNA profile should have been destroyed. An argument on these grounds failed in *King*, but in a 5:4 decision. Such an argument might be more successful in other jurisdictions due to their requirements for destruction of samples and profiles.

3.9.2 The Police Perform a Dragnet

Dragnets are permitted in most jurisdictions, although they are generally not effective in finding a match to the crime scene sample. The key feature of a dragnet is that those asked to submit samples provide voluntary consent for this.

In this case, Mr B refused to provide consent. He gave several, commonly used, reasons for doing this, relating to lack of probable cause and privacy. The police attempted to convince him to comply with their request by discussing possible negative consequences for him not providing consent, and as a result he reluctantly agreed. This form of possible coercion by the police has been reported in the United States and in the United Kingdom, and civil suits have been filed as a result.

3.9.3 The Familial Testing

When the dragnet was unsuccessful, the police turned to familial testing. Familial testing requires only a partial match to the crime scene sample to be established, and has attracted criticism for its inaccuracy and its ability to produce 'false positive' results. In the United Kingdom familial testing is considered routine, but in other countries a different approach is taken. United States Federal policy is not to permit familial testing, although individual states can create their own rules. It appears to be an acceptable practice in Australia and in New Zealand, however in the latter jurisdiction a Police-designed Protocol must be followed.

This case highlights some of the ethical issues relating to familial testing. The obvious issue is privacy. Once Mr B is identified as being related to one of the offenders, his family is placed under investigation, even to the extent of the police following minors and surreptitiously collecting a Coke can to obtain a DNA sample. The testing may affect Mr B's standing in the family, as he may not have wanted them to know that he had been arrested in the past. Further, he has effectively become a genetic witness against his own nephew. While the B family is Caucasian, familial testing has been noted to have a disproportionate effect on non-Caucasian families.

3.9.4 Phenotyping for Race, Hair and Eye Colour

In the case study, the crime scene sample is phenotyped, meaning that racial, hair and eye colours are identified. While accuracy of tests for these traits is increasing, there is still a concern that a person's genetic make-up might not be reflected in his appearance. Phenotyping requires use of the DNA sample, and not just the profile. It is currently not permitted in most countries, with the United Kingdom and Holland being the notable exceptions.

In this case, the phenotyping was accurate in terms of eye colour, but not in terms of hair colour. This potentially could have misled the police into eliminating Child B as a suspect. If Child B had been non-Caucasian, the physical description might have provided racial tension within the community.

3.9.5 Call for Universal DNA Database

Following conviction, there was a call for a Universal Database to be created, to help the police investigate crime. Issues relating to privacy and resourcing have been discussed in this chapter.

4. The 'criminal gene'

4.1 INTRODUCTION

Chapter 2 discussed the rise of the eugenics movement, and its subsequent decline following World War II. A period of relative tranquility then followed in the United States, lessening the need for eugenic thought to re-emerge. In the 1960s, however, this tranquil period ended. In the United States, crime rates increased dramatically, with the per capita rate of reported violent offences tripling between 1960 and 1978. Between 1965 and 1970, violent crime grew more than 16 per cent per year. Again, it appears that society turned to genetics to explain this.

This chapter will begin by considering the first attempted return to a criminal gene argument, with XYY Syndrome. It will then discuss the growing scientific understanding of the interaction of genes and environment in understanding behavior. With this new understanding, it will consider some of the genes currently associated with criminal tendencies and discuss some of the scientific studies which attempt to understand the role genes play in the likelihood of engaging in criminal conduct.

4.2 THE RETURN OF GENETIC DETERMINISM: XYY SYNDROME

4.2.1 XYY Syndrome Emerges as Possible Genetic Link

In 1956 Swedish geneticists published research concluding that the normal number of chromosomes in human cells was not 48 as was previously thought, but was in fact 46.[1] Over the next five years, this announcement was followed by further publications of reports of individuals with chromosomal aneuploidies (additional or missing chromosomes). In 1959 individuals with 47XXY, 45X and 47XXX aneuploidies

[1] It had previously been thought to be 48: Tjio and Levan, 'The chromosome number of man' (1956) 42(1) *Hereditas* 1.

were identified,[2] and the following year 48XXYY was discovered. The first published case of a man with 47XYY was reported in 1961.[3]

The first suggestion that a chromosomal aneuploidy, specifically XYY, might be significant in terms of behavior appeared in 1964.[4] A study identified nine XYY patients at Carstairs State Hospital in Scotland,[5] a special security hospital for the developmentally disabled. The study reported that the patients' 'outstanding personality features were extreme instability and irresponsibility, and in their criminal behavior they did not appear to have considered any but the most immediate consequences of their actions'. They further demonstrated 'very little depth of feeling in their emotional responses, or in relationships with others'. At least five of the men had previous criminal convictions, and three of these had been convicted before the age of 10. The mean age for first conviction was 13 years, compared with 18 for the control group of XY men. Other notable characteristics were height (of the nine patients, six were reported as being over 6 feet tall), and below average intelligence (eight were classified as 'high-grade mental defectives'). The response to this study of nine men was immediate. One scientist commented that 'there are no born criminals, but persons with the XYY defect have considerably higher chances'.[6] Scientists began to identify and study other XYY men, and reported similar results. One study described XYY men as 'unstable and immature, without feeling or remorse, unable to construct adequate personal relationships … and committing apparently motiveless crimes …'.[7]

In 1969 Gibbens[8] summarized approximately 20 studies of XYY males in prisons or secured hospitals. These studies showed that while the

---

[2] The number refers to the number of chromosomes. Females are generally 46XX and males 46XY.

[3] Sandberg et al., 'An XYY human male' (1961) 278 *Lancet* 488.

[4] The man identified in 1961 was described in the study as 44 years old, 6 feet tall, and of average intelligence. His only recorded behavioral issue was his inability to keep employers satisfied with his performance as a manual worker. He was tested solely due to the fact that he had a daughter with Down's Syndrome.

[5] Jacobs, 'Aggressive behavior, mental subnormality and the XYY male' (1965) 208 *Nature* 1351.

[6] Lejeune, quoted in Richard Morris, *Perspectives in Abnormal Behavior* p. 226.

[7] Price and Whatmore, 'Behavioral disorders and the pattern of crime amongst XYY males identified at a maximum security hospital' (1967) Brit Med J 553.

[8] 'The delinquent and his brain' (1969) 62 J Royal Soc of Med 57.

natural birth occurrence of XYY syndrome was approximately 0.1 per cent (or one in 975 births), the pooled frequency of the XYY men in the studies (and therefore in jail) was 72/3813, or 1.89 per cent, and the median for each study was 2.05 per cent. The studies suggested, therefore, that the number of XYY males in these secured facilities was over 20 times the natural birth occurrence. XYY syndrome therefore became linked with an increased likelihood of criminality. Characteristics of XYY were commonly listed as height (over 6 feet tall), low IQ, and aggressive behavior. They also often had acne scarring.

4.2.2 XYY Syndrome in the Courts 1965–1968

In 1965, Daniel Hugon was charged with the murder of a prostitute in a hotel in Paris, France. His lawyer argued that it was relevant to the case that Hugon was an XYY male. The judge responded to this argument by adjourning the trial and appointing a three man medical commission to consider whether, or to what extent, XYY syndrome could absolve a man of legal responsibility. The commission found Hugon competent to stand trial, accepting that XYY syndrome did bring on 'troubles of comportment and humor', but not that it made men 'killers'. Hugon was subsequently found guilty of murder. The effect to which the scientific evidence of XYY Syndrome affected his sentence is unclear. The case report stated that due to 'extenuating circumstances' which were described as 'unspecified'[9] the prosecution suggested a sentence of 5–10 years for the murder, and the jury settled on 7 years.[10]

In 1967, XYY Syndrome made newspaper headlines as a result of two cases. In the United States, Richard Speck, who had been convicted of the torture, rape and murder of eight student nurses, was falsely reported as being XYY syndrome by the *New York Times* in a story on XYY syndrome which ran over three consecutive days.[11] This 'identification' as XYY appeared to be based on his appearance and previous criminal history. Speck was over 6 feet tall, acne scarred, had a below average IQ and a history of violence against women. Speck was not, however, XYY. He had undergone chromosomal analysis the previous year, as a result of a geneticist suggesting possible XYY Syndrome to Speck's lawyer due to

---

[9] And therefore possibly not XYY, which had been specified at least in the pre-trial pleadings.

[10] It has been noted that immediately after this trial, an attorney for a man convicted of murdering a young girl filed a demand for analysis of his client's chromosome pattern, to assist with an appeal.

[11] *The Times* also published similar stories.

his physical characteristics, but this analysis had revealed that Speck was 46XY. Nevertheless, the story was front page news for three days, attracting significant public attention. In the second case an Australian, Robert Tait, was (correctly) identified as being XYY. Tait had been convicted in 1962 of murder, committed while on parole for sexual assault, and in 1967 was part of a study of inmates at Pentridge Prison, Melbourne, which revealed his XYY status.

In 1968 in Australia, XYY Syndrome was successfully raised in court, and had a notable impact on the trial. Lawrence Hannell was found not guilty by reason of insanity of the murder of 77-year-old Mary Redfern, due to his XYY status.

4.2.3 XYY Syndrome Reconsidered

In the mid- to late-1960s, XYY Syndrome became a popular topic of discussion. Numerous scientific studies were published,[12] cases discussed its impact on criminal responsibility, and the media reported the stories.[13] One scientist, Lederberg,[14] described the studies as providing 'one of the most tangible leads for connecting genetic constitution with behavior in man'. By the end of the 1960s, however, interest waned, and a backtracking in the scientific reporting could be seen. Several reasons for this can be identified. First, the rarity of the condition meant that the majority of the discussion had already occurred.[15] Second, scientists began publishing reports of 'well-adjusted XYY individuals',[16] which suggested that it was not merely genetics that resulted in the high levels of offending rates of XYY males, but that the environment also appeared to play some role.[17]

---

[12] Fox, 'XYY offender, a modern myth' (1971) 62(1) J Crim Law and Criminology 59, comments that by 1971 there were over 200 articles. It should be noted that many were duplicate publications, the Scotland study, for example, appears as at least four different articles.

[13] Witkin, for example, describes the 'prominent attention' given in the press to these stories: 'Criminality in XYY and XXY men' (1976) 193 *Science* 547.

[14] 'The genetics of human nature' (1973) 40(3) *Social Research* 375.

[15] West, 'Psychological contributions to criminology' (1988) 28 Brit J Criminology, 77.

[16] See, for example, Brown, 'Males with an XYY sex chromosome complement' (1968) 5 J Med Genet 341, and Hook 'Behavioral implications of the human XYY genotype' (1973) 179 *Science* 139.

[17] Corning, for example, commented that 'social learning' could facilitate or inhibit violent behaviors amongst XYY males: 'Towards a general theory of violent aggression' (1972) 11 *Social Science Information* 7.

The third, and strongest, reason for the decreased scientific interest, was peer criticism. Following the initial hype over the over-representation of XYY men in the prisons or secure units, more attention began to be paid to the studies themselves.[18] The original Jacobs study when read properly failed to actually show a significant increase in violence among XYY men. The nine XYY males had a cumulative total of 89 convictions. Of these, only eight were offences against another person (the remainder being offences against property). This average of 0.9 violent offences per XYY man was substantially less than the average of 2.6 in the control group of XY males (although the control group had only an average of 7.7 property convictions). Similar results were found in studies in 1967[19] and 1972,[20] demonstrating a failure to show that XYY men were more violent than XY men.

Most significantly, scientists began to criticize the methodology of the earlier studies. Witkin[21] and Hook[22] both commented on the low numbers of participants in the studies, and Witkin pointed specifically to a number of reports of XYY that were based on observations of a single individual only.[23] In addition, a number of studies did not include control groups, meaning there was no comparison with which to judge the criminality of the XYY man. Freyne further commented that factors like intelligence, education level and socio-economic factors were often not taken into account in studies. When these were factored in, the elevated crime rate

---

[18] Noel, in a 1974 study of seven XYY and 28 XXY men, found no evidence of below-average intelligence or increased criminality among the XYY men: 'The XYY syndrome: Reality or myth?' (1974) 5(5) *Clinical Genetics* 387. Thielgaard in 1983 found that there was only a slight IQ deficit in XYY men, and that the only area where impulse control appeared to differ between XYY and control males was in the area of spousal violence: 'Aggression and the XYY personality' (1983) 6 Int J Law and Psych 413.

[19] Price and Whatmore, 'Behavioral disorders and the pattern of crime amongst XYY males identified at a maximum security hospital' (1967) Brit Med J 553.

[20] Owen, 'The 47 XYY male: A review' (1972) 78 Psychol Bull 209.

[21] 'Criminality in XYY and XXY men' (1976) 193 *Science* 547.

[22] Hook, 'Behavioral implications of the human XYY genotype' (1973) 179 *Science* 139.

[23] One example is J. Cowie, 'XYY constitution in prepubertal child' (1968) 1 Brit Med J 748. The study discusses one child, eight years of age. This child was described as having 'a particular interest in sharp-pointed objects … he rammed a screwdriver into a little girl's abdomen'.

among XYY men lowered.[24] Reviewers of the studies also commented that the higher proportion of XYY men in prisons or secure hospitals could be explained by the admission criteria for the studies. One common characteristic of XYY is above-average height. Hook describes the methodology of two of the seven studies as selecting participants by height. Witkin found a similar methodology in another study, which began by identifying all men born in Denmark between 1944 and 1947 (28,884 men) and then applied a cut-off height of 184cm. This reduced the number down to 4558, 12 of which were XYY. Finally, the criminal convictions of this group were considered, and it was found that five of the 12 XYY men (or 41.7 per cent) had convictions, compared to only nine XY men. In other words, the studies admitted subjects by a height criterion that would by definition result in an increased occurrence of XYY men.[25]

A similar backtracking occurred in the courts. In 1968 in Germany, Ernst-Dieter Beck was sentenced to life imprisonment for the murder of three women. At trial, scientists argued that his XYY status meant that he was unable to control his impulses. The court disagreed, finding that he was aware of what he was doing. In 1969 a similar argument was rejected in the US in the case of Sean Farley, who was convicted of rape and murder in New York, with the jury rejecting the defence of insanity.[26]

A detailed consideration of XYY occurred in 1975 in *People v Yukl*.[27] Charles Yukl had been charged with the murder of a 23-year-old woman, and it was noted that he had already served time for a similar, brutal murder. Yukl planned to plead insanity, on the basis of XYY Syndrome. The court rejected his request to introduce evidence of his XYY status, commenting that the studies were not convincing:

---

[24] In a 2012 study, involving 161 XYY men and up to 100 controls per individual (who were selected for having the same month and year of birth) it was noted that when controlled for socio-economic status, the conviction risk of both groups was similar.

[25] For example, Power comments that a New York prisoner who is over 6 feet tall and had been in a max. security hospital has a 1-in-4 chance of being XYY: 'Subnormality and crime II' (1969) 9 Med, Sci and Law 162.

[26] These cases were discussed in Fox, 'XYY offender, a modern myth' (1971) 62(1) *Journal of Criminal Law and Criminology* 59.

[27] 372 N.Y.S. 2d 715, (Sup Ct 1975). The case also considered other XYY cases, notably *Millard v State* 8 Md App 419 (1970) 261 A 2d 227, *People v Tanner*, Court of Appeals of California, second district division three, December 17, 1970, and *People v Farley* (Sup Ct, Queens County, Indictment No. 1827 [April 30, 1969]).

> [T]he sampling, thus far, has been inadequate and inconclusive. A built-in bias exists because samples comprised of institutionalized persons will, of course, contain more than a fair number of violent and aggressive types. The statistical significance to be attached to the results of these studies is in doubt until such time as adequate control group data can be compiled.

A recent case referring to XYY was *Re SLD*.[28] In this case, a 13-year-old boy kidnapped and murdered a 3-year-old girl. While he was identified as being XYY, the judge commented that:

> For a while it was theorized that the XYY karyotype … was associated with a predisposition to violent criminal behavior. More recent studies however contradict that proposition and I do not place any reliance upon it as an indicator of future dangerousness.

4.2.4 Conclusion

Nelson,[29] writing in 1975, summed up the reporting of XYY Syndrome well. He considered the link between XYY and criminality to have resulted from 'breathtakingly atrocious methodology' and that 'uncritical publicising of such alleged links, both separately and in connection with sensational murder trials, fixed the association in the public mind, and the more careful scientific work since has done little or nothing to alter it.'[30] The mid-1970s effectively signaled the end to arguments of a link between XYY and criminality, although there are still the occasional references to such a link.[31]

---

[28] [2002] NSWSC 758.

[29] 'Nature/Nurture Revisited II' (1975) 19 Journal of *Conflict Resolution* 734.

[30] In fairness, Price and Whatmore had in fact pointed out in their study that 'It is reasonable to question what part mental subnormality may play in their disturbed behavior. It is well to remember that the men we have described may represent a selected group of XYY males, and that others found in the ordinary population, or even in penal populations, may show different features from those described above.'

[31] In 1988 Elliott comments that 'the 'prejudices' of some social scientists against genetic determinism is because it implies human weaknesses are unalterable. '… however, this pessimism ignores the great power of social forces to mold behavior in both normal and abnormal personalities.': 'Violence a product of biosocial interactions' (1988) 16 J Am Acad Psychiatry Law 131.

4.3 A GENE X ENVIRONMENT SHIFT

With the decline of eugenics in the 1930s, scientists began to move from a pure genetic determinism theory of behavior to a gene x environmental theory, which considered an effect (or a behavior) to be the cause of the interaction of both genes and the environment. This new theory of behavior was attractive for several reasons. First, it started with the assumption that people are all created equal, in contrast to the eugenics movement which divided people into genetically fit and unfit categories. Second, it allowed for the concept that behavior can be altered through learning and rehabilitation. If a person's conduct is the result of a learned behavior, then this behavior can also be unlearned, allowing for inappropriate behavior to be modified. If conduct is purely the result of genetics, there can be no rehabilitation.

Scientists began to use twin studies to understand the interaction between genes and environment, and the extent to which each influenced behavior. By comparing monozygotic (identical) twins (who have the same genes and are presumably raised in the same environment) to dizygotic (fraternal) twins (who have different genes but are presumably raised in the same environment) the link between behavior, genes and the environment could be considered. Hundreds of twin studies have suggested that between 37 and 67 per cent of variance in antisocial behavior can be attributed to genetic factors, depending on social environments. Two studies, one in 2002, the other in 2003 suggested that in an impoverished social environment, shared environment accounted for 60 per cent variance in IQ and the contribution of genes was close to zero. In an affluent environment, the result was the opposite. This suggests that pre-existing genetic tendencies are either activated or exacerbated by environmental factors.

While these studies demonstrated a link between genes, the environment, and behavior, they are not able to identify which genes cause or influence behavior, and specifically which genes might result in criminal behavior. It is highly likely, however, that there is more than one gene involved in determining behavior. Han Brunner,[32] for example, has commented that:

> Because genes are essentially simple and behavior is by definition complex, a direct causal relationship between a single gene and a specific behavior is

---

[32] 'Abnormal behaviour associated with a point mutation in the structural gene for Monoamine Oxidase A' (1993) 262 *Science* 578.

> highly unlikely. … thus the concept of a gene that directly encodes behavior is unrealistic.

It is, therefore, more realistic to understand behavior as being the result of the combined effect of several genes, each contributing a small-moderate effect and interacting with the environment.

4.4 A BASIC GUIDE TO GENETICS

Before this chapter moves on to consider genes that have been identified as possibly being associated with criminal conduct, it may be beneficial to provide a brief guide to genetics. The human genome is the complete set of genetic information for a human. It consists of DNA sequences within 23 chromosomal pairs in cell nuclei, as well as DNA in the mitochondria. These chromosomes contain approximately 20,000–25,000 genes. Genes are the functional or working units of DNA. They provide sets of instructions for coding for a particular function or trait.

When scientists or academics talk about identifying particular genes that might code for a specific behavior, they are generally not talking about whether a gene is actually present in the genome or not. The focus is instead on whether a person has a specific type of the relevant gene. Some genes are polymorphic, meaning there are several different variations of that gene. Each variant is known as an allele. One such way in which two copies of the same gene can vary is the number of times a short DNA sequence repeats in the gene, called the Variable Number Tandem Repeat (VNTR). If the VNTR occurs in the coding region, this might alter the type of product being produced. If the VNTR occurs in the promoter region, this might influence the amount of the product being produced.

4.5 IDENTIFYING RELEVANT GENES FOR BEHAVIOR

The starting point in identifying genes that might affect behavior is to accept that there is no specific gene that makes someone a criminal, and to instead focus on identifying behavioral traits that might increase a person's likelihood of engaging in anti-social behavior, and consider genes relating to these traits. The obvious traits to consider are aggressiveness and impulsiveness.

Aggressiveness can be defined as either 'behavior produced to cause physical harm or humiliation to another who wishes to avoid it'[33] or as 'behaviour which is intended to increase the social dominance of the organism relative to the dominance position of other organisms.'[34] It originally developed as an evolutionary response to a potential threat. Over time, cortical functioning developed that inhibited this response in situations where it was not considered desirable or appropriate. Aggressive behavior, in the absence of a direct threat, is today considered to be a result of this inhibiting function failing to occur properly.

Impulsivity is the tendency to act without foresight.[35] Impulsive actions tend to be associated with one of two negative situations. The first is the failure to adequately process and respond to sensory evidence or social cues (known as attentional impulsivity). An example of this might be the failure to understand another person's facial expression as indicating fear, but instead understanding it as indicating anger and responding to this as if it were a threat. The second is the failure to regulate motor responses following a perceived threat (known as impulsive action) for example a stress response to a situation. Impulsive actions might also be expressed as aggressive actions.

Two molecules that have been associated with both impulsiveness and aggression are serotonin and dopamine. Neurons releasing these molecules are prominent in brain regions that regulate impulse control, and the higher the levels of serotonin and dopamine in the brain, the more likely a person is to engage in impulsive, and potentially aggressive, behavior. Serotonin has been specifically linked with sensitivity to punishment and pleasure, while dopamine has been implicated in reward sensitivity and sensation seeking. The amount of serotonin and dopamine present in brain regions might therefore result in some people being more readily shaped by either rewards or punishments, or more likely to engage in risky behaviors, than others. Genes that regulate serotonin and dopamine are therefore potential candidates for understanding a link between genes, the environment and behavior. Several relevant genes will be discussed below.

---

33 Baron and Richardson, *Human Aggression* (1994) (US: Springer 2004).

34 Ferguson and Beaver, 'Natural born killers: The genetic origins of extreme violence' (2009) 14 *Aggression and Violent Behavior* 286.

35 It is often associated with addictions, ADHD, bipolar and ASPD.

4.6 MONOAMINE OXIDASE-A (MAO-A)

Monoamine Oxidase-A (MAO-A) is an enzyme encoded by the MAOA gene. Its role is to degrade oxidase neurotransmitters, which include serotonin and dopamine. Dodge[36] described the function of MAO-A in this way:

> when humans are faced with threat or provocation, we naturally experience rage and an impulse to act aggressively, but activation of the MAO-A enzyme enables us to withhold that response. If the MAOA gene does not produce enough enzyme, this results in higher levels of serotonin remaining and a higher likelihood of acting aggressively.

The MAOA gene is found on the short arm of the X chromosome. In 1998,[37] scientists reported the identification of a 30 base pair VNTR polymorphism of the gene.[38] In layman's terms, the scientists discovered that the gene has several different variants, or alleles, which are distinguished from each other by the amount of times a 30 base pair sequence repeats. Those people whose base pair sequence repeats 2 or 3 times are described as having Low MAOA,[39] and those with the 3.5 or 4 repeat variants are described as having High MAOA. There are also 5 and 6 repeat variants, but these are rare and their effect is not clear.[40] A person with Low MAOA has transcription rates which are between two and 10 times more efficient than a person with High MAOA. As an example of this, a person with the two repeat (Low) variant will produce only 25–30 per cent of the MAO-A enzyme produced by a person with the four repeat High variant. Producing less enzyme results in less serotonin being

---

[36] Dodge, 'Mechanisms of gene-environment interaction effects on the development of conduct disorder' (2009) 4(4) Perspect Psychol Sci 408.

[37] Sabol, 'A functional polymorphism in the Monoamine Oxidase A gene promoter' (1998) 103(3) *Human Genetics* 273.

[38] In 2011 a new polymorphic VNTR was found, which consists of a 10-bp repeat. It is thought that this will provide more accurate information than the 30-bp repeat, but hasn't been fully studied yet.

[39] Beaver argues that the 2 repeat should be in a category of its own, as these people are at far greater risk of being arrested, and therefore mask the results for the 3s: 'Exploring the association between the 2 repeat allele of the MAOA gene promoter polymorphism and psychopathic personality traits, arrests, incarceration and lifetime antisocial behavior' (2013) 54 *Personality and Individual Differences* 164.

[40] There are conflicting reports as to whether the 5 repeat sequence fits better as Low or High, and the 6 repeat has been identified so rarely that a determination cannot be made.

degraded. The higher level of serotonin therefore in the brain will result in the person having an increased chance of acting impulsively or aggressively when compared to a person with High MAOA.

Dodge[41] described Low MAO-A activity as being 'associated with a pattern of autonomic arousal and defensive information processing that is characterized by hypervigilance to hostile cues, hostile attributional biases, selection of self-defensive goals, and the experience of self-righteous anger. All of these processing responses lead to highly aggressive behavior.' This does not mean, however, that a person with Low MAOA will automatically act in this manner. Statistics, which will be discussed in more detail later, suggest that one in three Caucasian males, and potentially two in three Asian males, have the Low MAO-A allele. Yet, the majority of these people do not engage in aggressive behavior. The majority of studies on MAOA have failed to detect a direct link (known as a significant main effect) between the Low MAOA form of the gene and aggressive behavior. The studies show instead that the link arises only when the gene interacts with environmental stresses. A person with the Low MAOA gene, who has also been raised in a negative environment, is more likely to behave aggressively or impulsively than a person without one or both of these factors. Some of these studies will be discussed below.

4.6.1 The Brunner Study (1993)[42]

The link between MAOA and impulsive aggression was first identified in the Brunner study. In 1978 a woman asked Brunner and his team for help in identifying a potential genetic condition in her family. She explained that for generations some men in her family had been prone to unprovoked aggressive outbursts. This trend had occurred so frequently that in the 1940s her uncle had compiled a record of nine affected family members, and she had subsequently identified five more. As examples, one man had raped his sister and while subsequently serving time in a mental institution had attacked his warden with a pitchfork. Another had tried to run his boss over with a car after being told that his work was not acceptable. A further two were arsonists. It had been noted that all of the affected men were mildly retarded. This could be contrasted with other,

---

[41] Dodge, 'Mechanisms of gene-environment interaction effects on the development of conduct disorder' (2009) 4(4) Perspect Psychol Sci 408.

[42] 'Abnormal behaviour associated with a point mutation in the structural gene for Monoamine Oxidase A' (1993) 262 Science 578.

unaffected, male family members who tended to be successful and had average to above average IQs.

The fact that no women appeared to have been affected led Brunner and his team to first look at the X chromosome. They theorized that a genetic defect on an X chromosome would affect males, who have one X and one Y chromosome, but may not affect females who have two X chromosomes since their second X chromosome could compensate for any genetic defect on the first. For ten years Brunner failed to identify a causative gene. The breakthrough came in the late 1980s, when the discovery of new informative markers enabled the team to locate genes that cause hereditary diseases. Using this approach, they were able to identify the MAOA gene region as the likely site of the defect. Urine samples of affected men confirmed that the MAOA gene was not functioning correctly. In fact, it was completely absent in these men, meaning no MAO-A enzyme was being produced. There were therefore high levels of serotonin and dopamine remaining in the brain. This could logically explain the men's behavior. Neurotransmitters like serotonin and dopamine affect flight or flight responses to stress. Affected men in the family were effectively in high gear all the time, and therefore unable to handle additional stress.[43]

Brunner concluded that there was a 'relation between isolated complete deficiency of MAO-A activity and abnormal aggressive behavior in affected males'. He further wondered if this relationship was confined only to a complete MAOA deficiency, given the range of variation of MAOA activity in the population.

4.6.2 Knockout Mice and Subsequent Studies

A knockout mouse is a mouse which has had a gene muted or 'knocked out'. Studies on mice which have had the MAOA gene knocked out showed dramatically elevated serotonin levels in the brain and an increased reactivity to stress. When subject to resident-intruder tests they also showed enhanced male aggressiveness. These studies therefore confirmed Brunner's conclusion on the role of the MAOA gene, and in particular, the effect of its absence.

Attempts to replicate the findings in the Brunner study among other male human populations, however, soon revealed a problem. No person outside the original family could be identified as having a complete

---

[43] To support this, it was noted that the two arsonists in the family had acted following the deaths of close relatives.

MAOA deficiency, suggesting that this was abnormality unique to this particular family. Scientific attention therefore shifted to consider Brunner's suggestion that low amounts of MAOA could also result in similar impulsive aggressive behavior, and began to compare individuals with Low and High MAOA to determine any effect on behavior.

4.6.3 Caspi (2002): Genes × Environment[44]

The Caspi study was a longitudinal study examining the impact of childhood maltreatment on the probability of the development of anti-social behavior in adolescence and adulthood. It followed 1037 children born in a particular year in Dunedin, New Zealand, interviewing them every two years. When the team became aware of Brunner's study, they genotyped the MAOA polymorphism of the cohort members.

The results for the Caucasian male members of the cohort suggested that the MAOA gene moderated the impact of childhood maltreatment on the development of anti-social behavior in males. Where there was no reported maltreatment, Low MAOA males were less likely than High MAOA males to engage in antisocial behavior. As the severity of maltreatment increased, however, this result changed significantly. The likelihood of antisocial behavior increased steadily among the High MAOA males, but increased dramatically among the Low MAOA males. While only 12 per cent of the cohort was identified as Low MAOA, this group accounted for 44 per cent of violent convictions. Further, 85 per cent of those with Low MAOA who were severely maltreated developed antisocial behavior (Figure 4.1, p. 88).

The Caspi study concluded that the presence of the Low MAOA gene coupled with childhood maltreatment made a male more likely to engage in antisocial behavior than a male without one of these two factors.

4.6.4 Haberstick (2005) and Huizinga (2006): Failure to Replicate Findings[45]

The Haberstick study utilized data from the National Longitudinal Study of Adolescent Health (Add Health), a study of twin or sibling pairs

---

[44] 'Role of genotype in the cycle of violence in maltreated children' (2002) 297 Science 851, 852.

[45] Haberstick, 'MAOA and antisocial behaviour in the presence of childhood and adolescent maltreatment' (2005) Am J Med Genet B Neuropsychiatr Genet 59; Huizinga, 'Childhood maltreatment, subsequent antisocial behaviour and the role of MAOA genotype' (2006) 60(7) Biol Psychiatry 677.

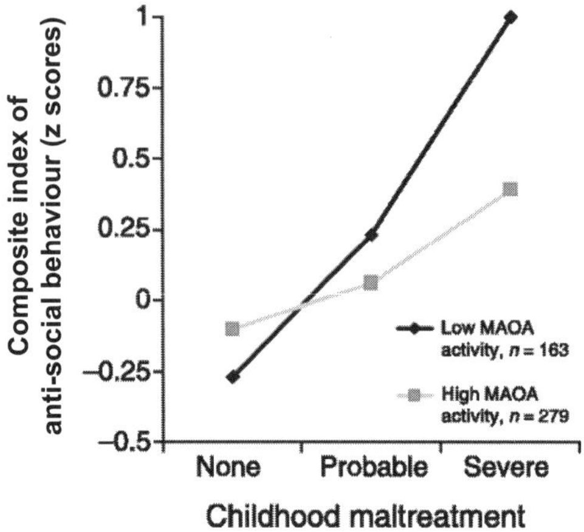

Source: A. Caspi, 'Role of genotype in the cycle of violence in maltreated children' (2002) 297 *Science* 851, 852.

Figure 4.1 Means on the composite index of anti-social behavior as a function of MAOA activity and a childhood history of maltreatment

comprising 5470 individuals from grades 7–12 who had a full biological sibling between the ages of 12–20. This particular study isolated the results from 774 Caucasian males, in an attempt to replicate the Caspi study.

The Huizinga study followed 277 Caucasian males as part of the Colorado National Youth Survey Family Study who were between the ages of 11 and 17 in 1976. The males were interviewed at a frequency of once a year from 1977–81, then every three years thereafter about any maltreatment suffered.[46] As with the Caspi study, the participants were subsequently genotyped to determine whether they had Low or High MAOA.

In both of these studies there was a failure to replicate the Caspi results. Childhood maltreatment was identified as a risk factor for anti-social behavior, but the differences between Low and High MAOA seen in Caspi were not present in either study.

[46] Maltreatment was measured through self-reporting, following the question 'have you been beaten up?' by parent or step-parent.

4.6.5 Spatz-Widom (2006): Females and Non-Caucasians[47]

The Spatz-Widom study was a specialized study which matched maltreated and non-maltreated children, following them into young adulthood to assess the impact of maltreatment on the risk of violent or antisocial behavior. It began with 1196 individuals in 1989, and was still following 896 in 2002, 631 of which gave permission for DNA testing.

The findings in relation to Caucasian males replicated the Caspi results, showing a link between childhood maltreatment, Low MAOA and subsequent antisocial behavior. Interestingly, though, this study also considered the female and non-Caucasian members of the cohort. The effect on Caucasian females was found to be equivalent to that of Caucasian males, resulting in the authors suggesting that High-MAOA 'buffered or protected them from an increased risk of becoming violent and/or antisocial in later life.' For the non-Caucasian cohort members, however, the results differed, showing no interaction between the gene, environment and behavior. The study commented that 'even though it is the rare case that suggests that a single gene can have a direct and universal impact on a behavioral phenotype, the lack of a GxE [gene and environment] interaction for non-white individuals in the current study was unexpected'. One explanation provided was that the MAOA gene might impact differently on people of different races. Alternatively, it could simply mean that using the VNTR polymorphism as a proxy for overall MAOA expression in non-whites was not an appropriate measure.[48]

4.6.6 Sjoberg (2007) and Aslund (2011): Females, Revisited[49]

In 2007, Sjoberg conducted a study of 119 females, and in 2011, Aslund studied 882 females. In both, they found that it was the High MAOA allele (or more correctly, having at least one chromosome with the High allele) that was linked to aggression in females when coupled with childhood maltreatment. These studies therefore failed to replicate the

---

47 'MAOA and the cycle of violence' (2006) 60(7) Biol Psych 684.

48 In other words, that the method used to identify Low MAOA in Caucasians might not be the appropriate method for non-Caucasians.

49 Sjoberg, 'Adolescent girls and criminal activities, role of MAOA-LPR genotype and psychosocial factors' (2007) 144B(2) Am J Med Genet B Neuropsychiatr Genet 159; Aslund, 'Maltreatment, MAOA and delinquency' (2011) 41(2) Behav Genet 262.

Spatz-Widom study results which indicated that the Low MAOA gene affected Caucasian males and females in the same way.

4.6.7 McDermott (2009): The Hot Sauce Study[50]

The McDermott study is notable for the fact that it went beyond interviewing participants to actually testing aggressive responses in a controlled environment. The research question being asked in the study was whether or not people are purely self-interested utility maximizers. In other words, would people pay money to cause physical pain to others who have stolen from them?

Participants were given the opportunity to win money through correctly answering vocabulary questions in a test. Next, they were told that a person located in another room had stolen either 20 per cent or 80 per cent of their winnings. The participants could use some of their remaining winnings to punish the thief by purchasing shots of hot sauce (Tabasco sauce) and forcing him to drink these. If the thief failed to drink he would forfeit the money, however it would not be returned to the participants. The number of shots purchased in each scenario was recorded, and the MAOA level of the participants measured.

When 20 per cent of the winnings were taken (20 per cent being intended to indicate a low level of threat or aggressive act towards the participant) 12 per cent of Low MAOA and 6 per cent of High MAOA individuals chose to purchase the maximum amount of shots permissible. The difference in responses between groups in this situation was not considered particularly significant. When 80 per cent of the winnings were taken (intended to indicate a high level of threat or aggression) 44 per cent of Low MAOA individuals gave the maximum, compared to only 19 per cent of High MAOA. The study therefore suggested that when faced with a low level of threat or aggressive act there was no significant difference in response between Low and High MAOA, but when faced with a higher level, the Low MAOA group responded significantly more aggressively. This was a similar result to the Caspi study.

---

[50] 'MAOA predicts behavioral aggression following provocation' (2009) PNAS 2118.

4.6.8 The Christchurch Study (2012): A Gene Main Effect?[51]

This longitudinal study traced 1265 children born in Christchurch, New Zealand in mid-1977. Similar to the Dunedin study, its aim was to examine the effect of childhood maltreatment on anti-social behavior. Towards the end of the study, 395 males were genotyped to determine their MAOA status. This study is notable due to its conclusion: 'we found a general tendency for the overall rate of antisocial behavior to be higher in the low activity MAOA group than in the high'. In other words, the study suggested a gene main effect, that it was the presence of the gene that indicated the future anti-social behavior, and the role of the environment was not considered significant. The authors referred to five other studies that have observed this, suggesting that this was not a unique finding.

4.6.9 Choe (2014): African-Americans and 'Harsh Parenting'[52]

The recent Choe study is notable for two outcomes. First, it found that the Low-MAOA polymorphism is the risk variant for African-Americans. Second, it used a different measure of childhood maltreatment than other studies, which it referred to as 'simple punitive discipline' or 'mild forms of harsh parenting'. Despite this variant, it found the same interactive effect with the gene as with the harsher forms.

4.6.10 Tiihonen (2014): MAOA and Recidivist Offenders[53]

This study considered results from over 500 violent, incarcerated offenders. It found that there was a 'strong main effect for Low [MAOA] genotype, but that maltreatment did not modify the risk in any way. The authors considered the difference between this result and that in the Caspi study, and commented that Caspi had focused on young people, and here the participants were adult prisoners. The authors further pointed out that the majority of violent crime in Finland is committed under the influence of alcohol. It was possible that this was the 'environment' factor in these cases. They noted that 'the low dopamine

---

[51] 'Moderating role of the MAOA genotype in antisocial behavior' (2012) Br J Psychiatry 116.

[52] 'Interactions between MAOA and punitive discipline' (2014) 2(5) Clinical Psychological Science 591.

[53] Tiihonen, 'Genetic background of extreme violent behavior' (2014) Mol Psychiatry 1.

metabolism rate due to Low MAOA may result in higher levels of aggression during alcohol or stimulant intoxication'.

4.6.11 The Variation between Studies

The studies discussed above were chosen as representative of the results of numerous published MAOA studies. One notable factor when comparing the studies is a lack of consistency between the findings. As further evidence of this, in 2009 Weder[54] surveyed all available MAOA studies and found in relation to Caspi's results four replications, four partial replications, four negative findings, and one opposite finding. Fergusson[55] repeated the exercise in 2011 and found ten replications, five negative findings and three reversals. There are two reasons why there might be this level of disagreement or inconsistency between studies. The first is that the studies differ in research design and measurement methods, and this has affected the overall results. Second, there may simply be an absence of a stable gene x environment interaction.

4.6.11.1 Variations in research design

As has already been seen in the discussion of XYY syndrome, the selection criteria for participants may impact the results. Selecting people because of their history of antisocial behavior and then testing them for Low MAOA might overemphasize the frequency of Low MAOA people engaging in antisocial behavior in the community as a whole in the same way that selecting people by height overemphasized the frequency of XYY males in prisons or secured hospitals. Studies that simply take a representative sample of the community, for example everyone born in Dunedin or Christchurch in a particular time period, are therefore more likely to accurately reflect society.

Another common way in which research design has influenced the participants studied is by only selecting specific sub-groups. Many of the studies isolated results from Caucasian males from the overall participant pool. Other studies focus on other races. The reason for this is population stratification, a recognition that the way genes are expressed can vary between different racial or ethnic categories. The fact that some studies suggest that Low MAOA is the risk allele in Caucasians, and other studies suggest that High MAOA is the risk allele in African-Americans

---

[54] 'MAOA genotype, maltreatment, and aggressive behavior' (2009) 65(5) Biol Psych 417.

[55] 'Moderating role of the MAOA genotype in antisocial behavior' (2012) 200(2) Br J Psych 116.

does not mean that one study contradicts the other. It may simply mean that the gene expresses differently among different racial groups. For this reason, one study commented that 'pooling together all racial groups is unadvised.'[56] Another commented that 'just as there is some evidence revealing that environmental factors may have different effects for different racial and ethnic groups, there is also the possibility that genetic effects may be moderated by race and/or ethnicity.'[57] Studies appear to take a binary approach to race, defining participants either by observation or by self-designation as Caucasian or non-Caucasian. The impact on mixed-race may differ.

Another reason for considering racial groups separately is the differing frequencies of the Low and High alleles between different racial groups. In Caucasians, the Low form occurs in approximately 33 per cent of males, in non-Caucasians, the Low form occurs far more frequently, in approximately 66 per cent. The two repeat allele, which appears to be the one most closely linked to impulsive aggression, occurs in only 0.1 per cent of Caucasians, but in 5–6 per cent of non-Caucasians.

Isolating males from females in studies is also common. As has been seen above, the MAOA gene is found on the long arm of the X chromosome. Females, having two X chromosomes and therefore two MAOA genes, by necessity need to be considered separately. The effect of having two MAOA genes is unknown. Generally with females, genes on one of the X chromosomes will simply be inactivated, and studies that have measured the amount of MAOA in females suggest that this might be occurring. Females with two High MAOA alleles do not appear to produce double the amount of MAOA compared to a male with one High MAOA allele. On the other hand, approximately 15 per cent of x-linked genes escape inactivation, and recent studies have suggested that MAOA might be one of these genes. If this is the case, it is clear that the two categories (Low and High) are not necessarily appropriate in studying the effect of MAOA on females. In a Swedish study[58] in fact, females were

---

[56] 'Intersection of genes and neuropsychological deficits in the prediction of adolescent delinquency and low self control' (2010) 54(1) Int J Ther Comp Criminology 22.

[57] Beaver, 'The association between genetic risk and contact with the criminal justice system in a sample of Hispanics' (2011) 27(1) J Contemp Crim Just 81.

[58] Melas, 'Genetic and epigenetic associations of MAOA and NR3C1 with depression and childhood adversities' (2013) 16 Int J Neuropsychopharmacology 1513.

separated into three categories: Low/Low, Low/High, and High/High.[59] Approximately 14 per cent were Low/Low, 45 per cent were Low/High and 40 per cent were High/High.

4.6.11.2 Variations in measurement methods

The Caspi study suggested that a Caucasian male with the Low allele who had suffered childhood maltreatment was more likely to engage in antisocial behavior than a Caucasian male with the High allele, or with the Low allele but no childhood maltreatment. Some studies have replicated this result, while others have failed to do so.

While the method of classification of the allele as High or Low is generally agreed upon in the studies[60] the definition of childhood maltreatment is not, which might explain the differing results. Some studies define maltreatment in terms of physical incidents only, while others also include verbal and/or sexual maltreatment. The Christchurch study went further, additionally considering the impact of maternal smoking during pregnancy, school failure,[61] IQ and material deprivation.

The measure of classification of severity or the necessary frequency of the incidents also varies. One study asked participants if they had been physically hit at least one time in the past year. Another asked participants how often they had been physically hit in the past month, with the options being: never, once, a little, or a lot. The latter two options are clearly subjective.

Further, how this information is obtained can affect the accuracy or fairness of the classification. For example, in longitudinal studies occurring from birth, it is the parents that will be asked about any maltreatment for the first few years. The first five years of life may be the critical period for predicting future antisocial behavior,[62] but asking the parents if they subject their child to mild or severe maltreatment is likely to result in answers that are unsafe in terms of reliability. On the other hand,

---

[59] In the actual study, the authors use S (Short) and L (Long) to refer to the Low and High alleles respectively. The abbreviations have been changed in this chapter for consistency.

[60] Except for debates over whether the VNTR works for race, or whether the 30br VNTR is the right location, and on how to classify the less common 2, 5, 6 repeats.

[61] This was explained as leaving school without qualifications.

[62] One study of 189 showed that those with childhood maltreatment under the age of five were more likely to show antisocial behavior between the ages of 15–20.

young children might unintentionally exaggerate[63] or minimize[64] the severity. Some studies ask older children to report back on maltreatment as a child, which also contains a level of unreliability. One study attempted to address the reliability issues in self-reporting by using observation by trained personnel. Children attended a day camp over five days, for seven hours a day, and were therefore observed for 35 hours for signs of childhood maltreatment.

The description of the later conduct also differs. Some studies discuss antisocial behavior, while others refer to conduct disorder or antisocial personality disorder, all of which have subtle differences in meaning. Further, the measure of this behavior also differs. Some studies use the objective measure of criminal convictions, while others use self-reporting. The Christchurch study pointed out the unreliability of simply using criminal convictions: actually being arrested and convicted depends on external factors, being the actions of law enforcement (whether the subject is actually caught), the nature of the offending (whether it is too low a level of offending to result in an arrest, or whether the subject is merely given a warning instead) and the response of the justice system (whether the subject is given an alternative punishment to conviction?[65]). Self-reporting of behavior is a more accurate measure as it removes these external factors. As an example of the potential difference in results depending on whether the measure is engagement in the act, arrest or conviction, a 2006[66] Swedish study of 81 boys showed 37 per cent having been arrested (and therefore probably even fewer being convicted), but 87 per cent had self-reported as having engaged in criminal acts.

4.6.12 Other Studies on MAOA

Other studies have suggested that Low MAOA has links to other behaviors. In the presence of a negative childhood environment it can also increase the likelihood of alcoholism, of joining a gang, and of carrying and using weapons while in a gang. A third group of studies

[63] For example, a light smack might be reported as more if the child felt it was highly undeserved or had never been smacked before.

[64] For example, a child might not report behaviours because he did not want to get his parents into trouble.

[65] These alternative punishments might include diversion, discharge without conviction, or ASBOs.

[66] 'Role of MAOA genotype and psychosocial factors in male adolescent criminal activity' (2006) 59(2) Biol Psychiatry 121.

however, have pointed to pro-social behaviors associated with Low MAOA, for example engaging in cooperative behaviors, and even voting. Further, these studies demonstrate that Low MAOA individuals are more likely to take financial risks, but only when it is advantageous to do so. One study[67] concluded that Low MAOA individuals 'perform better in risky financial decision making because they exhibit an improved ability to select the optimal response when it is advantageous.'

While the Low allele tends to be associated with external behaviors like aggression and risk taking, the High allele tends to be associated with internal behaviors. High MAOA individuals who suffer childhood maltreatment exhibit a greater likelihood of developing anxiety, neuroticism and panic disorders. In a 2009 study of 114 children, 74 of which had been removed from their parents care due to neglect or abuse, there was a strong link between High MAOA and inattention. In addition, 70 per cent of the children suffering the neglect or abuse were diagnosed as having Post Traumatic Stress Disorder.

4.6.13 Brain Scan Studies on MAOA

In addition to the studies discussed above, some scientists have used brain scans to understand whether there is a link between Low MAOA and impulsive behavior. These scans have mostly focused on the limbic system of the brain, which contains the amygdala. The amygdala processes external stimuli and their emotional significance, accesses emotional memories, and triggers defensive or aggressive behaviors where appropriate. Information provided to the amygdala to enable it to carry out this processing is modulated by neurotransmitter systems, including dopamine and serotonin. Low MAOA results in less serotonin being degraded, and therefore more serotonin remaining in the amygdala, making it hyper-reactive and more likely to react in an aggressive manner. The impact of this has been identified in several studies. In Meyer-Lindenberg's study[68] participants were shown pictures of faces with sorrowful or fearful expressions. Functional Magnetic Resonance Imaging (fMRI) was used to measure the activity in the amygdala. Those participants with Low MAOA and a history of maltreatment showed hyper-responsiveness of the amygdala, indicating a likely aggressive

[67] Frydman, 'MAOA-L carriers are better at making optimal financial decisions under risk' (2010) Proc R Soc B 1.

[68] 'Natural mechanisms of genetic risk for impulsivity and violence in humans' (2006) 103(16) PNAS 6269.

response. In the Eisenberger study[69] participants played two virtual ball games. Again, fMRI was used to measure the reaction. In the first game, the participant believed he was playing with two other people. The game involved throwing the ball to one of the other players, and the participant received the ball 50 per cent of the time. This game was called 'inclusion'. In the other game, 'exclusion', the participant received the ball only seven out of 60 times (or approximately 12 per cent of the time). Participants then self-reported their feelings and the fMRI scans were analysed. In 'exclusion', Low MAOA participants showed significant activation in the anterior insula and the dorsal anterior cingulated cortex, both of which are associated with rejection-related distress. This finding was therefore consistent with the previous study, and suggests that the impulsive aggression displayed by Low MAOA results from a heightened sensitivity to negative emotional experiences, rather than a decreased sensitivity.

4.6.14 What Do Studies Tell Us?

The language that we use to explain the results of the MAOA studies needs to be carefully chosen. In New Zealand, when a small cohort of 17 Maori men were identified as having a significantly higher frequency of the Low allele than is found in Caucasian men, this was linked to the fact that Maori are overrepresented in the New Zealand prison system. The author of the study suggested that MAOA was a 'violence gene', which quickly became rephrased as a 'warrior gene'[70] and resulted in a strong backlash due to racial implications. Following a couple of recent cases in Italy and the United States, the term 'murder gene' appeared frequently in the media.

This language is unhelpful for several reasons. First, any description of this gene as predisposing an individual to violent behavior is inaccurate. The studies don't focus on individual predisposition, but on whether one group of individuals are more likely than another group to engage in antisocial behavior. Individuals with (a) Low MAOA and (b) childhood maltreatment are more likely to engage in (c) antisocial behavior, than other individuals without (a) or (b). This does not mean that in an individual case (a) + (b) = (c). We cannot genetically test a person, assign

[69] 'Does rejection hurt? An FMRI study of social exclusion' (2003) 302(5643) *Science* 290.

[70] The author claimed later to have been mis-quoted, and that he was in fact presenting a counter argument to his opinion: Rod Lea, 'MAOA, Addiction And The Warrior Gene Hypothesis' (2007) 120 NZMJ 5.

him or her a score based on his level of childhood maltreatment and then use this to accurately predict whether he will engage in antisocial behavior.

Second, any description using the wording 'genetic predisposition', or suggesting such a result, is inaccurate. It is not just genetics which is relevant, but genetics plus environment. In addition, it is not technically a predisposition. This word suggests that people with the Low allele will always be more predisposed to violence than people with the High allele. This is not what Caspi and subsequent studies have suggested. Consider the graph from Caspi's study again. A genetic predisposition is something that consistently increases the probability of individuals from one group, as opposed to members of the other group, developing a particular trait. If the Low allele created a genetic predisposition, the line representing the Low allele would always be higher than the line representing the High allele. But this is not the case. The lines representing the two groups cross. At the lower end of the childhood maltreatment axis, it is the High allele group which are more likely to engage in antisocial behavior. As we move along the axis, there is a rank change, and the Low group becomes the more likely group. This cannot therefore be a genetic predisposition.

4.6.15 Conclusion

The studies discussed above suggest that there is a link between levels of MAOA and incidents of antisocial behavior, particularly where there has been a negative childhood environment. The studies do, however, lack consistency. This may be due to the difference in function of MAOA between racial or gender groups, or due to difference in research design. It may also suggest that there is an additional key factor in understanding behavior that we are not yet aware of, perhaps another gene or triggering environmental factor. Brain scan studies similarly suggest a connection between MAOA and antisocial traits, and provide a chemical justification for this conclusion.

Other studies on MAOA provide us with an important lesson. It is not accurate, despite the numerous studies on MAOA behavior, to automatically label Low MAOA as a crime gene, or a bad gene. There are some pro-social behaviors associated with having this gene, just as there are anti-social behaviors linked to having the High MAOA gene. This is an important fact to remember in the subsequent discussions in this book. Exactly how to describe the presence of Low MAOA will be discussed further at the end of this chapter, once some other genes that have potential links to antisocial conduct are discussed.

4.7 OTHER GENES

In the last few years, attention has begun to shift from a strong focus on MAOA to also considering other genes with links to serotonin and dopamine. Studies on these are at a more preliminary stage, but there are some indications that these other genes also affect behavior.

4.7.1 Serotonin

4.7.1.1 Introduction

Serotonin is a neurotransmitter which is involved in the regulation of emotions through maintaining mood balance and reducing impulsive behaviors. Low levels of serotonin therefore mean that this inhibiting feature is not occurring, and more aggressive behavior or impulsive actions may result.

4.7.1.2 Relevant genes

There are several genes that are linked to the regulation of serotonin. The most commonly discussed serotonin gene is 5-hydroxytryptamine transporter (5HTT, also known as SLC6A4). Serotonin is synthesized from tryptophan and is then released into the synapse. It must then be removed from the synapse for re-use. This removal occurs through a serotonin transporter like 5HTT. The amount of serotonin a transporter is able to remove depends on a polymorphism in the transcriptional control region of the gene, known as 5-HTTLPR. There are two alleles, the short allele, which contains a repeat sequence of 14 base pairs, and the long allele, which contains a repeat sequence of 20-23 base pairs.[71] Each person inherits one gene from each parent, meaning a person might be Short-Short (SS), ShortLong (SL), or LongLong (LL).

The short allele results in less serotonin being recycled, meaning there will be more serotonin remaining in the synapse, and less available for reuse. In studies on monkeys and mice, the short allele has been associated with increased aggression and impulsivity and conduct disorders, although there have been some non-replication studies.

---

[71] The difference between the alleles has also been described not in terms of the repeat sequence, but in terms of total number of base pairs, with the short allele containing 484 base pairs, and the long allele containing 528 base pairs.

As with MAOA, environment appears to play a key role. Van Ijzendoorn,[72] considering the data from a number of studies from 2004–2012, highlighted that the short allele operated similarly to Low MAOA. Similarities with the Caspi graph were noted. Those with the SS allele profited more significantly from positive environments, but were more vulnerable to negative environments. While as a group they were less likely to engage in criminal conduct in the absence of a negative environment (for example childhood maltreatment), they underwent a rank change with SL and LL alleles as the effect of the negative environment increased.

In support of the idea that the SS individuals have a greater susceptibility to environment, one study[73] on moral behavior found that S carriers rated 'unintentional harm' as less acceptable than L carriers. It was suggested in the study that this was due to the fact that they reacted more strongly to fearful stimuli. A brain scan study by Hariri[74] confirmed this, finding that fMRI scans showed that S carriers had greater neuronal activity of the amygdala in response to fearful stimuli.[75]

While 5HTT is the serotonin gene receiving the most attention, there are also other potentially relevant genes being discussed. One is the Tryptophan Hydroxylase (TPH) gene. This encodes the TPH1 enzyme, which is involved in the synthesis of serotonin. The gene contains two alleles, and there have been suggestions that the low allele results in less serotonin being produced. Cichetti,[76] however, has commented on the lack of studies, particularly in relation to the relevance of environment, on this gene.

Another potentially relevant group of genes, which like 5HTT are only just beginning to be studied in relation to behavior are the 5-Hydroxytryptamine Receptor genes. This is the name given to genes which encode a family of serotonin receptors that mediate serotonin dependent effects. There are seven types of these receptors, numbered

---

[72] 'Serotonin Transporter Genotype 5HTTLPR As A Marker Of Differential Susceptibility?' (2012) Transl Psychiatry 147.

[73] Abigail Marsh, 'Serotonin Transporter Genotype (5-HTTLPR) Predicts Utilitarian Moral Judgments' (2011) 6(10) PLoS One. 2011 e25148.

[74] 'Serotonin Transporter Genetic Variation And The Response Of The Human Amygdala' (2002) 297 Science 400.

[75] This heightened, rather than lowered, sensitivity to negative emotional experiences was also seen in the MAOA fMRI studies, above.

[76] Cichetti, 'The effects of child maltreatment on early signs of antisocial behavior: Genetic moderation by Tryptophan Hydroxylase, Serotonin Transporter, and Monoamine Oxidase-A-Genes' (2012) 24(3) Dev Psychopathol 907.

5-HTR1 to5-HTR7. Among these, 5-HTR1A and 5-HTR1B are considered as major candidates for association with aggression, and this has been confirmed in rodent studies.

4.7.2 Dopamine

4.7.2.1 Introduction

Dopamine is a neurotransmitter with links to behavior. It is a regulator of reward behavior, releasing pleasurable sensations in the brain. Low levels of dopamine mean that behavior is less rewarded, requiring individuals to seek out pleasure, whether through legal or illegal means, to elevate the dopamine to a normal level. This suggests that polymorphisms in certain dopamine genes may be linked to antisocial behaviour via pleasure/reward pathways in the brain.

4.7.2.2 Relevant gene DAT1

DAT1 (or SLC6A3) is a dopamine transporter gene which codes for the dopamine transporter protein DAT. The protein transports dopamine from the synapse back to the presynaptic neuron for re-use. The amount of dopamine the transporter is able to remove from the synapse depends on the polymorphism in the transcription region of the gene. There are two alleles, one which repeats a 40 base pair sequence 9 times, and one which repeats 10 times. As people will inherit one allele from each parent, individuals will be classified as 9R (having 2 × 9R alleles), 10R (having 2 × 10R alleles) or 9/10R (having 1 × 9R and 1 × 10R).[77]

The allele most associated with antisocial behavior is 10R. It facilitates more efficient transportation and re-uptake of dopamine, resulting in reduced dopaminergic activity, and therefore reduced reward sensation.

In the Add Health[78] study, people with 10R and 9/10R had trajectories for serious and violent delinquency which were twice as high as for 9R. Interestingly, there does not appear to be a different effect between racial groups. While 10R had a 'stronger significance' amongst Caucasians, one study found it to be 'consistently predictive for antisocial behavior' amongst both Caucasian and non-Caucasian subsamples.[79]

---

[77] There can also be 6, 7, 8 and 11R sequences, but these are rare. In the Add Health study, for example, 96% had 9 or 10R.

[78] National Longitudinal Study of Adolescent to Adult Health.

[79] Here, antisocial behaviour was measured by police contact.

4.7.2.3 Relevant gene DRD4

Another potentially relevant gene is Dopamine Receptor D4. This codes for a dopamine receptor, D4, which controls neural signaling. The gene has multiple alleles, which repeat a 48 base pair sequence between 1 and 11 times. The most common alleles are 4 and 7. Anyone with a repeat of 5 or less is usually designated as having the Short allele, and 6 or more as Long.

The long allele, particularly the 7 repeat, known as DRD4-7, may be considered to be the risk allele, as it codes less efficiently. Studies on DRD4-7, especially in presence of adverse social constraints and low parental quality, have shown it to be associated with externalising behavior, including shorter tempers, thrill seeking and lower effortful control.

4.7.2.4 Relevant gene DRD2

Another potentially relevant dopamine receptor is DRD2. This receptor contains a polymorphism in the A1 allele, which erases a particular site, known as Taq1. The A2 allele does not erase this site. The A1 allele is also described as the 178 genotype, and the A2 as the 304 genotype. Again, individuals inherit one from each parent.

The A1 allele is recognized as a contributor to Reward Deficiency Syndrome, in which a lack of dopamine means that the reward pathways in the brain are not activated. Such an individual therefore must engage in higher levels of excitement or stimulation in order to activate these pathways. This might occur through increased risk taking, or aggressive and impulsive actions.[80]

The Add Health study showed that the 178/304 genotype is associated with higher levels of delinquency than the 304/304 or 178/178 genotype. A 2011 study[81] also found a significant association between A1 and delinquency, but interestingly this occurred only amongst those who had been victims of crime themselves (which can be described as a specific type of negative environmental influence).

4.7.3 Catechol-O-Methyl Transferase (COMT)

COMT is a gene that produces an enzyme which degrades catecholamines such as dopamine. It therefore plays an important role in the

---

[80] It has also been linked with alcoholism and pathological gambling.

[81] Beaver, 'A Dopamine Gene (DRD2) Distinguishes Between Offenders Who Have And Have Not Been Violently Victimised' (2011) Int J Offender Ther Comp Criminal 251.

regulation of dopamine levels in synapses, particularly in the prefrontal cortex where the dopamine transporter is poorly expressed. The gene has a polymorphism which results in a functional single amino acid substitution consisting in a valine to methionine change (Val158Met). In other words, one allele codes for the production of the amino acid methione and the other for valine. The Met 158 allele of the COMT Val158Met polymorphism produces only approximately half the enzymatic activity of the Val 158 allele. This lower activity points to the likelihood that the Met allele is the risk aggressive personality trait.

In studies it has been associated with emotionality, impulsivity, hostility, anger, violence, aggression, and the risk of committing homicides and suicides by violent means. Novelty-reward seeking, and motor impulsivity within a simulated real-life decision making. In a brain scan study, the Met allele enhanced the reactivity and connectivity of hippocampus and ventrolateral prefrontal cortex during the presentation of faces displaying negative emotions.

4.7.4 Conclusion

The functions of the genes discussed above suggest a logical link between particular alleles and antisocial behavior, and some studies have supported this suggestion. The limited number and nature of these studies, however, should be kept in mind. The MAOA studies provide an important lesson on the importance of replication studies to ensure the validity of the conclusions reached by early studies.

4.8 A 'CRIMINAL GENE' OR SOMETHING ELSE? THE IMPORTANCE OF LANGUAGE

While this chapter began with the title 'the "Criminal Gene"' it should appropriately end by evaluating the choice of language used to describe the various alleles of the genes discussed within it. While the media prefers the sensational terms 'crime gene', 'murder gene' or 'warrior gene', many scientific studies instead talk about 'risk' alleles, by which they mean the allele which increases the chance of antisocial behavior when childhood maltreatment is present. Focusing on the idea that some people are more vulnerable because they possess alleles that don't function correctly is known as a diathesis stress perspective. Some scientists are beginning to reject this perspective and therefore a 'risk' label. Ellis,[82] for example, has noted that if the risk allele truly was dysfunctional it would have disappeared over time due to evolution. The fact that the different variants still remain suggest there must be some advantage to each of them. The label of 'risk' allele, with its negative connotation, might not therefore be appropriate.

One author has suggested that a better descriptive term for the relationship between environment and one particular gene allele might be an 'interactive predisposition', which he defines as 'the presence of a genetic difference between various groups [which] both increases and decreases the probability of individuals from one group, in comparison to individuals from the other group, developing a particular phenotypic trait, depending on the environmental conditions experienced.'[83] This is, however, a complicated definition.

Other authors have focused not on the negative aspects of one allele but on the beneficial aspects of the other. The latter might be described as a resiliency gene, one that makes its carriers more resilient to negative childhood experiences. A study on the LL allele of 5HTT described it as 'protective against childhood adversity'.[84] Using terms like 'resiliency' or 'protectiveness' shifts the focus to beneficial aspects, avoiding the carriers of the other allele being characterized as a victim. This conceptual shift is interesting, and may have implications for how genetic arguments are responded to in the justice system or in public policy discussions.

Another author has suggested rebranding Low MAOA as a 'plasticity allele' or a 'susceptibility' allele.[85] This label is attractive for both its accuracy and its relative neutrality. Plasticity suggests that its carriers are simply more influenced by their environment. If a Low MAOA individual's environment as a child is 'good' or 'supportive' (in other words, little to no childhood maltreatment) this person will be likely to act in a similar manner, resulting in him being less likely to engage in antisocial behavior. As his childhood environment moves closer to becoming 'bad' or 'adverse' (in other words, severe childhood maltreatment) he will

---

[82] Ellis et al., 'Differential susceptibility to the environment: An evolutionary-neurodevelopmental theory' (2011) 23 Psychology, 7, 23.

[83] Tabery, 'From a genetic predisposition to an interactive predisposition' (2009) 34 J Medicine and Philosophy 27, 35.

[84] Reif, 'Nature and nurture predispose to violent behaviour: serotonergic genes and adverse childhood environment' (2007) 32 Neuropsychopharmacology 2375, 2379.

[85] Bielsky, 'The nature (and nurture?) of plasticity in early human development' (2009) 4(4) Perspectives on Psychological Science 345.

again be likely to act in a similar manner, moving up the scale of probability of engaging in antisocial behavior.

A benefit to a label of 'plasticity' is that this accurately reflects the information in the studies. Simply labeling something as a 'risk' allele does not explain the change in rank when the individual is subject to a supportive environment, therefore it misrepresents the scientific evidence. It also does not allow for this to be acknowledged, or emphasized. It depicts the allele as the less desirable allele, whereas this is not necessarily the case. In a supportive environment, these people are less likely to commit crime than people with the other allele. Another benefit is that this perspective allows for people with the allele to modify their behavior. The diathesis stress perspective suggests that a person with the particular allele who has suffered childhood maltreatment will always be more likely to react aggressively in a stressful situation. A plasticity perspective suggests that a subsequent change in environment might reduce the likelihood of acting aggressively. As examples of this, Bakermans-Kranenburg's study[86] concluded that children with L-DRD4 (which some would term the 'risk' allele) showed the largest decline in conduct problems in response to positive parental training. Brody[87] showed similar results with children with S-5HTTLPR following family based intervention. A further study suggested that individuals with both S-5HTTLPR and L-DRD4 showed greater desistance from crime following marriage.

It is important that whatever term is ultimately chosen, it accurately reflects what the studies are describing. This requires consideration of the rank change depending on childhood environment, and also possibly the fact that the brain scan studies are indicating that the displayed aggression is defensive (resulting from fear or anxiety) rather than offensive.

4.9 RECONSIDERING THE CASE OF CHILD B

In the scenario, evidence is presented at trial that both Child A and Child B had the Low MAOA gene. Child B had additionally suffered childhood maltreatment severe enough to result in several hospital admissions. Child A did not appear to suffer any childhood maltreatment.

---

[86] 'DRD4 genotype moderates the impact of parental problems on unresolved loss or trauma' (2011) 13(3) Attachment and Human Behavior 253.

[87] 'Participation in a family-centered prevention program decreases genetic risk for adolescents' risky behaviors' (2009) 124 Pediatrics 911.

The MAOA gene was first linked to antisocial behaviour in 1993 in a study by Brunner. Since then studies, notably by Caspi, have suggested that individuals with the Low MAOA gene who have suffered childhood maltreatment are more likely to engage in antisocial behaviour than individuals without one or both of these factors. The Low MAOA gene appears in approximately one in three Caucasian males. Frequency amongst other racial groups appears to be higher. The Caspi study has been replicated by some studies, but not by others. A notable non-replication is the Christchurch study, in which the effect of the environmental factor of childhood maltreatment was not considered to be relevant, finding instead a gene main effect. These non-replications may be due to inconsistency in research design or measurement, but may also indicate that more research into the link between MAOA and antisocial behaviour is needed.

In this case, Child A is Low MAOA but has suffered no childhood maltreatment. According to the Caspi study, this places him in a group with a lower risk of engaging in antisocial conduct. When his Low MAOA status was raised in court, the judge noted the lack of an environmental influence and rejected the evidence. This approach is in line with the Caspi study, but may be challengeable as a result of the Christchurch study. In Child B's case, the evidence was accepted due to proof of childhood maltreatment.

4.10 CONCLUSION

Cesare Lombroso wrote in 1911 that 'the most horrendous and inhuman crimes have a biological, atavistic origin'.[88] While this chapter began by discussing XYY Syndrome, a genetic condition thought in the 1970s to result in criminality and therefore to support Lombroso's claim, it then moved on to show the rise of behavioral genetics, which argues against a purely atavistic or genetic origin.

Today, scientists generally accept that behavior results from the interaction of genes and environment. Scientists also generally agree on the difficulty in determining which genes are relevant to which behavior, which forms of environmental conditions are relevant, and the degree to which the genes and environment interact. This chapter has discussed some genes which appear to have a link to aggression and impulsive conduct, and therefore potentially to criminality. The studies discussed,

---

88 Cesare Lombroso, 'Criminal Man' (1911) (trans. M. Gibson) (Duke University Press 2006).

however, have made it clear that understanding exactly how the relevant genes and environmental factors interact is complicated. While this behavioral science knowledge is therefore useful in understanding potential causes of criminal conduct in general terms, among a particular subset in society, it is of less use when focusing on one particular individual. Behavioral genetics arguments in court, the subject of the next chapter, therefore need to be carefully considered.

5. The 'criminal gene' argument in the courts

5.1 INTRODUCTION

The previous chapter discussed several genes which have been associated with antisocial behavior. It considered the basic function of these genes, in order to explain the origin of this link, and then discussed scientific understanding of the role of these genes and their interaction with specific environmental conditions in human behavior.

This chapter will consider the current use of a genetics arguments in court. It will begin by discussing the admissibility of behavioral genetic evidence, and will then consider its use during both the trial and the sentencing phase of court proceedings.

5.2 ADMISSIBILITY OF EVIDENCE AT TRIAL

5.2.1 Relevance of Information

In order for evidence to be considered by a judge or jury in criminal proceedings it must first be admissible. The starting point for admissibility is generally that evidence is admissible if it is relevant.[1] 'Relevant evidence' can be defined as 'evidence that, if it were accepted, could rationally affect (directly or indirectly) the assessment of the probability of the existence of a fact in issue in the proceeding'.[2] An alternate definition is evidence which has 'any tendency to make a fact more or less probable than it would be without the evidence [where] the fact is of consequence in determining the application'.[3] One additional requirement

[1] See for example, s7 Evidence Act 2006 (NZ), s56 Evidence Act 1995 (Australia), Rule 402 US Federal Rules of Evidence. The UK does not have a specific rule admitting relevant evidence.

[2] Section 55(1) Evidence Act 1955(Australia).

[3] Rule 401, US Federal Rules of Evidence.

is that the evidence must be based on conditions that existed at the time the cause of action arose.

There is often a provision in evidence laws which allows for the exclusion of otherwise relevant evidence if its use would be unfair. In New Zealand and Australia, the test for exclusion is whether the probative value of the evidence is outweighed by its unfairly prejudicial effect on the proceeding.[4] In Australia evidence can additionally be excluded if it might be misleading or confusing, or cause or result in an undue waste of time.[5] In the United Kingdom, the court may refuse to allow evidence which 'would have such an adverse effect on the fairness of the proceedings that the court ought not to admit it'.[6] In the United States, Rule 403 states that 'the court may exclude relevant evidence if its probative value is substantially outweighed by a danger of one or more of the following: unfair prejudice, confusing the issues, misleading the jury, undue delay, wasting time, or needlessly presenting cumulative evidence'.

In determining whether genetic evidence can be introduced at trial in light of the previous discussion, the first question is whether the information is relevant. If we take the definition of relevance as 'affecting (directly or indirectly) the assessment of the probability of the existence of a fact in issue in the proceeding' this requires us to first identify 'a fact in issue'. This fact in issue could be described generally as whether the defendant had reduced mental capacity or was unable to achieve the required mental state. More specifically, it could be described as whether a person's genetic makeup, particularly in the presence of a negative childhood environment, affected that person's ability to control his impulses and/or resulted in him acting aggressively in the particular situation. Phrasing the issue this way, genetic evidence appears relevant in determining criminal responsibility.

The remaining question is whether the introduction of this evidence would have an adverse effect on the fairness of the proceeding, or result in unfair prejudice. With genetic information there is a clear concern that a defence argument that genetics affected the ability to control impulses might be then used by the prosecution to suggest that this might require a longer sentence in order to protect society from the inevitable reoffending. The use of genetic evidence as a 'double edged sword' will be considered in more detail below.

---

[4] Section 8(1) Evidence Act 2006 (NZ), s135 Evidence Act 1995 (Australia).

[5] Section 135 Evidence Act 1995 (Australia).

[6] Section 78 Police and Criminal Evidence Act 1984 (UK).

5.2.2 Evidence by Family Members

While mere opinion evidence is generally not admissible in court[7] there are exceptions to this. In New Zealand, s24 allows a witness to state an opinion if it 'is necessary to enable the witness to communicate, or the fact-finder to understand, what the witness saw, heard or otherwise perceived'. In Australia, s78 uses similar language, and in addition allows a lay opinion if it is 'necessary to obtain an adequate account or understanding of that person's perception of the matter or event'.

In the United Kingdom the provisions in the Criminal Justice Act 2003 relating to non-expert opinion are more detailed. This form of opinion is permitted in relation to the defendant's bad character in several situations.[8] One is where the opinion is 'important explanatory evidence'. This phrase is further defined in s102 as being evidence that 'without it, the court or jury would find it impossible or difficult properly to understand other evidence in the case'. Its value for understanding the case is substantial. A second situation is where the opinion is 'relevant to an important matter in issue between the defendant and the prosecution'. Again, this is further defined in a latter section. Section 103 suggests this might include, inter alia, 'the question whether the defendant has a propensity to commit offences of the kind with which he is charged'.

It is clear that one of the best ways to discuss the gene and environment interaction in a particular individual is through family members presenting evidence on the childhood of the individual, and on any relevant familial history of antisocial behavior which might suggest a genetic link. Such evidence would enable the family member to explain what they had seen, heard or perceived about their family's history, enabling the criteria in the New Zealand and Australian legislation to be satisfied. It would also likely meet the definition of 'important explanatory evidence' in the United Kingdom legislation, allowing the judge or jury to better understand the context of the genetics and environment argument being raised by the defence. It would further assist in understanding an important matter at issue between the defence and prosecution, being whether there was any impairment of mental responsibility resulting from the genetic and environmental factors.

---

7 Section 23 Evidence Act 2006 (NZ), s76 Evidence Act 1995 (Australia).

8 Section 101 Criminal Justice Act 2003 (UK).

5.2.3 Expert Opinion Evidence

If a person is considered an expert in his or her field, he may provide his expert opinion to the court, provided certain additional rules are met. These rules relate to 'assistance', 'relevant expertise', 'impartiality' and 'evidentiary reliability'.[9]

First, the expert opinion evidence must be of 'substantial help' to the fact-finder in ascertaining any fact that is of consequence to the determination of the proceeding.[10] In the United Kingdom, it was stated in *R v Turner*[11] that expert opinion 'is admissible to furnish the court with … information which is likely to be outside the experience and knowledge of a judge or jury'. Expert opinion evidence is unnecessary, however, if the judge or jury could 'form their own conclusions without help'.

Second, the expert must be giving an opinion which is based on a fact within the general body of knowledge that makes up the expertise of the expert,[12] or is 'wholly or substantially' based on that knowledge.[13] The expert must therefore be someone with specialized knowledge or skill based on experience, training or study. In the United States for example, Rule 702 requires an expert witness to be 'qualified as an expert by knowledge, skill, experience, training or education'.

Third, the expert must be able to give impartial evidence on the matters within his or her field of expertise. In the United Kingdom, Rule 33.2 Criminal Procedure Rules 2010 states that an expert has an overriding duty to give opinion evidence which is objective and unbiased. In the United States this requires that 'the expert has reliably applied the scientific principles and methods to the facts of the case'.[14]

Fourth, there may be a requirement that the subject matter be of acceptable standard. This may require that it is recognized as a science, and that the underlying evidence is generally accepted. This requirement would not, however, necessarily preclude evidence in a new area of

---

9 These four rules are taken from the UK common law, see the Law Commission (LawCom No 325) *Expert Evidence in Criminal Proceedings In England and Wales* (2011), [2.2].

10 Section 25(1) Evidence Act 2006 (NZ).

11 [1975] QB 834.

12 Section 25(3) Evidence Act 2006 (NZ).

13 Section 79(1) Evidence Act 1995 (Australia).

14 Rule 702(d).

science being admissible. In *R v Atkins* the English Court of Appeal observed that:[15]

> [W]hile there should be proper anxiety about new areas of expertise; and problems could arise where experts overstated their case … the remedy was not to prevent experts from expressing informed opinion, but:
>
> (i) to have evidence examined and criticised by an expert of equal experience and skill;
> (ii) to subject the evidence to rigorous testing by cross-examination; and
> (iii) to ensure careful judicial exposition to the jury of the difference between, on the one hand, arithmetical measures and, on the other, subjective, but informed, judgments.

In determining whether the opinion is generally accepted, individual jurisdictions might either apply the 'reliability' test or create a more specific test. As an example of the former test, the United Kingdom Court of Appeal in *Reed*[16] commented that 'expert evidence of a scientific nature is not admissible where the scientific basis on which it is advanced is insufficiently reliable for it to be put before the jury' but that 'there is no enhanced test of admissibility for such evidence'. As an example of the latter test, South Australia applies the *Bonython*[17] test which requires that 'the subject matter of the opinion forms part of a body of knowledge or experience which is sufficiently organized or recognized to be accepted as a reliable body of knowledge or experience'.[18] 'Acceptability' in this situation might fall to be judged by the court or by the scientific community.

The rules in relation to this fourth requirement in the United States appears more complicated. Until 1993, the test for admissibility of scientific evidence was found in *Frye v United States*,[19] which allowed scientific evidence that was 'sufficiently established' and had 'gained general acceptance in the particular field in which it belongs'. This test was criticized in the 1960s and 1970s for effectively imposing a 'waiting period' before evidence reached this standard of acceptance. In 1974 the situation was complicated when the Federal Rules of Evidence were introduced. Rule 702 states:

---

[15] *R v Atkins and Atkins* [2009] EWCA Crim 1876 [27]. Cited in New Zealand in *R v Shepherd* [2011] NZCA 666.

[16] [2009] EWCA Crim 2698, [2010] 1 Cr App R 23, [111].

[17] [1984] 38 SASR 45.

[18] At 47.

[19] 293 F 1013, 1014 (DC Cir 1923).

> A witness who is qualified as an expert by knowledge, skill, experience, training, or education may testify in the form of an opinion or otherwise if:
>
> (a) the expert's scientific, technical, or other specialized knowledge will help the trier of fact to understand the evidence or to determine a fact in issue;
> (b) the testimony is based on sufficient facts or data;
> (c) the testimony is the product of reliable principles and methods; and
> (d) the expert has reliably applied the principles and methods to the facts of the case.

It was not made clear whether the absence of the 'general acceptability' wording of *Frye* meant that Rule 702 was replacing *Frye,* or whether this was a differently worded codification of that test. The situation was not completely clarified until 1993 when the Supreme Court in *Daubert v Merrell Dow Pharmaceuticals*[20] confirmed that the requirement that science be based on reliable scientific principles and required federal courts to follow Rule 702, and that this replaced *Frye*.[21] Under *Daubert*, it is the judge and not the scientific community taking the gatekeeper role.[22] The judge is to make a 'preliminary assessment of whether the testimony's underlying reasoning or methodology is scientifically valid and properly can be applied to the facts at issue'. This might involve a consideration of such factors as testability, peer review and publication, the existence of methodological standards (including the error rate of the methodology), and general acceptance within the scientific community. Overall, it is a 'flexible' test, with the focus 'solely on principles and methodology, not on the conclusions they generate'.

Expert opinion evidence from behavioral geneticists, who could discuss any genetic testing and the impact of the gene and environmental interaction, or from neuroscientists, who could discuss fMRI scans showing MAOA or serotonin levels would appear to be of 'substantial help' to a judge or jury. The technical nature of the scientific knowledge

---

20 509 US 579 (1993).

21 It should be noted that some states still follow *Frye*. One of the reasons for the change was that 'general acceptance' takes time, effectively imposing a 'waiting period'. It was also regarded as an 'elitist and unhelpful' approach. When Rule 702 was subsequently drafted in 1974 the *Frye* test of 'general acceptance' was not mentioned.

22 Zick describes the effect of Daubert as taking 'the decision-making process out of the hands of the scientific community and placing it in the hands of the trial judge' and that Daubert converted trial courts from 'passive recipients of scientific and technical data' into engaged evaluators of scientific technique: 'Constitutional empiricism: Quasi-neutral principles and constitutional half-truths' (2003) 82 N C L Rev 115, 181.

would mean that it is outside of the common general knowledge of these individuals. This would satisfy the first criterion for admissibility of expert opinion evidence. The second and third criteria, that the evidence is within the expertise of the expert, and that he can give impartial evidence, are more subjective but it can be noted that both behavioral genetics and neuroscience are recognized scientific fields with people that are classified as experts.

The fact that research into the interaction between Low MAOA and the environment, or Low Serotonin levels is a new area of science will not necessarily be a barrier to admissibility. Particularly in relation to MAOA and childhood maltreatment, multiple studies have been conducted. While they are not producing consistent results and many questions still remain, this will probably not prevent the evidence being admissible. The lack of consistency in the studies is more a matter for believability, and therefore the weight given to this evidence, than of admissibility.

Genetics evidence does appear to meet the standard for admissibility at trial stage, although it will not necessarily follow that judges or juries will be persuaded by it, or will give it any more weight than any other piece of evidence. The interests of justice suggest that while care must be taken that this evidence does not unfairly prejudice the defendant, it should be allowed to be presented in court at the trial stage. Whether or not it will be (or has been) successful will be discussed below.

5.3 GENETICS EVIDENCE DURING THE TRIAL: TO NEGATE MENS REA

5.3.1 Mens Rea

The term 'mens rea' refers to the state of mind that is required as part of an element of a crime, and might be phrased as intention, knowledge, recklessness or negligence. Generally, mens rea requires that the person consciously desire a result, or know that the result is almost certain to follow from his conduct.

If a crime has a specified mens rea element, the accused cannot be convicted of that crime unless that element is established. In *Landrigan*, a case which will be discussed further below, the judge commented that 'it is highly doubtful that the sentencing court would have been moved by the information that Landrigan was a remorseless violent killer because he was genetically programmed to be violent'. The use of the language, 'genetically programmed' raises an interesting issue. If an individual killed because he was genetically programmed to kill, or to put it another way, because his genes gave him no choice in a given situation but to kill, can he fairly be said to have met the mens rea element of intention to murder? Or are his actions in fact unintentional and more analogous to acting as an automaton? Even if we accept that the judge's choice of wording in *Landrigan* is not scientifically accurate, the overriding question remains the same. The scientific studies discussed in the previous chapter suggest that certain individuals, while not 'programmed to kill', can be described as perhaps having a 'genetic propensity' for violence, or due to their genetics and environmental background, are simply more likely to act impulsively or aggressively. Does this affect their ability to meet the mens rea requirement? This section will consider some examples where this kind of argument has been raised.

5.3.2 Application to Genetics

5.3.2.1 Serotonin cases

Bernet et al.,[23] in an article considering MAOA and SLC6A4, discuss several cases in which the presence of low levels of serotonin have been raised in court in an attempt to negate mens rea. While these cases do not specifically refer to a genetic reason for low serotonin (for example, the 5HTT gene) they do provide good examples of how such an argument might be run.

In *State v Jon Hall*, Hall was convicted of the first degree murder of his estranged wife. On appeal, an expert witness presented evidence that Hall had low levels of serotonin in his brain. Another expert witness testified that there was a 'correlation between low levels of serotonin in the brain and violent acts' to the extent that in his opinion, Hall was 'unable … to achieve the mental state' necessary for criminal liability. The prosecution presented expert evidence that the serotonin testing in this case lacked accuracy, and the conviction was affirmed.

In *Tennessee v Godsey*, the defendant was charged with premeditated first degree murder following a bar fight. Expert and lay evidence of low serotonin levels, alcoholism, brain damage, mental retardation and intermittent explosive disorder were introduced. Godsey argued that these factors resulted in his having diminished capacity (which under Tennessee law would operate to negate the mens rea). The jury appeared to

---

[23] 'Bad nature, bad nurture and testimony regarding MAOA and SLC6A4 genotyping at murder trials' (2007) 52(6) J Forensic Sci 1362.

agree to some extent and found him guilty of second degree murder, sentencing him to 25 years' imprisonment.

In *State v Payne*, the defendant was charged with first degree premeditated murder and first degree felony murder. An expert witness argued that Payne had statistically low serotonin levels and that therefore his 'capacity to control impulse once it had occurred [was] virtually non-existent'. The argument was therefore that Payne could not be found guilty of first degree murder because of his low serotonin levels. The court informed the jury that his mental condition could have prevented him from forming the mens rea for the offence, and the jury agreed, finding Payne guilty of the lesser offence of second degree murder.

These cases can be compared to *Police v Uncapher*, where an argument on appeal that Uncapher's low levels of serotonin prevented him from forming the mens rea for murder was rejected, due to evidence of premeditation.

Despite the argument being unsuccessful in two of these four cases, the fact that the argument is being made is interesting. In two of the cases, *Hall* and *Uncapher*, factual problems (in *Hall*, problems with the testing, and in *Uncapher*, evidence of premeditation) prevented the need to consider the impact of the serotonin argument. The cases suggest that these type of arguments are beginning to appear in the US courts, and *Payne* and *Godsey* suggest they may succeed in appropriate cases.[24]

5.3.2.2 *State v Waldroup*[25]

In October 2006, Davis Bradley Waldroup Jr was living in a trailer in an isolated area on Kimsey Mountain having separated from his wife, Penny, whom he believed to have had an extramarital affair. On the day in question, Penny drove out to the trailer to drop off their four children for a visit. She took a friend, Leslie Bradshaw,[26] for support, and was sufficiently worried about seeing Waldroup to tell another friend to call the police if she had not returned by a certain time. When they arrived, Waldroup appeared carrying a rifle and a photograph of a bear he had killed with the rifle, which he said he wanted to show the children. He attempted to talk to his wife, and when she refused to speak to him took the keys from the car and threw them away, preventing her from leaving. He then shot Leslie Bradshaw eight times with the rifle and sliced her

---

24 Further, it should be remembered that in none of the cases was genetic testing carried out. This might have strengthened the argument.

25 No E2010-01906-CCA-R3-CD, 2011 WL 5051677 (Tenn Crim App Mar 29 2011).

26 This was the woman with whom he believed his wife had an affair.

head open with a sharp object, likely a machete. Next, he shot Penny in the back as she attempted to flee, cut her with a penknife and struck her with a shovel and a machete. He pulled her into the house and told his children to say goodbye to their mother, as this was the last time they would see her. He finally took her into the bedroom and attempted to have sexual intercourse with her. When a policeman arrived (having been called by the friend who had not heard from Penny by the appointed time), Penny ran from the trailer and begged the officer to protect her children.

Waldroup was charged with two counts of especially aggravated kidnapping (preventing both women from leaving by discarding the car keys while carrying a rifle), one count of first degree murder (of Leslie Bradshaw) and one count of attempted first degree murder (of Penny Waldroup). The trial was heard by a jury.

The defence argued that genetics was relevant. Defence Attorney Wylie Richardson stated early that 'it wasn't a who done it … it was a why done it'. The prosecution had described the crime scene in vivid terms: 'there are murders and then there are … hacking to death, trails of blood',[27] and the defence used genetics as a way of countering that image:

> I think if that wasn't out there, then all the jury would have seen are all these terrible pictures where he took a machete and hacked at his wife. And they would have thought, he's the worst of the worst and that's what the death penalty is for, the worst of the worst. But because they heard all the mental issues, they understood what was going on in him and understood why he did what he did.

Genetic tests introduced by the defence showed that Waldroup, a Caucasian male, had the Low MAOA gene. Further, evidence was introduced to show that he had been severely abused as a child, and had also recently encountered 'stressful life experiences'.[28] As a result of these two factors the defence argued that he was 'unable to engage in the reflection and judgment necessary to premeditate the crimes'.

The defence's evidence appeared to convince at least some of the jury members. One juror later commented to newspapers that 'evidently, it's just something that doesn't tick right. … Some people without this would

[27] The Judge, Carroll Ross, commented that this was 'one of the most senseless, brutal slayings [he had] ever witnessed in [his] entire career'.

[28] Waldroup also had both long and short alleles of the SLC6A4 gene. According to William Bernet, the expert witness, this put him at an increased risk of depression and suicidality.

react totally different than he would. A diagnosis is a diagnosis, it's there. A bad gene is a bad gene.' Another commented 'there was more to his whole life that led to that moment' and when asked if the jury decision was swayed by genetics, replied, 'Oh, I'm sure … and his background, nature vs nurture'.

Waldroup was sentenced to 32 years' imprisonment. This comprised two consecutive sentences of 20 years for especially aggravated kidnapping and 12 years for aggravated kidnapping, a concurrent term of 12 years for the attempted second degree murder of his wife, and six years for the voluntary manslaughter of Leslie Bradshaw. In all convictions the judge awarded the maximum sentence available.

It is the conviction for the voluntary manslaughter of Leslie Bradshaw which is the most interesting, and appears to best show the impact of the MAOA argument. Under Tennessee law, criminal homicide is defined as the unlawful killing of another person, which may be: first degree murder (a premeditated and intentional killing of another); second degree murder (a knowing killing of another); or voluntary manslaughter. Voluntary manslaughter is defined as 'the intentional or knowing killing of another in a state of passion produced by adequate provocation sufficient to lead a reasonable person to act in an irrational manner'. The key element is provocation. It is unclear exactly what Leslie Bradshaw did to provoke her killing. Waldroup believed her to have had an affair with Penny, resulting in the breakdown of his marriage, but he was already aware of this fact prior to the day in question. On that day, she did not appear to be doing anything to provoke the attack, apart from being present. According to the facts taken from the judgement, 'Ms Bradshaw was standing near the passenger-side door. Appellant was standing by the driver's side of the van. Appellant began to yell at Ms Bradshaw and blamed her for the demise of his marriage to Mrs Waldroup. Appellant, while standing by the driver's side door, raised the rifle and began to fire'.

It appeared that the jury was sufficiently convinced by the genetic argument and evidence of abuse as a child to conclude that Waldroup's actions were not intentional or premeditated.[29] This precluded a finding of first degree murder. Why the evidence also precluded second degree murder is unclear. The conviction for voluntary manslaughter is a difficult fit on the facts. It requires acceptance that Bradshaw, by her mere presence, provoked the attack. The only reason for this result must be that while the jury accepted that Waldroup knowingly killed her and was therefore deserving of some punishment, the explanation of the Low

---

[29] It could be noted that the jury deliberated for only 11 hours.

MAOA gene and childhood maltreatment was so persuasive that they returned a verdict of the least serious crime available.

Judge Carroll Ross sentenced Waldroup to the maximum six years imprisonment for voluntary manslaughter, while making his feelings about this result clear through his advice to Waldroup to 'think twice about appealing. The state might not mind trying this again and asking for the death penalty. You might not be as fortunate with a jury next time'.[30]

5.4 GENETICS EVIDENCE DURING THE TRIAL: AS A DEFENCE

5.4.1 Insanity

5.4.1.1 Introduction

The criminal law begins with a presumption that all individuals are sane at the time they committed the relevant act. If this is not the case, the individual has the burden of demonstrating this and rebutting the presumption. A defence of insanity reflects an argument that an individual is mentally incapable of understanding or perhaps controlling his or her conduct. It is therefore more appropriate that this person receive treatment than punishment.

The insanity defence arose from the M'Naghten case in 1843. The M'Naghten Rule states that an individual is to be regarded as sane unless it is proven that 'at the time of committing the act, the accused was laboring under such a defect of reason, from disease of the mind, as not to know what he was doing was wrong'. This is still the law in the United Kingdom.

In New Zealand, the test is codified in s23 Crimes Act:

> No person shall be convicted of an offence by reason of an act done or omitted by him when laboring under natural imbecility or disease of the mind to such an extent as to render him incapable
>
> (a) Of understanding the nature and quality of the act or omission; or

---

[30] Despite this, Waldroup appealed in March 2011, with the decision being given in August 2013. The appeal was only on the basis that the facts did not support the two kidnapping charges. The court of criminal appeals in Tennessee agreed, reversing this ruling and remanding these charges to the trial court for a new trial.

(b) Of knowing that the act or omission was morally wrong, having regard to the commonly accepted standards of right and wrong.

It is generally recognized that this is a codification of the M'Naghten Rule.[31]

In Australia, the test differs by state, but all are recognized as being based on the M'Naghten Rule. Six States or Territories[32] and the Commonwealth also include a volitional element, allowing insanity to be argued where the individual was unable to control his actions. As an example, in Western Australia the law states (with the volitional element in italics):

> A man is not criminally responsible for an act or omission on account of unsoundness of mind if at the time of doing the act or making the omission he is in such a state of mental impairment as to deprive him of capacity to understand what he is doing, *or of capacity to control his actions*, or of capacity to know that he ought not to do the act or make the omission.

In the United States, four states do not have an insanity defence.[33] Of the rest, approximately half of the states apply the definition in the Insanity Defence Reform Act 1984:

> It is an affirmative defense to a prosecution under any Federal statute that, at the time of the commission of the acts constituting the offense, the defendant, as a result of a severe mental disease or defect, was unable to appreciate the nature and quality or the wrongfulness of his acts. Mental disease or defect does not otherwise constitute a defense.

The other states use the American Law Institute Model Penal Code, which relevantly states:

> A person is not responsible for criminal conduct if at the time of such conduct as a result of mental disease or defect he lacks substantial capacity either to appreciate the criminality [wrongfulness] of his conduct or to conform his conduct to the requirements of the law.

Generally, therefore, an insanity defence has two criteria. First is the existence of a mental disease or defect, and second is a consequential

---

31 While it seems to vary, due to 'render him incapable' the courts have not interpreted it this way.

32 Western Australia, Queensland, Tasmania, South Australia, ACT and Northern Territory.

33 Utah, Montana, Idaho, Kansas.

inability to understand what he is doing, or to understand that it is wrong, or (in some jurisdictions) to control his actions.

5.4.1.2 XYY Cases and the insanity defence

The idea of behavioral genetic evidence being used to establish a defence of insanity was first tested with XYY syndrome. In an early case, *People v Farley*[34] Judge Farrell permitted expert evidence of XYY to go to the jury. The jury rejected this evidence, however, and found him guilty of murder. Subsequent United States cases appeared less willing to consider a link between XYY and insanity. In *Millard v. State*,[35] the judge declined to allow the jury to consider insanity. While it was accepted that the defendant had XYY syndrome, this in itself did not result in a finding of insanity, and a link between the two was 'not based on reasonable medical certainty'.

In the same year, a Californian Appeal court reached the same result in *People v Tanner*.[36] The court refusal to grant the defendant's motion to replace his guilty plea with a plea of insanity on the basis that the causal link between XYY syndrome or aggressive behavior and insanity could not be established. The court considered that the evidence suggested 'only that aggressive behavior may be one manifestation of the XYY Syndrome' and not 'that all XYY individuals [we]re by nature involuntarily aggressive'.

One successful example in Australia was that of Laurence Hannett who was acquitted of murder on the grounds of insanity after a psychiatrist testified that due to his XYY syndrome 'every cell in his body was abnormal'. While this case was cited in a subsequent case, *People v Yukl*, the court in that case nevertheless denied funding for genetic testing to establish XYY Syndrome on the basis of lack of causation between genetics and behavior.[37]

5.4.1.3 Application to genetics

None of the cases thus far involving evidence of Low MAOA or serotonin have attempted to argue insanity as a defence, likely learning from the XYY cases. Whether insanity could be successfully argued as a defence in a Low MAOA or serotonin individual is uncertain. The first criterion of insanity generally requires the presence of a mental disease

---

[34] Sup Ct Queens County, Indictment No 1827, April 30 1969], unreported, cited in *People v Yukl* 372 NYS2d 313 (NY Supp Ct 1975).

[35] 261 A 2d 227 (Md Ct Spec App 1970).

[36] 91 Cal Rptr 656 (Ct app 1970).

[37] *People v Yukl* 372 NYS2d 313 (NY Supp Ct 1975).

or defect, described in New Zealand as natural imbecility or a disease of the mind. This can be a difficult concept to define, and indeed the New Zealand Court of Appeal referred to 'disease of the mind' as being 'a term which defies precise definition and which can comprehend mental derangement in the widest sense'.[38] What is important is that there be an internal rather than external cause. The condition must have something to do with a person's psychological or emotional make-up, resulting in the impairment of the functioning and reasoning of the mind in a way that is not transitory, and not self-induced.[39] While it is generally mental disorders, for example hallucinations and delusions, that meet this standard, behavioral disorders can technically be included.

Based on this understanding, an insanity argument based on Low MAOA could succeed. It is caused by something internal, being a reduced amount of the MAOA enzyme being produced. It affects a person's psychological makeup, by making them more likely to act aggressively or impulsively. Further, the amygdala studies suggest that low MAOA affects the ability to reason (and interpret fearful faces) in a way that is not transitory or self-induced.

Classifying Low MAOA as a disease of the mind is also consistent with two categories of cases which have reached the same results. The first is a series of cases considering dissociative states following reactions to 'ordinary stresses and disappointments of life'. In a Canadian case, *Rabey v R*,[40] a student attacked a female when she rejected his romantic advances. Psychiatric evidence suggested that his attack was carried out in a state of dissociation caused by a psychological blow following discovery of the young woman's rejection of him. The majority commented that 'any malfunctioning of the mind or mental disorder, while having its source primarily in some subjective condition or weakness internal to the accused (whether fully understood or not) may be "a disease of the mind" if it prevents the accused from knowing what he is doing'. The dissociation in this case was considered to have its source primarily in the accused's psychological or emotional makeup. This case was approved by the High Court of Australia in *R v Falconer*,[41] which phrased the question as to whether the reaction was 'one of an unsound

---

[38] *R v Cottle* (1958) NZLR 999, 1011.

[39] *R v Kemp* [1957] 1 QB 399. In this case, Lord Devlin commented that 'the law is not concerned with the brain but with the mind, in the sense that "mind" is ordinarily used, the mental faculties of reason, memory, and understanding'.

[40] [1980] 2 SCR 513 (SCC).

[41] (1990) 171 CLR 30 HCA.

mind, or the reaction of sound, healthy mind to external factors'. Similarly, in New Zealand, cases have accepted this approach. In *Police v Bannin*,[42] it was commented that 'If the primary cause of the state of abnormality was internal to the accused, for example … psychological inability to cope with the ordinary stresses of life … the condition will be classified as a disease of the mind. The contrary will be true if the principal cause was external to the accused …' Similarly in *R v Yesler*,[43] the accused's actions were considered an extreme reaction to 'ordinary stresses that can be expected in life, and therefore cause lay in internal psychological, psychiatric or emotional make-up'.

The second category of cases relate to diabetes. In *R v Quick*,[44] a diabetic nurse assaulted a disabled patient while suffering from hypoglycaemia (low blood sugar caused by excessive insulin). The High Court judge considered that Quick's actions were a consequence of a disease of the mind caused by his diabetes. The Court of Appeal disagreed, finding that the cause was external 'by his use of the insulin prescribed by his doctor'. In *R v Hennessy*[45] however, the person was hyperglycemic (elevated blood sugar caused by failure to take insulin). In this case, the Court of Appeal found this to be a disease of the mind, as his actions were caused by an internal inherent defect.

The obvious challenge to classifying Low MAOA or serotonin as an internally caused disease of the mind is that it is not Low MAOA alone that predisposes an individual to the conduct. There must also be childhood maltreatment. In the language of the insanity defence, while the MAOA might be considered an internal cause, the environmental factor would be an external cause. The courts have addressed the consequences of the presence of a combination of both internal and external factors in self-medication cases. In these cases, a person with psychological issues (an internal factor) has self-medicated with drugs or alcohol (an external factor) resulting in the behavior in question. In determining whether an insanity defence could apply, courts in the United Kingdom,[46] Australia[47] and New Zealand[48] have phrased the test

---

42 [1991] 2 NZLR 237.

43 [2007] 1 NZLR 240.

44 [1973] EWCA Crim 1.

45 [1989] 2 All ER 9.

46 *AG for Northern Ireland v Gallagher* [1963] AC 349.

47 *R v Falconer* (1990) ALJR 20, *DPP (Vic) v Whelan* (2006) 177 A Crim R 449.

48 *Police v Bannin* [1991] 2 NZLR 237, *R v Lipsey-McCarthy* CA 237/04 28 October 2004.

as either 'would the disease itself, ignoring the intoxication, be considered disease of the mind?' or 'what is the primary or principal cause?' or whether the action was 'caused or contributed to' by the disease of the mind. A genetics argument would appear to meet this test. Ignoring the external (environmental) case, the internal cause of Low MAOA or serotonin would still be a disease of the mind. It may be considered a 'principal' cause, but should satisfy a 'contributed to' test.

It would appear, therefore, that the first criterion for insanity would be able to be satisfied in the United Kingdom, Australia, and New Zealand. The situation in the United States is slightly trickier. For those states adopting the M'Naghten Rule, the approach would be the same. In the other states, which have adopted the Model Penal Code, the situation is complicated by the definition of 'mental disease or defect' which specifically 'do[es] not include an abnormality manifested only by repeated criminal or otherwise antisocial conduct'. Since the consequence of Low MAOA or serotonin claimed would be antisocial conduct, this might preclude the use of this defence.

The second criterion for insanity relates to the effect of the mental disease or defect. The jurisdictions discussed above all refer to one effect as being equivalent to the M'Naghten 'not to know what he was doing was wrong' through either being unable to understand the nature and quality of the act, or not knowing that the act was morally wrong. This is the more problematic criterion. The cases suggest that the individuals are aware of the nature and quality of the act. Waldroup, for instance, was able to use three different weapons, tell his children that effectively he was about to kill their mother, try to convince her to shower to remove the blood, and attempt sexual intercourse with her. He was able to explain coherently to the police officer that he had killed Bradshaw, and show him the body. His defence focused on his inability to control his impulses, rather than a belief that what he was doing was acceptable. This would suggest, therefore, that this criterion and therefore the defence, would not succeed.

In the United States, the Model Penal Code uses an alternative second criterion, that the individual is unable to 'conform his conduct to the requirements of the law'. This has been described as an 'irresistible impulse' test. To satisfy this, it would be necessary to show that the impulse was uncontrollable rather than uncontrolled. In other words, the action would not have occurred but for the defect. This will be challenging to establish, as the action is correctly a result of the gene plus environment, and even then, this makes the impulsive action more likely to occur. The causal connection between the gene and the action will probably not be sufficient.

Some Australian states also add an alternative second criterion, being that the unsoundness of mind deprives him 'of capacity to control his actions'. This also seems to be an application of the irresistible impulse test, although the High Court of Australia in *Falconer* interpreted it to require an unconscious involuntary action due to the mental disease. Again, this will be difficult to prove, for the reasons discussed above. In addition, there has been no evidence thus far of the actions being unconscious. The individuals are aware of what they are doing. It appears unlikely therefore, that a defence of insanity would be available in a genetics argument.

5.4.2 Diminished Responsibility

5.4.2.1 Introduction

Diminished responsibility operates as a partial defence, reducing murder to manslaughter. Such a partial defence recognizes that while a person might not be legally insane, they are suffering from some form of abnormality of mind which substantially impairs their judgement or responsibility for actions. It is accepted as a defence in the UK, in four states in Australia and in several US states. It is not a recognized defence in New Zealand.

5.4.2.2 Elements of diminished responsibility

In the UK, s2 of the Homicide Act 1957[49] states that:

> **Persons suffering from diminished responsibility**
>
> (1) A person ('D') who kills or is a party to the killing of another is not to be convicted of murder if D was suffering from an abnormality of mental functioning which–
>
> a) Arose from a recognized medical condition;
> b) Substantially impaired D's ability to do one or more of the things mentioned in subsection (1A); and
> c) Provides an explanation for D's acts and omissions in doing or being a party to the killing
>
> (1A) Those things are–
>
> a) To understand the nature of D's conduct;
> b) To form a rational judgment;
> c) To exercise self-control.

[49] As inserted by s52 Coroners and Justice Act 2009.

The first requirement of the partial defence is therefore an 'abnormality of mental functioning'. Under the previous s2 Homicide Act, this was phrased as an 'abnormality of mind', which was defined by Lord Parker in the UK Court of Appeal in *R v Byrne*[50] as being 'a state of mind so different from that of ordinary human beings that the reasonable man would term it abnormal'. In the Australian states which have a diminished responsibility defence, three (New South Wales,[51] ACT[52] and Queensland[53]) also refer to 'abnormality of mind', while the Northern Territory[54] requires that the 'mental capacity be substantially impaired'.

The second requirement is that this abnormality arises as a result of a recognized medical condition. In New South Wales, this is phrased as 'resulting from an underlying condition'. ACT and Queensland use 'arising from a condition of arrested or retarded development of mind or any inherent cause or whether induced by disease or injury' and the Northern Territory requires it to arise 'wholly or partly from an underlying condition'.

Third, it must substantially impair the person's ability to understand the nature of his conduct, to form a rational judgment or to exercise self-control. In New South Wales this is phrased as 'to understand events or to judge whether a person's actions were right or wrong, or to control himself or herself'. In ACT, it must simply 'substantially impair his or her mental responsibility for the act or omission'. In Queensland, it must impair capacity to understand what he is doing, to control his actions, or to know he ought not to act.

Fourth, the UK is alone in requiring that the impairment provides an explanation for the action. In the United Kingdom, ACT, and Queensland it is specified that a person meeting these criteria shall not be convicted of murder, but of manslaughter. In New South Wales and the Northern Territory, this is a matter of discretion, requiring that the impairment be so substantial that this result should occur.

5.4.2.3 Application to a genetics argument

The potential success of an argument of diminished responsibility in relation to Low MAOA or serotonin is difficult to predict. Such an argument may well satisfy the requirements of subsections (a)–(c) of the UK legislation, or the Australian equivalents, but it may have difficulties

---

50 [1960] 2 QB 396, 403.
51 Crimes Act 1900 (NSW) s23A.
52 Crimes Act 1900 (ACT) s14.
53 Criminal Code 1899 (Qld) s304A.
54 Criminal Code Act s159.

with the initial wording of the section, which requires the condition to be an 'abnormality'. In previous chapters, the prevalence of the Low MAOA allele has been discussed, suggesting that it occurs in 1 in 3 Caucasian males, and up to 2 in 3 Asian males. If the definition of abnormality in *R v Byrne* continues to apply in the United Kingdom, requiring that the abnormality be so different from that of ordinary human beings that a reasonable person would consider it an abnormality, it is not clear that this will be satisfied. If the gene's interaction with environment is taken into account (in other words, if the abnormality is not simply the Low MAOA allele but the Low MAOA allele and childhood maltreatment) this might lower the rate of occurrence, potentially allowing it to be seen as abnormal. The wording of the legislation, however, refers to 'abnormality of mind' and to 'inherent causes' suggesting that the external factors might not form part of the classification of abnormality.[55] On this analysis, diminished responsibility will probably not be available. It is worth, however, considering the remaining criteria on the chance that this analysis is incorrect.

The second requirement is that Low MAOA or serotonin is an established medical condition. This should be satisfied. It can be tested for, and numerous studies have been conducted on its effect on behavior. As it relates to the amount of an enzyme produced in the brain, It is also likely to be either an underlying or inherent condition. Third, it must impair the individual's ability to do certain things. The United Kingdom section includes 'exercise self-control' as part of the list, as do the NSW and Queensland equivalents. This appears to fit with an MAOA argument. The ACT and Northern Territory on the other hand, refer to mental responsibility and mental capacity respectively being impaired. These are more difficult concepts to define, but lack of control might satisfy these. Whether Low MAOA operates as a substantial impairment is a matter of judgment on the facts of each case, and at this point, the external environmental factors would become important and require close consideration. Finally, the United Kingdom requires that the abnormality explain the defendant's actions. The scientific studies discussed above have demonstrated a causal link between Low MAOA or serotonin and lack of control when particular environmental conditions are present, which would in appropriate cases provide an explanation.

---

55 A comparison can be drawn with the mixed causes cases discussed above under insanity, where the question was whether it was a disease of the mind when the external clause was not considered.

5.4.2.4 Conclusion

Diminished responsibility, in those jurisdictions which have codified such a partial defence, may be available for use in a genetics type case. If the facts of the *Waldroup* case are considered, diminished responsibility might have been arguable. He was shown to have Low MAOA, an established medical condition. His actions on the day, with the use of numerous weapons, indicate a loss of self-control, which the jury appeared to see as explained by the Low MAOA (and perhaps his childhood maltreatment). In fact, given that diminished responsibility reduces murder to manslaughter, diminished responsibility would have provided a more legally understandable and defensible result than the actual sentence of voluntary manslaughter. Again, the main issue would have been whether the abnormality requirement was met.

5.5 GENETICS EVIDENCE DURING APPEAL: INEFFECTIVE COUNSEL

In the United States, the majority of genetics arguments occur during appeals on the basis that trial counsel was ineffective. This argument is based on the 6th and 14th Amendments. The 6th Amendment protects the right to a fair trial, which includes the right of an accused 'to have the assistance of counsel for his defence'. In *McMann v Richardson*[56] the Supreme Court held that part of this right is the right to 'effective' assistance of counsel. The 14th Amendment prevents deprivation of any person of 'life, liberty, or property, without due process of law'. In capital cases, due process has also been held to require effective counsel.[57]

In order to establish that counsel was ineffective, the Supreme Court in *Strickland v Washington*[58] established a two-part test. First, counsel's performance must be 'deficient', and second, this deficiency must have 'prejudiced' the defendant. This latter part requires proof of a 'reasonable probability' that the verdict would have been different with effective counsel, or that the ineffectiveness 'so undermined the proper functioning of the adversarial process that the trial cannot be relied on as having produced a just result'. The starting point is a presumption that counsel acted competently.

---

56 397 US 759 771 (1970).

57 *Powell v Alabama* 287 US 45 (1932).

58 466 US 669.

5.5.1 Application to Genetics Cases

In Denno's[59] study of 33 genetics cases from 2007–11, she comments that 'most' included claims of ineffective counsel. In 10 of these cases the defendants were successful in having their death sentences vacated, and in seven of these the failure to investigate or present behavioral genetics evidence was noted as the decisive factor.

It is clear that such an argument cannot succeed unless the defendant actually provides evidence of a genetic test showing Low MAOA or serotonin (a 'positive' test) during the appeal. A lack of a chance to obtain a test will not be sufficient.[60] In addition, the defendant must also demonstrate how the positive test result would have affected the outcome of the case. In *Landrigan v Stewart*, discussed in more detail below, the claim eventually failed as it was felt that genetic evidence would not have made a difference to the result.

The mere fact that counsel obtained a positive test does not mean that counsel is ineffective for failing to introduce this as evidence. In *Martin v State*[61] counsel had received the positive test results, but ultimately recommended that his client accept a plea deal. This was seen by the appeal court as a legitimate decision. In *US v Duran*,[62] discussed further below, it was explained that 'tactical and strategic choices made by defence counsel need not be perfect' and that an appellant must 'surmount a very high hurdle' to prevail in these circumstances.

5.5.2 Genetic Testing or Social History Evidence?

One trend that appears to be emerging from these cases is that genetic evidence forms only part of the larger category of explaining the defendant's background. While the courts overwhelmingly feel that the defendant's personal and familial history is a relevant factor that an effective counsel would investigate and present evidence on, it is not

---

[59] Deborah Denno has published two pieces of research studying genetics cases: 'Behavioral genetics in criminal cases: 1994–2007' in *The Impact of Behavioral Sciences on Criminal Law*, Farahany (ed.) (2009) (Oxford University Press 2011), and 'Courts' increasing consideration of behavioral genetics evidence in criminal cases: Results of a longitudinal study' (2011) *Michigan State Law Review* 967.

[60] *State v Kirkland* 140 Ohio St.3d 73, 5 NE 3d 818 (Ohio, May 13, 2014), *State v Tenace* NE 2d 2006 WL 664327 (Ohio App 6 Dist 2006, March 17, 2006), *Taylor v Florida* 887 So 3d 749 (March 8, 2012).

[61] Unrep SW 3d 2007 WL 2811995, Tenn Crim App 2007.

[62] 201200440 (NMCCA 2014).

clear that this requires specific genetic testing to be performed and presented in court.

In *Hawkins v Wong*,[63] for example, the Ninth Circuit Court of Appeals found that there should be an evidentiary hearing to determine whether counsel was ineffective for failing to hire a social historian who arguably could have shown that the defendant 'was born into a family marked by extreme pathology and dysfunction over multiple generations.' This testimony would likely have revealed a genetic predisposition to alcoholism and mental illness which, coupled with the accused's childhood of abuse, neglect and abandonment, would have helped in understanding his actions.

In *State v Ferguson*,[64] the failure to introduce genetic evidence of a genetic predisposition to a personality disorder did not lead to counsel being considered ineffective as sufficient evidence had been produced in other ways. Specific testimony on genetics by expert witnesses was not required where counsel could explain this link to the jury,[65] or where the jury could infer a genetic link.[66] In other cases, claims for ineffective counsel have been successful where there was a failure to investigate the defendant's background, but the language has been unclear as to whether this was a failure to consider genetics, social information, or a combination of the two. Where the jury had heard genetic evidence during the trial, it was not necessary to reintroduce it at sentencing.

5.5.3 Steven Mobley

In 1991 Steven Mobley[67] entered a Domino's Pizza store with the intention of robbing it. Having done so, and as he was leaving, he turned and shot the manager who was on his knees begging for his life.[68] Mobley was arrested three weeks later, after robbing a dry cleaning store. When he realised he was being chased by police he threw his pistol out of the car window. This was subsequently retrieved by the police, and when Mobley realised it would additionally link him to the Domino's robbery, he confessed to both robberies and the murder.

---

[63] 2010 WL 3516399 (ED Cal Sept 2 2010).

[64] 887 SW 2d 585.

[65] *Hodges v Bell* 548 F Supp 2d 485 (MD Tenn 2008).

[66] *Woodall v Simpson* 2009 WL 464939 (WD Ky 2009).

[67] Also Known As 'Tony', his middle name.

[68] Mobley boasted of this to his cellmates. Physical evidence from the scene supports the claim that the victim was on his knees.

Mobley's lawyers were in a difficult position. According to one of his court-appointed lawyers, they soon 'realised that they had no legal defence to the armed robbery and murder charges because of Mobley's numerous confessions'.[69] There was also no traditional 'mitigating' evidence that they could offer the jury. Mobley was 25, Caucasian, his father was a multimillionaire, and he had no history of neglect or sexual or physical abuse. He did, however, have a history of severe personality and behavioral issues.[70] His court-appointed lawyers knew of four generations of his family having engaged in violent and aggressive acts,[71] and when they became aware of the publication of the Brunner study,[72] they admitted this into evidence and sought court funding of $1000 for MAOA testing. The funding was denied, and Mobley convicted and sentenced to death.

The sentence was appealed before the Georgia Supreme Court, and the lawyers again argued that following the Brunner study, the trial court should have allowed Mobley to be tested for genetic deficiencies. The appeal court declined this application, stating that the MAOA argument 'will not have reached a scientific stage of verifiable certainty in the near future and Mobley could not show that such a stage will ever be reached'.[73] The following year, Mobley's new lawyer argued that previous counsel was inadequate for two slightly contradictory reasons. The first reason was for raising the 'unorthodox mitigating defence that attempted to show a possible genetic basis for Mobley's conduct'[74] and for continuing to present a genetic argument in mitigation even though funding had been declined on the basis that the argument was exotic. The second reason was for refusing to accept Mobley's father's offer to fund the genetic test. The Habeas Corpus Court accepted this first argument and vacated the sentence,[75] but it was reinstated by the Georgia Supreme Court, which considered counsel to have acted adequately.[76] Fletcher J

---

69 Quoted in Deborah W. Denno, 'Revisiting the legal link between genetics and crime' 69 L. & Contemp. Probs. 209, 209 (2006).

70 These included thieving as a child, and prison sentences for forgery and numerous robberies. While awaiting trial, he reportedly sodomised his cellmate and tattooed Domino on his back, and taunted and threatened prison guards.

71 These included murder, rape, extreme spousal abuse, alcoholism, explosive temperaments and antisocial conduct. Like the Dutch family, however, there were also high achievers among the male family members.

72 Discussed in Chapter 4.

73 *Mobley v State* 455 S.E.2d 61, 66 (Ga 1995).

74 *Turpin v Mobley* 502 S.E.2d 458, 463 (Ga 1998).

75 Ibid, 461.

76 Ibid, 467.

accepted that counsel had decided against presenting genetic evidence as they considered that there was only a slim chance it would succeed. In addition, it was commented that counsel had been 'able to present the genetics theory', sufficiently through the testimony of a family historian. There was no evidence that a genetic expert could add anything to this. The test in *Strickland* was therefore not satisfied. Mobley's sentence stood, and he was executed in 2005.

5.5.4 Jeffrey Landrigan

Jeffrey Landrigan was born Billy Hill. His biological father had allegedly raped his biological mother the first time they met, although they subsequently became step-siblings and married. After Landrigan's birth, his biological father was convicted of murder and sentenced to death. His biological mother abused drugs and alcohol during his pregnancy, and when he was six months old, Landrigan was adopted. His adoptive mother was an alcoholic, and his childhood was abusive. He turned to drugs and alcohol early, notably overdosing in class in 8th grade. In 1986 Landrigan killed his best friend, and was sentenced to prison in Oklahoma. There, he was reintroduced to his biological father following a chance comment by an inmate that Landrigan looked like a man on death row. During his time in prison he repeatedly stabbed another inmate before escaping in 1989. It was during this escape that he committed another murder, for which he was sentenced to death.

One of his grounds of appeal was ineffective counsel. He argued that counsel failed to 'explore additional grounds for arguing mitigation evidence', which included the 'biological component' of his violent behavior.[77] The District Court rejected the claim, stating that even if counsel was deficient, there was no demonstrated prejudice to Landrigan from this. A subsequent appeal to a three-man appellant panel[78] also denied relief, finding a genetics argument 'rather exotic' and not relevant. In addition, the panel found that even if this argument had been introduced, it would not have affected the outcome of the trial, as Landrigan had expressed no remorse for his actions, and further, he had refused to allow testimony from family. It was doubtful that he would therefore have allowed this evidence to be admitted.

The case was then appealed to the Ninth Circuit Court of Appeals. The majority of this court felt that counsel had failed to reasonably investigate

---

77 App to Pet for Cert F-3.

78 *Landrigan v Stewart* 272 F3d 1221, 1223 (9th Cir 2001).

any potential mitigating evidence. This included a failure to speak to witnesses, and particularly to follow up on a letter sent by Landrigan's birth mother which suggested that Landrigan had 'mental health issues, had begun drinking at an early age, and that his adoptive mother was an alcoholic who would walk around nude in front of him'. Further, the letter pointed out that Landrigan's biological father was on death row and the 'blood link to Darrel [and] I are what has messed up his whole life'.[79] A 1998 neuropsychological evaluation stated that Landrigan's genetic make-up, in utero drug exposure, and abusive childhood resulted in disorderly behavior that was 'beyond the control of Mr Landrigan' and left him unable to 'function in a society that expects individuals to operate in an organized and adaptive manner'.[80] As a result of this additional information, the court had 'grave doubts'[81] that Landrigan had received effective assistance of counsel. The next issue was whether this was relevant, as Landrigan had refused the introduction of mitigating evidence through refusing to allow his natural mother and ex-wife to testify. The court determined that while Landrigan had refused this testimony from these people, he would have allowed the genetic evidence if he had known about it. This was sufficient basis for an evidentiary hearing.

The minority disagreed, finding that even if this evidence had been identified, it would not have made a difference to the final result. They pointed to the fact that the mitigating effect of any genetic evidence would not outweigh its aggravating effect. Further, they disagreed with the finding that Landrigan would have permitted this evidence. They pointed to the fact that attempts by counsel to soften the details of the murder of his best friend, the attack on the inmate, or evidence that Landrigan had been a good father and husband for a period of time were sabotaged by Landrigan, who went out of his way to introduce contrary versions of events,[82] even to the extent of telling the court to 'bring on' the death penalty.

A final appeal was heard by the Supreme Court in 2007. The majority disagreed with the majority in the Court of Appeals, instead preferring the conclusion of the minority in the Court of Appeals, that Landrigan would not have permitted the mitigating evidence.[83] While both the

---

[79] *Landrigan v Schriro* March 6, 2006, [6].

[80] Ibid, [6].

[81] Ibid, [7].

[82] *Landrigan v Schriro* pp. 2352–55.

[83] Landrigan's behavior in interrupting mitigating evidence 'confirms what is plain from the transcript of the colloquy: that Landrigan would have

majority and the minority in the Supreme Court agreed that counsel had been ineffective, the majority felt that the second requirement of prejudice was not met.

5.5.5 Schurz[84]

A recent example is *Schurz*. Eldon Schurz was sentenced to death for a murder which was, in the words of the trial judge, 'especially heinous and depraved'. On the evening in question, Schurz had taken (without consent) a can of beer from a group of men. He later returned to the group to take more beer and overheard a newcomer saying that if he had been there when Schurz had taken the first can, he would have stood up to Schurz. Schurz responded by attacking the newcomer with 'a barrage of punches' and then splashed gasoline on him and set fire to him. The victim was described by the appeal court as an 'unrecognizable, charred husk' who nevertheless managed to answer a few questions before dying.

A jury convicted Schurz of first degree murder and the judge sentenced him to death. He subsequently appealed on numerous grounds, including that counsel was ineffective for failing to present evidence of a 'genetic predisposition' to substance addiction. The appeal judge rejected this, noting firstly that counsel was not deficient in presenting mitigating evidence, commenting 'you can't always get what you want. But Eldon Schurz just about did. He wanted the judge who sentenced him to hear a laundry list of mitigating evidence, and his attorney dutifully presented it'. Although the evidence presented had not included genetic evidence, this did not prejudice the result as this evidence was 'so speculative that it comes nowhere close to showing deficient performance, much less prejudice'.

5.5.6 *US v Duran*[85]

Duran was a private in the Marine Corps, who had been convicted of attempted murder, maiming and assault on a sentry, following an attack on a Gunnery Sergeant with a home-made machete. On appeal, Duran

---

undermined the presentation of any mitigating evidence that his attorney might have uncovered'. The court also agreed with the colourful language in the initial Court of Appeal panel *Landrigan v Stewart* 272 F3d 1221, 1226 (CA 9 2001) 'in the constellation of refusals to have mitigating evidence presented … this case is surely a bright star'.

84 State v Schurz 176 Ariz 46, 859 P2d 156 (1993).

85 201200440 (NMCCA 2014).

argued that counsel had been ineffective due to failure to pursue testing for Low MAOA. He made the interesting argument that behavioral genetic testing in cases such as his were now part of 'reasonable professional assistance', on the ground that both state and federal courts were now increasingly recognizing this evidence in cases. In addition, he cited three cases in which an ineffective counsel argument was accepted due to failure to test. The Government argued in response that 'the science on the connection between this MAOA gene and aggression is not settled'.

The court considered the cases mentioned by Duran, and considered that:

> We believe that these cases stand for the broader proposition that trial defense counsel, in capital cases, must reasonably investigate and present evidence of an accused's mental health in mitigation, and not for the proposition espoused by the appellant, that behavioral genetics testing is the 'prevailing professional norm' in cases involving a violent offender.

It concluded that 'we decline the appellant's invitation to create a presumption that defence counsel must seek behavioral genetic testing in cases involving violent crime or risk a finding of ineffective assistance'.

5.6 ADMISSIBILITY OF EVIDENCE AT SENTENCING

5.6.1 Introduction

It should be noted that a different standard of admissibility applies in sentencing than at trial stage, due to the fact that determination of appropriate sentence is a different objective than determination of guilt. The focus in determining admissibility at sentencing is generally discussed in relation to principles of sentencing, or mitigating or aggravating factors in sentencing.

In the United Kingdom, relevant factors in sentencing include 'any such matters as, in the opinion of the court, are relevant in mitigation of sentence'.[86] Notably, evidence of 'mental illness or disability' is considered a factor 'indicating significantly lower culpability'.[87] In Australia, the Crimes Act contains a list of matters to be taken into account, including the 'nature and circumstances of the offence' and 'the character

---

[86] Section 166(1) Criminal Justice Act 2003.

[87] Sentencing Guidelines Council, Overarching Principles: Seriousness (Dec 2004) p. 7.

… and mental condition of the person'. The court can take into account any evidence relating to these matters that is 'relevant'.[88] In New Zealand, the principles of sentencing require the court to take into account 'the gravity of the offending in the particular case, including the degree of culpability of the offender,'[89] and also 'any particular circumstances of the offender than mean a sentence or other means of dealing with the offender that would otherwise be appropriate would, in the particular circumstances, be disproportionately severe'. Further, the offender under s27 'may request the court to hear any person or persons called by the offender to speak on … the personal, family, whanau, community and cultural background'[90] and how this might have related to the commission of the offence.

A similar approach to admissibility is taken in the United States. In 2006, the US Supreme Court set the standard for mitigating evidence as being evidence relevant to 'any aspect of the defendant's character or record and any of the circumstances of the offence that the defendant proffers as a basis for sentence less than death'. Where the US differs from the other countries discussed above, however, is in the fact that in approximately 32 states the death penalty is available as a sentence. In those states it has been noted that 'death is different', suggesting that the admissibility standard is lowered further. In *Lockett v Ohio*,[91] it was commented in relation to death penalty cases that 'the Eighth and Fourteenth Amendments require that the sentencer, in all but the rarest kind of capital case, not be precluded from considering, as a mitigating factor, any aspect of a defendant's character or record and any of the circumstances of the offence that the defendant proffers as a basis for a sentence less than death'. In *Hitchcock v Dugger*,[92] the Supreme Court stated that the sentencer may not refuse to consider 'any relevant evidence'.

5.6.2 Evidence of Future Dangerousness during Sentencing

When considering a sentence, a judge may be either permitted or required to take into account whether the convicted person is likely to be of future danger to society. As will be discussed in the next chapter, one

---

[88] Section 16A Crimes Act.

[89] Section 8 Sentencing Act.

[90] 'Whanau' is a Maori term, which is used to refer to a person's extended family.

[91] 438 US 586, 604.

[92] 481 US 393, (1987).

of the justifications for punishment is to incapacitate the offender for the protection of society. If it is clear that the offender is highly likely to offend in the future, a longer sentence may be justified.

In the United Kingdom, s225 Criminal Justice Act 2003 allows for the imposition of a 'sentence of imprisonment for public protection' for serious offences. Subsection (4) clarifies that this is a sentence 'for an indeterminate period'. In considering imposing such a sentence, s225(1) states that the section applies where a person is aged over 18, and 'the court is of the opinion that there is a significant risk to members of the public of serious harm occasioned by the commission by him of further specified offences'. Section 229(2) states that in making the decision as to future dangerousness under s225, the court:

> (a) Must take into account all such information as is available to it about the nature and circumstances of the offence;
> (aa) may take into account any information as is available to it about the nature and circumstances of any other offences of which the offender has been convicted by a court anywhere in the world;
> (b) May take into account any information which is before it about any pattern of behavior of which any of the offences mentioned in paragraph (a) or (aa) forms part; and
> (c) May take into account any information about the offender which is before it.

In addition, the Sentencing Guidelines Council list the following as aggravating factors:

> Previous convictions, particularly where a pattern of repeat offending is disclosed.
>
> Failure to respond to warnings or concerns expressed by others about the offender's behavior.

In New Zealand, the court can take into account as an aggravating factor 'the number, seriousness, date, relevance and nature of any previous convictions of the offender'. This factor would clearly be used to predict the likelihood of future dangerousness. In addition, the court can impose a sentence of preventive detention 'to protect the community from those who pose a significant and ongoing risk to the safety of its members' for certain violent or sexual offences. When considering whether to impose such a sentence, the court must consider:

(a) Any pattern of serious offending disclosed by the offender's history; and
(b) The seriousness of the harm to the community caused by the offending; and
(c) Information indicating a tendency to commit serious offences in the future; and
(d) The absence of, or failure of, efforts by the offender to address the cause or causes of the offending; and
(e) The principle that a lengthy determinate sentence is preferable if this provides adequate protection for society.

In Australia, the list of sentencing principles requires consideration of whether 'the offence forms part of a course of conduct consisting of a series of criminal acts of the same or a similar character' as well as 'the deterrent effect that any sentence or order under consideration may have on the person' and 'the prospect of rehabilitation'. While not specifically using words like 'indeterminate sentence' or 'preventative detention', the ability to increase the sentence due to future dangerousness is clear from the language in the sentencing principles.

5.7 GENETICS EVIDENCE DURING SENTENCING: GENERAL

As has been suggested above, the standard for admissibility of evidence differs between the guilt and sentencing phases of a trial. As such, evidence that might not have been admissible in terms of guilt might be considered admissible as a mitigating factor. In sentencing, the aim for the defence is to provide mitigating evidence. This may include evidence presented to humanise the defendant, and to show how his background and pre-existing conditions contributed to the events leading to the conviction. The prosecution's role is to identify aggravating factors, for example relating to the seriousness of the offending or the defendant's likelihood of reoffending.

5.8 GENETICS IN SENTENCING: US NON-CAPITAL CASES

The majority of cases in the US using mitigating evidence during sentencing have occurred in the context of death penalty cases. Deborah Denno has published two studies of genetic cases argued in the US, the first from 1994–2007 and the second from 2007–11. In her first study, she identified six out of 27 cases heard between 1994–2004 which used genetics arguments in non-capital sentencing cases. In the next three years this increased to 11 out of 21. From there, however, enthusiasm appears to have dropped off. She points to only one case in her 2007–11 study, *Morris v Malfi*. This was an unsuccessful appeal against a sentence of life imprisonment for carjacking and first degree murder, based on a possible genetic link to psychopathy.

5.9 GENETICS IN SENTENCING: US CAPITAL CASES

Appeals of sentencing in capital cases are more common, with Denno pointing to 37 out of 48 cases from 1994–2007 and 32 out of 33 from 2007–11 …[93] As she comments, however, there is little evidence that this kind of argument is successful. Some of these cases will be discussed below.

5.9.1 Mobley

In *Mobley*, the facts of which have been discussed above, counsel attempted to introduce evidence of a probable genetic explanation for his actions. This is evidenced through a comment to a newspaper that 'there is no legal defence to his crime … there is only the mitigating factor of his family history. His actions may not have been a product of totally free will. Murder, rape, robbery, suicide, you name it, the Mobley family has had it'. While no specific genetic evidence was admitted, due to the court declining the application for funding for genetic testing, information about Mobley's family was introduced through a relative, who was known as the family historian. Counsel argued that 'four generations of Mobley men' had engaged in criminal actions. This evidence alone failed to mitigate, and Mobley was sentenced to death.

5.9.2 *Creech v Hardison*[94]

In 2010, Creech had been convicted of the first degree murder of another inmate. This was carried out through an assault with the use of a battery filled sock and through Creech stomping on the victim's face and neck.

---

[93] Deborah Denno, 'Behavioral genetics in criminal cases: 1994-2007' in *The Impact of Behavioral Sciences on Criminal Law*, Farahany (ed.) (2009), and 'Courts' increasing consideration of behavioral genetics evidence in criminal cases: Results of a longitudinal study' (2011) *Michigan State Law Review* 967.

[94] No CV 99-0224-S-BLW, 2010 WL 1338126 (D Idaho Mar 31 2010).

During the penalty phase, he offered mitigating evidence from a psychologist that it was likely that he was 'biologically or genetically' predisposed to violence. The court, however, sentenced him to death, finding that the mitigating evidence did not outweigh the aggravating factors. On appeal, Creech introduced further evidence from a neurological examination showing bilateral brain damage. The appeal court did not consider that this new evidence would have impacted the result, stating that 'while a neurologist's opinion that Creech has brain damage may be more specific than [the psychologist's] testimony' it still offered 'only a modest counterweight' to the aggravating factors. The nature of the crime was seen as 'highly aggravating', while any biological factors were only 'mitigating'.

5.9.3 *State v Schurz*[95]

In 1989, the defendant murdered the victim by splashing him with gasoline and setting him on fire. The facts are discussed in more detail above. On appeal, he claimed that evidence of his genetic predisposition to addiction and mental illness should have been introduced. The court noted that neither of these factors prevented the defendant from controlling, comprehending or understanding his actions. Further, the aggravating factor of a 'heinous murder, lighting a defenceless, trapped man on fire' was an 'exceedingly powerful one' and would not have been outweighed by any mitigating factor the genetic evidence might have had.

5.9.4 Rene Patrick Bourassa Jr[96]

In June 2010, Bourassa was arrested for the murder of 80-year-old Lillian Wilson in Arkansas. She had been found beaten to death inside a church, and her purse and car keys had been stolen. Four days later, Bourassa was arrested in Washington, still driving her car. He confessed to the murder, and even re-enacted it for the police on video. When informed that the charges against him would include capital murder, and therefore

---

[95] No 07-99025 (9th Cir 2013).

[96] The facts are taken from two newspaper stories: Chad Day, 'Beliefs of victim help killer get life' Arkansas Online April 14, 2012, and George Brown, 'Man convicted of capital murder for killing woman with cross' WREG.com, April 13, 2012.

the potential for the death penalty, he pled not guilty. At trial, the focus of the defence was not on denying the murder but on avoiding the death penalty.

The Prosecution stated that 'there is something in this world called pure evil and it was rampant at Central Methodist Church that Sunday morning'. Bourassa explained that his car had broken down near the church, and that he had been sleeping in the church for several days. When Wilson had entered the church he had hidden, but she had seen him. Over the course of the next hour, he had alternated between beating her with a brass cross from the communion table and talking to her. He said 'the only thing in my mind is I can't let her go because I won't make it far … I was swinging, not looking … I can't stand the sight of blood, it makes me sick … I set the pew on top of her … she kept telling me her dad bought the cross …'. He claimed that he had only intended to knock her out, but Wilson, injured but still alive, brought up Bourassa's mother. Defence counsel commented that 'you can see the rage that took over at that moment. … Is that someone really thinking straight to do that?'

Expert testimony showed that Bourassa had Low MAOA. In addition, he had suffered sexual assaults at four years of age and again in the 5th grade. His mother testified to a history of mental illness and suicide on both sides of the family. She commented 'it was my fault. I shouldn't have ever had kids' although it is unclear if this comment was in relation to genetics, or Bourassa's difficult childhood.[97]

After four hours of deliberation, the jury found him guilty of aggravated robbery, theft, commercial burglary, fraudulent use of a credit card and capital murder. The following day, they deliberated for two hours over sentencing, deciding in reverse order of seriousness and imposing the maximum sentences for the first four convictions. In relation to the murder conviction they decided on life in prison without parole. How much of a role the genetics argument played is unclear. One newspaper reported that '[t]he relatively lenient verdict in Bourassa's trial was the result of a criminal defence argument that has, in recent years, become de rigueur in capital cases nationwide: shifting the blame for behavior, just ever so slightly, away from the individual defendant, and toward uncontrollable biological factors'.[98] One juror commented that some jurors were swayed by the 'pages' of mitigating evidence which 'weighed heavily' in favour of life in prison rather than death. Others, like himself,

[97] His father had left them when Bourassa was two years old, and her mother remarried 33 days later. She subsequently attempted suicide several times, and finally the court gave custody to his father.

[98] Elijah Wolfson, 'My genes did it!' www.newsweek.com, March 5, 2014.

had been swayed by the fact that they felt the victim would not have wanted the death penalty.[99]

5.9.5 Conclusion

The trend in these cases appears to be to accept the validity of genetic evidence, but to give it the same weight as other evidence. In most cases, the mitigating effect of the genetic evidence was outweighed by the aggravating nature of other factors.

5.10 GENETICS IN SENTENCING: ITALY

The presence of the Low MAOA gene has been raised as a mitigating factor in two Italian cases.

5.10.1 Abdelmalek Bayout

In 2007, Abdelmalek Bayout was attacked by a group of youths, who insulted him by calling him a 'faggot' for wearing black eyeliner around his eyes for religious reasons, and then physically assaulted him. Following the attack, Bayout left the scene and went to a cultural centre where he changed clothes. He then bought a knife and went looking for his attackers. He subsequently attacked Walter Perez, whom he wrongly believed to be one of his attackers, killing him.[100]

Bayout was convicted of murder, and was initially sentenced to nine years, two months imprisonment. This reflected a reduction of approximately three years from the judge's starting point due to evidence of mental illness. He appealed the sentence, and in May 2009 the Trieste Appeal Court heard evidence that Bayout had Low MAOA. Judge Reinotti commented that this was 'particularly compelling [evidence, that] would make him particularly aggressive in stressful situations', and further reduced the sentence by one year. Bayout's lawyers did not consider his race to be a relevant factor in understanding the effect of MAOA, and the only evidence of childhood maltreatment relied on was

---

[99] Chad Day, 'Beliefs of victim help killer get life' *Arkansas Online* April 14, 2012. Interestingly, the Methodist Book of Discipline, which advocates against capital punishment, was introduced into evidence. The victim's son afterwards commented that the sentence was 'curious'.

[100] *Bayout v Francesco* 2009 RGS Assise App. 6/2008 RGNR 1685/2007, RG. Sent 5, dd 18 Settembre, 2009.

evidence of 'culture shock' from his move from his native Algeria to Italy 16 years before, when he was in his early twenties.

5.10.2 Stefania Albertani

In July 2009, Stefania Albertani went to the police to report a fraud that had supposedly been committed by her sister in 2007. During the discussion, she mentioned that her sister had either died or disappeared two months ago. A search of the sister's credit card statement showed that the sister's card had been used to top up Stefania's own mobile phone after this time, and the police opened an investigation. A week after the initial discussion, the police searched the Albertani residence. They then searched another house owned by the family after learning that Stefania had insisted for the past few months that her parents not use the house. On arrival at the house, the police 'faced an unexpected "strong smell of rotting flesh" and had found a burnt skeleton positioned in the immediate vicinity of the iron door to the rear of the house'.

As part of the ongoing and subsequent investigations, Stefania and her parents were monitored through the use of surveillance devices in their home. In October 2009, the surveillance devices picked up the sound of the mother screaming and crying for help and a drawer opening. The police intervened to find the mother 'on the ground, cyanotic, partially conscious [and] wearing a flaming apron that was burning her body'.[101] Stefania had attempted to strangle her mother with a belt (taken from the drawer) and had then set fire to her. The police soon learned that this sequence of events had taken place immediately after she had tried to kill both parents in the garage by setting fire to their car with them inside.

At trial, clinical evidence was introduced which suggested that Albertani had acted under the influence of an undefined psychotic pathological condition, which made her less than fully aware of her actions. This was not convincing, and she was convicted and sentenced to lifetime imprisonment.

She appealed the sentence, this time offering evidence of brain scans and genetic testing. The brain scans showed that she had alterations in the grey matter of two brain regions: the anterior cingulate gyrus, which is involved in inhibiting behavior, and the insula, which is linked to aggression. Genetic testing showed the presence of three genes linked to

---

[101] *Background and summary of the case* available online at euilegaltheory.files.wordpress.com/2011/11/background-and-summary-of-the-case.docx. This is taken from the Police record of arrest on 7 October 2009.

impulsive and aggressive actions, one of which was the Low MAOA gene. The expert witness explained that:

> We started neither from neuroimaging nor from genetics. On the contrary, we performed a thorough clinical examination and then we used these techniques [brain scan and genetic testing] to complete the picture with objective measures that strengthened our conclusions.

The judge considered this evidence to be 'more reliant [than the evidence at trial] on objectivity and evidence'.[102] Based on this evidence the sentence was reduced to 20 years, which is to include at least three years in a mental hospital undergoing treatment.

5.11 GENETICS IN SENTENCING: THE DOUBLE-EDGED SWORD

5.11.1 Introduction

While genetics evidence has been discussed above in relation to sentencing as a mitigating factor, it should be kept in mind that it could also potentially be seen as an aggravating factor. It is easy to imagine how a behavioral genetics argument could backfire. Evidence from the defence that a sentence should be reduced because a defendant's Low MAOA and childhood maltreatment made him less able to control his compulsive aggression can also easily lead to an argument for the prosecution that this very reason should require a longer sentence.

In *Landrigan*, the initial Court of Appeals panel explained this:[103]

> It is highly doubtful that the sentencing court would have been moved by information that Landrigan was a remorseless, violent killer because he was genetically programmed to be violent, as shown by the fact that he comes from a family of violent people, who are killers also.

---

[102] Fabio Turone, 'Medical tests help reduce sentence of woman accused of murder' 2011 BMJ 343.

[103] The judgment cites *People v Franklin* 167 Ill 2d 1, 26, 212 Ill Dec 153, 656 NE2d 750, 761 (1995): 'Although this evidence could have evoked compassion in the jurors, it could have also demonstrated defendant's potential for future dangerousness and the basis for defendant's past criminal acts'.

> [a]lthough Landrigan's new evidence can be called mitigating in some slight sense, it would also have shown the court that it could anticipate that he would continue to be violent.

As a result of Landrigan's long history of violent crime and 'flaunt[ing] his menacing behavior,' the panel commented that his 'assuring the court that genetics made him the way he is could not have been very helpful'.

Despite this obvious potential use as an aggravating factor, prosecutors have rarely adopted such an argument. Denno identifies three examples from 48 cases in her 1994–2007 study, but none in the 2007–11 study. She concludes that 'these results challenge arguments that such evidence will be legally detrimental to a defendant'.

One example of genetics being used as a double-edged sword is found in *Creech*, discussed above. In determining sentence, the District Court commented that Creech may have been biologically predisposed to violence. In addition, Creech had, 'by prior conduct and by conduct in the commission of the murders at hand ... exhibited a propensity to commit murder which will probably constitute a continuing threat to society'. These factors were relevant in justifying the death penalty, although the actual impact of the genetic evidence is unclear. While it is mentioned as part of aggravating factors, his prior conduct was sufficient evidence of propensity.[104]

It is interesting to note that in this case the genetic information appears to have been used as both a mitigating and an aggravating factor. Despite this, Creech appealed on the basis that this genetic evidence was not sufficiently considered. The Supreme Court dismissed the appeal, agreeing with the District Court decision.

While there is little evidence at present that genetic evidence has been used as an aggravating factor, this is still an option available to the prosecution. If the trend of increasing use of a genetics argument continues, this might result in the prosecution beginning to look more closely at its potential use as an aggravating factor.

5.12 CHRISTMAS TREE EFFECT / CSI EFFECT

One final point about the use of genetic evidence is the potential impact of the 'Christmas Tree' or 'CSI' effect. The Christmas Tree effect

---

[104] Creech had four previous convictions for murder in three different states, with other first degree murder charges pending. In addition, he had claimed responsibility for approximately 40 murders.

describes the idea that some kinds of evidence are so interesting and new that they have a greater effect on jurors than might otherwise be deserved. Presentation of this evidence is likened to the lights on a Christmas tree, so shiny and interesting that it dominates everything, blinding the jurors from considering the validity of the genetic evidence. The alternative name, the CSI effect, refers to a perception that due to the popularity of the television programme, jurors expect to be provided with scientific evidence as part of the prosecution case and give undue weight to this.

A 2006 study[105] showed that jurors do expect and demand scientific evidence. The study showed that jurors would even acquit if this evidence is absent, particularly where the rest of the evidence is circumstantial. This expectation is not directly due to jurors watching CSI, but is 'the result of broader changes in popular culture related to advancements in both technology and information distribution'. The study suggested that there was an expectation that prosecutors will obtain and present scientific evidence in cases.[106]

At present, genetics evidence seems to be neither subject to the Christmas Tree nor CSI effects, despite the media's intense interest in it. It has not generally been seen as shiny, new information by judges, and often appears to carry no more weight than the more commonly presented social history evidence. There was a level of shininess attached to evidence by the jury in the *Waldroup* case and perhaps by the Italian judge in *Bayout*, but what is interesting is that in these cases the evidence seems to have had the opposite effect to the DNA cases discussed by Judge Herlihy. Instead of the 'emotional desire to punish the criminal', it has operated to reduce the sentence. In terms of the CSI effect, there hasn't been any real demand for this evidence. Whether this will remain the position, however, in light of the more recent cases is unclear.

---

[105] Shelton, 'A study of juror expectations and demands concerning scientific evidence: Does the CSI-effect exist?' (2006) 9(2) *Vanderbilt Journal of Entertainment and Technology Law* 331.

[106] Ibid, at 368. The study also comments that jurors see DNA evidence as having 'a special aura of credibility', and that they expect DNA evidence to be 95 per cent accurate. Approximately 22 per cent of jurors expect to see DNA evidence in all criminal cases, and this number increases to 46 per cent in murder and 73 per cent in rape cases (at 357).

5.13 RECONSIDERING THE CASE OF CHILD B

In the scenario, the police seek and receive a court order to test Child B for Low MAOA. When the test is positive, it is subsequently used as an aggravating factor, resulting in a longer sentence being imposed on Child B than on Child A. The judge comments that he has given Child B the strongest sentence possible.

There are several issues with this scenario.

5.13.1 The Admissibility of the Evidence

Whether genetic evidence can be admissible in court has been a matter for debate. Rules relating to expert opinion evidence generally require that the evidence be of substantial help to the court, be based on the expertise of the person giving the opinion, be given impartially, and be of an acceptable standard. It is this latter criterion which might be the most difficult to establish. In earlier cases like *Landrigan* genetic evidence was seen as too exotic to be admissible. While more recent cases have been more accepting of this evidence, the most recent United States case of *Yepez* returned to considering it too 'young' to be admissible. Different rules to admissibility will obviously apply depending on whether the evidence is being introduced as a defence at the trial stage, or as a factor to be considered at the sentencing stage.

5.13.2 The Use of Genetic Evidence as a Defence

In this case, the lawyers for Child A attempted to introduce genetic evidence as part of a defence. While the judge accepted the scientific basis of the argument, the defence was rejected as there was no evidence of childhood maltreatment.

5.13.3 The Use of Genetic Evidence as a Double-edged Sword

A court order for DNA testing of Child B is sought and granted, and the police use the Low MAOA result, coupled with the childhood maltreatment, as an aggravating factor at sentencing. While the use of genetic evidence in this way, as a 'double-edged sword', has often been raised as a concern, it has yet to occur as a specific part of a prosecutor's argument of aggravating factors (not including general statements as to future dangerousness). This kind of argument must, however, be seen as likely to occur in the future as more cases are arising in which the defendant's MAOA status is raised by the defence in mitigation.

5.13.4 Sentencing

Both boys are convicted of murder. Child B's conviction for murder, and not some lesser offence like manslaughter, differs from the *Waldroup* case but is similar to the other cases which see the genetic evidence as relevant to sentencing only. Child B receives a substantially longer sentence than Child A. Interestingly, this is inconsistent with some of the genetics cases like *Bayout*, *Albertani* and *Bourassa*. It must be remembered, however, that the majority of cases considering genetic evidence in sentencing are appeals from death penalty cases. In these cases the maximum penalty has already been imposed before the genetics evidence is introduced. The judge's comments about Child B being 'genetically programmed to be a killer' do reflect other comments by judges in the *Landrigan* and *Waldroup* cases.

5.14 CONCLUSION

This chapter has considered the use of genetic arguments in court. One interesting trend seen in these cases is the reluctance of US judges to accept such evidence. The successful cases, *Waldroup* and *Bourassa*, have both involved juries. This can be contrasted with the two Italian decisions, where judges appeared to be convinced by the scientific expert opinion evidence. In Denno's surveys of genetic cases she notes that an increasing amount of cases introducing genetic arguments in her first survey, followed by a lower number in the second. The recent cases discussed in this chapter suggest that the popularity of such an argument is again increasing, likely fuelled by the fact that these arguments are beginning to be accepted. What can be seen in the United States thus far is a cautious use of genetics arguments. They appear more frequently in cases where the defendant has little to lose from introducing this evidence, and argues it either as part of an attempt to mitigate a potential death penalty sentence, or as an argument of ineffective counsel. While these arguments are not always successful, the facts of the cases discussed in this chapter can provide an explanation as to why. The murders committed tend to be extremely violent and/or cruel and therefore while the genetic evidence might be relevant, it is often insufficient to outweigh the aggravating features of the crime.

The two Italian cases have received significant attention in the media and in scientific and legal communities and it is probably these two cases that will result in genetic evidence being more commonly introduced and accepted in the future.

The next chapter will consider the effect that acceptance of this information might have on the criminal justice system as a whole.

6. The impact of a 'criminal gene' argument on punishment theory

6.1 INTRODUCTION

'It wasn't a who done it ... it was a why done it'. These words formed the basis of Bradley Waldroup's defence for the murder of Leslie Bradshaw and the attempted murder of Penny Waldroup. Having provided the jury with information relating to Low MAOA and childhood maltreatment, his lawyers summed up the jury's decision by saying 'they understood what was going on in him and understood why he did what he did'. In this case, discussed in the previous chapter, acceptance of the genetics evidence resulted in conviction of a lesser charge. This chapter will consider the effect on punishment theory of such acceptance.

In 1968, H.L.A. Hart wrote that before we can 'assess the extent to which the whole institution [of punishment] has been eroded by, or needs to be adapted to, new beliefs about the human mind' we must first answer three fundamental questions:[1]

1. What justifies our general practice of punishment?
2. To whom may punishment be applied?
3. How severely may we punish?

This chapter will consider the answers to these questions by looking at first, the concept of criminal responsibility and second, the justifications for punishment. It will then consider whether genetics arguments require us to rethink the answers to these questions.

[1] H.L.A. Hart, 'Punishment and responsibility' (1968) 3, quoted in Peggy Sasso, 'Criminal responsibility in the age of mind reading' (1999) 46 *American Criminal Law Review* 1191, 1196 (the wording of the three questions is taken from this article).

6.2 WHY DO WE HOLD PEOPLE RESPONSIBLE FOR CRIMINAL ACTS?

6.2.1 The Concept of Moral Blameworthiness

The criminal law serves to maintain the peace and good order of the community, through policies of predictability, efficiency and fairness. It is generally deontological in nature, adopting the approach that certain types of actions, for example murder, are intrinsically wrong. Criminal statutes are generally therefore structured as lists of acts which are impermissible.

The baseline, or foundational, component to imposing criminal responsibility is moral blameworthiness. People are considered to be rational actors who have the capacity to make decisions and to therefore choose to refrain from committing those acts prohibited by the criminal law. Morse[2] describes moral blameworthiness as requiring 'minimal rationality (a cognitive capacity) and minimal self-control or lack of compulsion (a volitional capacity)'. In simple terms, capacity for criminal responsibility requires a rational, self-determined action and some level of self-control. As H.L.A. Hart[3] explains, 'man's fate should depend on his choice and this is to foster the prime social virtue of self-restraint'. Without these attributes a person cannot be responsible, morally or criminally, for their actions. Hart continues that without this approach to criminal responsibility: 'We should lose the ability which the present system in some degree guarantees to us, to predict and plan the future course of our lives within the coercive framework of the law.'

Defences, in the form of justifications or excuses,[4] exist to mitigate the situations in which it is recognized that a particular individual either does not have the capacity for criminal responsibility in general,[5] or did not have this capacity in a particular situation.[6] Without these defences the law could not be considered just in imposing criminal responsibility, nor

---

[2] Stephen Morse, 'Excusing the crazy: The insanity defense reconsidered' 58 S. Cal L Rev 777, 781 (1985).

[3] H.L.A. Hart, *Punishment and Responsibility* (1968) (OUP: Oxford) p. 183.

[4] A justificatory defence accepts that the defendant acted out of necessity and acted reasonably. An excusatory defence accepts that while society does not necessarily approve of the individual's actions, it recognizes that there is a good reason why the person should not be considered culpable.

[5] For example, infancy and insanity.

[6] For example, automatism, compulsion, duress, necessity, provocation, intoxication.

would the justifications for punishing this individual, which will be discussed below, be satisfied. These defences are, however, generally limited to those factors affecting an individual's capacity to decide to violate a law which were specifically operating either at the time of, or closely preceding, the decisionmaking. Such factors would include evidence relating to the person's evaluative capacities (for example, a failure to correctly understand the relevant facts), or executive capacities (for example, whether he could conform his behavior to his intention, or whether he was acting involuntarily, like sleepwalking).

Factors relating to a person's background, including biological or environmental factors, are generally regarded by the law as not being sufficiently causative to affect this capacity and are therefore not relevant in determining criminal responsibility (although they may be relevant as mitigating factors in sentencing). This point has been seen most strongly in the United States, where a proposed defence of 'Rotten Social Background' has been considered but rejected.[7] While not denying the existence of some causal connection between the individual's background and the commission of the criminal act, the rejection of the Rotten Social Background defence reflects the fact that at the time of the decision to act, the person understood the situation and had the capacity to decide to carry out the act in question. In *Pohlot*[8] the court summarized:

> Criminal responsibility must be judged at the level of the conscious. If a person thinks, plans and executes the plan at that level, the criminality of his act cannot be denied, wholly or partially, because, although he did not realize it, his conscious was influenced to think, to plan and to execute the plan by unconscious influences which were the product of his genes and his lifelong environment.

The requirement of capacity for rational self-determined actions in order to justifiably impose criminal responsibility on an individual is often given the short-hand title 'free will'. The appropriateness of this abbreviation and its relevance to a genetics argument will be discussed further below.

---

[7] See, for example, 'The country has not adopted a rotten social background defence and is unlikely to do so anytime soon' Richard Delgado, 'The wretched of the earth', (2011) 2 Ala CR and CL L Rev 1.

[8] *US v Pohlot* 827 F2d 889, 906.

6.3 WHY DO WE PUNISH PEOPLE?

There are four recognized theories of why society punishes a person who has capacity for criminal responsibility yet who nevertheless decides to commit a criminal act. Three of these theories (deterrence, incapacitation and rehabilitation) are based on the utilitarian justification that punishment should prevent offenders from hurting people and should also serve as a warning to potential offenders of the consequences of engaging in a criminal act. The final theory, retribution, is based on the rationale that some individuals simply deserve to be punished. Where defences to criminal conduct exist, these generally reflect the fact that neither utilitarian nor retributive theories require punishment to occur.

The four punishment theories will be discussed below, before being considered in relation to a genetics-type argument.

6.3.1 Utilitarian Theories

Utilitarianism is an ethical theory which considers that the proper course of action is the one that maximizes utility. According to Jeremy Bentham,[9] who is credited with developing the theory, 'it is the greatest happiness of the greatest number that is the measure of right and wrong'. John Stuart Mill[10] expanded on this by explaining, 'Utility, or the Greatest-Happiness Principle, holds that actions are right in proportion as they tend to promote happiness, wrong as they tend to produce the reverse of happiness'. In determining where the Greatest Happiness arises, both the 'good' and 'evil' of decisions must be analysed.

In relation to crime, Bentham's starting position is that the object of the criminal law is to 'augment the total happiness of the community' and to 'exclude as far as may be, everything that tends to subtract from that happiness; in other words, to exclude mischief'. The punishment of an individual, however, should also be considered a mischief, and therefore, 'if it is at all to be admitted, it ought only to be admitted in as far as it promises to exclude some greater evil'. This suggests that punishment can only be used if it is of benefit to society, and is at a level that does not make the punishment itself the greater evil. The value of the punishment must not be less than the profit of the offence (Bentham's Rule One) but must be no more than is necessary to bring the person into conformity with the law (Bentham's Rule Five). This does not, however,

---

9 Jeremy Bentham, *A Fragment on Government* (Cambridge: CUP 1988).
10 John Stuart Mill, *Utilitarianism* (London 1864).

necessarily mean that the punishment must be proportionate to the crime. One exception to these Rules is where an act is 'conclusively indicative of a habit', in which case an increased sentence may be given to enable the punishment 'to outweigh the profit not only of the individual offence, but of such other like offences as are likely to have been committed with impunity by the same offender' (Rule Nine). There are therefore four situations in which punishment is not warranted: where it is groundless (where there is no mischief to prevent), where it is inefficacious (where it cannot prevent the mischief), where it is unprofitable or too expensive (where the mischief produced would be greater than that prevented), or where it is needless (where the mischief may be prevented without the punishment).

It should be noted that utilitarianism is aimed at achieving the greatest amount of happiness for the greatest amount of people, in other words for the benefit of society as a whole, as opposed to being for the benefit of the individual. Utilitarianism would therefore allow the punishment of innocent people if the harms that would be avoided by this punishment outweighed the harm caused to the innocent person by the punishment.[11]

Bentham does provide one exception: people who are not morally responsible for their actions should not be punished. This exception (on the grounds of inefficaciousness) would prevent punishment 'where the penal provision, though it were conveyed to a man's notice, could produce no effect on him, with respect to preventing him from engaging in any act of the sort in question'. As examples of those not morally responsible for their actions he refers to extreme infancy, insanity and intoxication.

The three utilitarian justifications for punishment will be discussed in turn.

6.3.1.1 Deterrance

Deterrance can be described as an example-based theory of punishment. It relies on the idea that a person contemplating committing a criminal act will be deterred by the level of punishment that has been imposed for committing that act on either himself (for previous crimes) or on other

---

[11] Rawls, for example, in criticising utilitarianism, discusses a practice which he calls telishment: a systematic programme of punishment of innocents. He argues that this must be acceptable to utilitarians. Utilitarians respond that this would result in unacceptable levels of insecurity, and would not therefore be permitted.

people committing similar crimes. According to Cesare Beccaria,[12] 'the purpose of punishment should be to create a better society, not to inflict revenge' and punishment should therefore be used to deter the individual, and also others, from acting. Oliver Wendell Holmes[13] saw deterrence as necessary from a societal perspective, even if this was resultantly unfair on an individual level: 'If I were having a philosophical talk with a man I was going to have hanged (or electrocuted), I should say, I don't doubt that your act was inevitable for you but to make it more avoidable to others we propose to sacrifice you to the common good'.

In economics language, deterrence employs as a starting point the assumption that an individual is a rational actor who seeks to maximize utility. Provided that the level of punishment imposed is sufficient to make the individual worse off than he was before committing the crime, he should rationally decide not to act. The only individuals who would decide to carry out the crime, therefore, are those that made the decision to act without having all of the correct information, those who failed to understand the consequences of acting, those whose unique circumstances meant that in this case the benefits did outweigh the harms, and those who have the correct information but are unable to adjust their behavior in accordance with this to refrain from acting.

The key feature of deterrence theory is a reliance on the classification of the individual as a rational actor. This can be a problematic assumption as it is clear that many criminals do not think rationally about the consequences of committing crimes. The theory also does not take into account individuals who may have capacity for criminal responsibility, but who are unable to modify their behavior to refrain from acting, in other words those who do not have 'free will'.[14] This has clear implications for behavioral genetic research.

6.3.1.2 Incapacitation

The second theory is incapacitation. Under this theory, a court may determine that because a particular individual is sufficiently likely to reoffend it is in society's best interests to protect itself by isolating this individual and therefore minimising his opportunities to reoffend. As

---

[12] Cesare Beccaria, *On Crimes and Punishment* (1764) (reprint) (London: Empire Books 2012).

[13] Holmes–Laski Letters: *The Correspondence of Mr. Justice Holmes and Harold J. Laski 1916–1935* 806 (Mark De Wolfe Howe (ed.)) (1953) (Cambridge, MA: Harvard University Press).

[14] See later.

Judge Hugo Black described it, 'isolation of the dangerous has always been considered an important function of the criminal law'.[15]

This is the one theory that focuses primarily on society and its needs rather than on the individual himself. The individual's mere presence as part of society justifies the punishment. As a result, the concept of 'free will' in order to impose punishment is minimized. Instead, the focus is on an assessment of likelihood of future offending.

6.3.1.3 Rehabilitation

This theory is based on the idea that 'human behavior is the product of antecedence causes, that these causes can be identified, and that on this basis, therapeutic measures can be employed to effect changes in the behavior of the person treated'.[16] The focus is less on punishment for the specific crime committed than on eliminating or drastically reducing any future offending.

6.3.2 Retributive Theory

The fourth theory of punishment is retribution. The beginnings of this theory lie with Immanuel Kant,[17] and his work on the metaphysics of morals. Kant disagreed with the utilitarian theory of promoting happiness, commenting that:

> Judicial punishment can never be used merely as a means to promote some other good for the criminal himself or for civil society, but instead it must in all cases be imposed on him only on the ground that he has committed a crime, for a human being can never be manipulated merely as a means to the purposes of someone else.

For this reason, punishment must be proportionate to the seriousness of the crime. Whereas utilitarianism would allow a disproportionate punishment in order to maximize happiness, Kant's approach would consider this as treating a person as a means to an end. Instead, the principle of equality must apply: 'only the law of retribution (jus talionis) can determine exactly the kind and degree of punishment'. Further, the individual himself must be deserving of punishment. This can be contrasted with Bentham, who considered this as a possible exception

---

[15] Powell v Texas, 392 U.S. 514, 539 (1968)

[16] Wayne LaFave and Austin Scott, Jr., *Substantive Criminal Law* 24 (2d ed.) (London: West Publishing Company 1986).

[17] Kant, *Groundwork of the Metaphysics of Morals* (1785) New Haven, CT; London: Yale University Press.

and not a starting point, or the other utilitarians who would find individual culpability irrelevant.

Provided that we have the capacity for 'pure practical reason' Kant considered that we should be held responsible for our actions. This would apply even if this capacity was not operating at the time of the act:

> As contingently rational beings, we do not necessarily have to exercise our free will and practical reason in every instance to be morally responsible. As long as we understand that morality commands us as a law, and that action should be governed by reason, we must be morally responsible when we fail to do so.

Kant identifies two situations in which an individual should not be considered morally responsible:

> The first [is where] the being is not a rational being and cannot recognize the action-guiding nature of reasons ... The second [is where] a being through no fault of his or her own, could not affect his or her actions through reason. Therefore, action is only determined by laws of nature and one's inclinations.

Kant's first reason relates to an impaired cognitive ability (for example, where the person acts as an automaton, or is unable to understand that actions are morally blameworthy), and the second to impaired volition (for example, where the person has a lack of impulse control). As he sees a person as subject to both the laws of nature and the universal moral law, both must be operative to justify moral responsibility being imposed.

His threshold for liability of capacity for pure practical reason does not exist on a spectrum. Someone who is affected by genetic or neurological conditions will still be liable for their actions provided they have some capacity for reason. A person's 'moral luck', the idea that some people are affected by conditions that impact on whether actions are moral or immoral, is irrelevant to his determination of moral responsibility (although it could be relevant to moral blameworthiness, or amount of punishment, without being inconsistent).

Under a retribution theory, punishment is administered because a person deserves it. For this reason it is also called 'desert' theory, on the basis that a person receives his 'just deserts' for his actions. According to Robinson,[18] there are three forms of punishment: vengeful (or the 'eye for an eye' approach); deontological (or the 'ultimate responsibility'

---

[18] Paul Robinson, 'Competing conceptions of modern desert: Vengeful, deontological and empirical' (2008) 67 Camb L J 145, 148.

approach); and empirical (in which punishment is measured by identifying what the community needs to reaffirm the collective consciousness).

Punishing someone through retribution can be regarded as restoring balance to the scales of justice or to society's 'moral order'. Indeed, Kant considered that a civil society has a moral obligation to exact retribution for crimes:

> Even if a civil society were to dissolve itself by common agreement of all its members, … the last murderer remaining in prison must first be executed, so that everyone will duly receive what his actions are worth and so that the blood-guilt thereof will not be fixed on people because they failed to insist on carrying out the punishment; for if they fail to do so, they may be regarded as accomplices in this public violation of legal justice.

Hegel[19] considered punishment to be showing respect for the moral autonomy of the criminal:

> In so far as the punishment which this entails is seen as embodying *the criminal's own right*, the criminal is *honoured* as a rational being. He is denied this honour if the concept and criterion of his punishment are not derived from his own act; and he is also denied it if he is regarded simply as a harmful animal which must be rendered harmless, or punished with a view to deterring him or reforming him.

A retribution theory can finally also be described from an empirical perspective. By punishing someone who fails to comply with certain moral and social norms, the community is itself affirming its commitment to those norms. As an example, Emile Durkheim stated that 'the law that has been violated must somehow bear witness that despite appearances it remains always itself, that it has lost none of its force or authority despite the act that repudiated it'.[20] The real function of the law is to maintain societal cohesion. According to this perspective, when someone damages this cohesion by breaking the law the community must respond through 'strengthen[ing] one another by giving mutual assurance that they are still in unison'. It should be recognized, however, that a person can only commit to these norms by having the capacity to accept them. If he does not (if he is not morally responsible) society does not need to punish him to reaffirm their beliefs.

---

[19] Georg Hegel, *Elements of the Philosophy of Right* (1820) (trans. H.B. Nisbet) (CUP 1991) p. 126.

[20] Ibid, p. 126.

The United States Supreme Court in *Furman v Georgia* found a more practical justification for retribution:[21]

> The instinct for retribution is part of the nature of man, and channeling that instinct in the administration of criminal justice serves an important purpose ... when people begin to believe that organized society is unwilling or unable to impose upon criminal offenders the punishment they deserve then there are sown the seeds of anarchy.

Punishment for retribution should be distinguished from punishment for vengeance. Retribution focusses on the level of punishment which the individual deserves, whereas vengeance focusses on the victim's desire for retaliation. To ensure a distinction between the two, retributive punishment imposes two requirements. First, the individual must be morally culpable, or a rational actor. If the individual was not able to make the decision to engage in the criminal action, or to control his behavior, then he is less morally culpable than a person who was able to make this decision and therefore a lesser penalty is required from him.[22] William Blackstone[23] wrote 'punishments are only inflicted for abuse of that free will which God has given to man'. Second, due to the focus on the individual, the punishment must be proportionate to his crime. According to John Rawls,[24] 'it is morally fitting that a person who does wrong should suffer in proportion to his wrongdoing'. Kant[25] agrees, commenting that punishment ought to be 'pronounced over all criminals in proportion to their internal wickedness'. Fondacaro[26] comments that both of these requirements are 'deeply grounded in common sense, folk psychology, religious principles and foundational legal presumptions and principles'.

A person who lacks 'free will' might therefore be considered to be less of a rational being, or to have less 'internal wickedness', and thus be deserving of a lesser sentence.

---

21 408 US 238 (1972).

22 Hegel comments that punishment on this basis in fact honours the criminal as a rational being.

23 William Blackstone, *Commentaries on the Laws of England* (Routledge-Cavendish 2001) 27.

24 John Rawls, 'Two concepts of rules' (1955) 64 Phil Rev 3, 4–5.

25 Immanual Kant, *Science of Right* (1790) (reprint) (trans. W. Hastie) (CreateSpace Independent Publishing).

26 Mark Fondacaro, 'Rethinking the scientific and legal implications of developmental differences research in juvenile justice' (2014) 17 New Crim L Rev 407, 425.

6.3.3 Application to Genetics

6.3.3.1 Introduction

In the previous chapter, several cases were discussed in which the punishment imposed was affected by a genetics argument. In these cases, Bourassa, Bayout and Albertani all had their sentences reduced. Waldroup, while sentenced to the maximum available, was convicted of a lesser offence. It is worth considering whether these reductions in sentence are justified under the punishment theories.

6.3.3.1.1 Deterrance The theory of deterrence focuses on two groups: the individual being punished, and society as a whole. In relation to both groups, the focus of punishment is on deterring any future criminal activity. In relation to the individual himself, deterrence theory would not justify punishment, or would at best see it as a weak justification. If the argument is that because of a combination of genetics and environment this person is more likely to act in an impulsive, aggressive manner, this argument suggests that the person's ability to act as a rational actor, or to act with the self-restraint that Hart requires, will be limited or non-existent. The idea of punishment will not therefore operate to deter this individual from reoffending, or will have only a minimal impact.

The reduced sentences in *Bayout* and particularly in *Albertani* (where part of the sentence was to be served in a mental health facility) would be justified. The maximum sentence in *Waldroup* would not.

In relation to society, however, punishment of the individual could still be justified. Although the individual himself may not be able to be deterred by the punishment, the rest of society (with the probable exception of the other MAOA members) could be deterred from acting in a similar way. This would justify the maximum sentence being imposed on Waldroup.

6.3.3.1.2 Incapacitation This is the strongest argument in favour of punishment. It can be seen in *Waldroup*, where the judge sentenced him to the maximum and warned him to 'think twice about appealing. The state might not mind trying this again and asking for the death penalty. You might not be as fortunate with a jury next time'.

It could also be seen in the comment of the judge in *Landrigan*,[27] that 'it is highly doubtful that the sentencing court would have been moved

[27] See below.

by the information that Landrigan was a remorseless violent killer because he was genetically programmed to be violent'.

While the language is extreme, it makes the point well. If the individual argues that the combination of his genes and environment means that he is far more likely to act impulsively and aggressively than others, then this is a strong predictor of future reoffending. In this case, society is justified in seeking protection from this individual, through incapacitation.

This theory would not justify the reduction of sentence in *Bayout* or *Albertani* (unless it was thought that the mental health treatment would reduce the likelihood of reoffending, thus reducing the need for incapacitation).

6.3.3.1.3 Rehabilitation The theory of rehabilitation assumes as a starting point that the circumstances leading to the offending can be addressed, and therefore the chances of their reoccurring in the future can be reduced or minimized. In relation to a genetics argument, this theory can be applied in two different ways. The first might be to say that there is no likelihood for rehabilitation. If the individual has the relevant gene and the environmental triggers have occurred, the chances of this individual reoffending are high. Under this understanding, rehabilitation will have little effect, and will not justify punishment. This might explain the reduction in sentencing in *Bayout.*

On the other hand, the possibility for treatment might be present. In the Albertani case, for example, part of her sentence was to be served in a psychiatric facility. Whether this would lower her chances of reoffending in the future is unclear, but it must be kept in mind that not all Low MAOA individuals who suffered childhood maltreatment commit antisocial acts. In the same way as other prisoners are offered anger management courses, Low MAOA offenders could be offered impulse or aggression management courses, or psychiatric or medical treatment to understand why they act aggressively and how to prevent this from happening in the future. Another alternative is pharmaceutical treatment. If the low amounts of MAOA could be artificially raised, resulting in the individual having amounts of MAOA equivalent to a natural High MAOA individual, then the Caspi study suggests that this individual will become less likely to engage in criminal behavior in the future. Synthetic MAOA as a treatment option may allow the goal of rehabilitation to be met. This will be discussed further in the next chapter.

6.3.3.1.4 Retribution The final theory is retribution. Whether this can justify punishment in a genetics case will depend on the form of punishment being imposed. If punishment is being imposed for vengeance, a genetics argument is of little relevance. An eye for an eye approach is not generally concerned with the moral agency of the offender, but with the need of the victim for vengeance. If punishment is imposed under a deontological theory, which relies on the individual being morally responsible for his actions, the genetics factor suggests retribution is not an appropriate reason to punish as moral responsibility will be lacking. Under the third option, empirical, the genetics argument is also irrelevant. The focus is on what society requires to restore the balance to the scales of justice, and to comply with Kant's idea of a moral obligation to exact retribution for crimes.

Interestingly, some scholars have pointed out that if we accept the deterministic argument that a person's genetics resulted in the relevant conduct (even taking into account the role of the environment) then we must also accept a sufficient level of determinism that gives society no choice but to punish the individual concerned. John Hart Ely,[28] for example, commented that if determinism is correct then 'we have no undetermined choice in the matter: we punish because we must. Indeed, we don't even have a choice about whether doing so should make us uneasy'. Similarly, Kolber[29] comments that 'one might wonder if it is humanly possible to deny our retributive impulses'. He refers to recent studies that suggest an 'intuitive sense of fairness runs deep in our primate lineage and that an adaptive tendency towards retributive punishment may have been a crucial development in the biological and cultural evolution of human sociality'. Based on this, he concludes that 'if retributivism runs that deep and is that useful, we might wonder whether we have any serious hope of, or reason for, getting rid of it'.

The four cases, *Waldroup, Bayout, Albertani* and *Bourassa*, do not appear to have evaluated punishment from an eye for an eye approach. The language in the decisions seemed to focus more on a moral responsibility perspective. An empirical viewpoint is perhaps also present, particularly so in *Bourassa* where a juror commented that the death penalty had not been imposed as the victim would not have wanted it. In none of the cases was it suggested that not punishing the individual would be appropriate. Even in *Waldroup* where the jury appeared heavily

---

28 John Hart Ely, 'Ely's Wager' (2002) 5 *Green Bag* 2d 393.

29 Adam Kolber, 'Will there be a neurolaw revolution?' (2014) 15 Colum. Sci. & Tech. L. Rev. 375, 816.

influenced by the genetics argument, the conviction of voluntary manslaughter suggested an acceptance that some level of punishment was required.

6.3.4 Is There a Dominant Theory?

With four different theories of punishment focussing on different end goals, it is reasonable that the measure of appropriate punishment in a given case might differ depending on which theory is seen to carry the most weight. This is especially true when it is considered that even among each individual theory there are differing approaches to the focus to be taken. One way of resolving the potential inconsistencies is to consider whether one or more theories is seen as dominant, or as carrying more weight than the others. Which theory or theories are considered dominant is a position that changes over time.

It is generally recognized that utilitarian theories were the most popular from the 1860s to the 1960s. In the United States, for example, rehabilitation was recognized as the 'self-professed goal' of the justice system. In *Williams v New York*[30] in 1949 it was commented that 'retribution is no longer the dominant objective of the criminal law. Reformation and rehabilitation have become important goals'. By the 1970s, however, this was beginning to change. In a 1976 death penalty case, *Gregg v Georgia*,[31] the plurality quoted *Williams*, but continued that 'neither is [retribution] a forbidden objective nor one inconsistent with our respect for the dignity of men'.

In 1984 the Senate Report for the Sentencing Reform Bill referred to 'the outmoded rehabilitation model' and the fact that 'almost everyone involved in the criminal justice system now doubts that rehabilitation can be induced reliably'.

In the 2012 case *Miller v Alabama*,[32] Justices Roberts and Alito in separate dissents reviewed the changing approach to sentencing and commented that:

> For most of the 20th century, American sentencing practices emphasized rehabilitation and the availability of parole. But by the 1980s, outcry against repeat offenders, broad disaffection with the rehabilitative model, and other factors led many legislatures to reduce or eliminate the possibility of parole,

---

30 337 US 241 (1949).
31 428 US 153 (1976).
32 567 US__ (2012).

imposing longer sentences in order to punish criminals and prevent them from committing more crimes.

Whitman[33] sees a 'great philosophical revival of retributivism' occurring in the last 40 years, while Alschuler[34] comments on incapacitation and deterrence becoming dominant goals by the late 20th century. The recent tentative drafts of the Model Penal Code,[35] beginning in late 2007, appear to support both conclusions. Despite commentary[36] that the draft 'continues the original Code's investment in utilitarian crime-reductive goals, including offender rehabilitation and the incapacitation of dangerous offenders', it is clear that retribution is, if not the dominant theory, then at least the starting point. The relevant provision on sentencing purposes begins with the purpose of rendering sentences 'within a range of severity proportionate to the gravity of the offences, the harms done to crime victims and the blameworthiness of offenders' (in other words a retributivist purpose) and is then followed by 'when reasonably feasible, to achieve offender rehabilitation, general deterrence, incapacitation of dangerous offenders …' (a utilitarianist purpose). The sentencing guidelines in 6B.03 begin with a retributivist approach of setting 'presumptive sentences for defined classes of cases that are proportionate to the gravity of the offences, the harms done to crime victims and the blameworthiness of offenders'. These sentences can then be 'tailored' in order 'to effectuate one or more of the utilitarian or restorative purposes in 1.02'. The commentary on the guidelines remarks on the change in approach from the 1970s–80s reforms which had a 'singular emphasis on the philosophy of just deserts' to a shift towards a 'hybrid approach of retributive and utilitarian goals in sentencing reform' which 'has become all but universal'.[37]

---

33 James Q. Whitman, *Harsh Justice: Criminal Punishment and the Widening Divide Between America and Europe* (OUP 2005) 23–24.

34 Albert W. Alschuler, 'The changing purposes of criminal punishment: A retrospective on the past century and some thoughts about the next', (2003) U. Chi. L. Rev. 1, 9.

35 American Legal Institute, Model Penal Code: Sentencing, Tentative Draft No. 1.

36 American Legal Institute Model Penal Code Draft (2007) p. 3.

37 The 2012 draft makes no alteration to these provisions. It does insert 6B.09 'evidence-based sentencing: Offender treatment needs and risk of re-offending', which requires consideration of needs for 'rehabilitative treatment' and 'future criminal conduct' but it is unclear whether this reintroduction of rehabilitation is intended to prioritize this as a sentencing theory.

This hybrid approach can also be seen in Australia, New Zealand and the United Kingdom. Warner[38] gives the example of s5 of the Australian state of Victoria's Sentencing Act 1991, which states 'the only purposes for which a sentence may be imposed are punishment … denunciation, rehabilitation, community protection and deterrence, or any combination of two or more purposes'. She concludes that 'having a list of conflicting purposes is something we appear to have to live with for the time being'. The United Kingdom Criminal Justice Act 2003 takes a similar approach. Section 142(1) lists purposes of sentencing as including punishment, reduction of crime by deterrence, reform and rehabilitation of offenders, protection of the public and reparation.[39]

The New Zealand legislation is also worded similarly. Section 7(1) Sentencing Act lists multiple purposes of sentencing. Some of these accord with the theories of retribution,[40] rehabilitation,[41] incapacitation[42] and deterrence.[43] Others seem to fall outside the scope of the four purposes relating to the promotion of responsibility for harm and providing for the interests of the victim and are based instead on restorative justice.[44] In addition, s7(2) makes it clear that there is no hierarchy of purposes, and this seems to be the position taken by judges. The writers of a leading criminal law text comment that instead of one theory taking precedence in New Zealand in all cases, different theories can be seen as taking precedence in different classes of crime.[45] In cases

---

[38] Kate Warner, *Theories of Sentencing: Punishment and Deterrence* NJCA Conference Paper (2014) http://njca.com.au/wp-content/uploads/2013/05/Warner-paper.pdf (accessed 25 March 2015).

[39] Andrew Ashworth in *Sentencing and Criminal Justice* (CUP 2010) p. 76, has criticized the approach of the UK legislation, for the reason that it amounts to giving judges and magistrates the freedom to determine policy or their own penal philosophy. For Hart, in *Punishment and Responsibility,* this was not an issue: 'No one expects judges or statesmen occupied in the business of sending people to the gallows or prison, or in making (or unmaking) laws which enable this to be done, to have much time for philosophical discussion of the principles which make it morally tolerable to do these things. A judicial bench is not and should not be a professional chair.'

[40] These include holding the offender accountable and providing reparation.

[41] These include assisting in rehabilitation and reintegration into society.

[42] These include protecting the community.

[43] These include denouncing the conduct and deterring the offender or others.

[44] J. Bruce Robertson and Jeremy Finn, *Adams on Criminal Law* (New Zealand: Thomson Reuters 2014).

[45] Ibid.

like drug dealing, immigration and passport fraud, for example, deterrence is the key principle. In sexual offending, on the other hand, deterrence is given the least weight and the focus is on incapacitation and rehabilitation.

Tonry[46] concludes that by the end of the first decade of the 21st century, 'there was no dominant sentencing paradigm in the US or other English-speaking countries'. He points to the fact that countries have parole boards, which he describes as 'the quintessential element' of indeterminate sentencing (or sentencing based on utilitarian principles), but also determinate mandatory minimum and three strikes laws. In addition, most countries have alcohol and drug and sexual offender treatment programmes, and are moving more towards restorative justice.

The lack of a dominant theory to help understand how a genetics argument might be approached can be seen as problematic as this might impact on consistency of sentencing. On the other hand, this might be seen as a positive development, as it will require the appropriate sentence for each case to be determined on the particular facts, rather than being determined purely on the basis of genetics.

6.3.5 Conclusion

This chapter thus far has discussed the four traditional justifications for punishment, and has suggested that there is no clear way to apply these to a genetic argument. Different outcomes could result depending on which theory, and even which sub-theory, is being applied. While in the United States it appears that retributivism is given priority, legislation in Australia, New Zealand and the United Kingdom expressly denies that any one theory of punishment, or principle of sentencing, takes priority over another. An approach like the one in New Zealand, where one theory might be preferred for a particular class of offending, might be problematic for a novel argument like the one being discussed here.

Hart,[47] quoted in the introduction to this chapter, concluded that '[t]ill we have developed this sense of complexity of punishment … we shall be in no fit state to assess the extent to which the whole institution has been eroded by, or needs to be adapted to, new beliefs about the human mind'.

The discussion above assumes that the traditional justifications for punishment can survive a genetics argument. This may not necessarily be

---

46 Michael Tonry, *Why Punish? How Much?* (New York: OUP 2011) p. 5.

47 H.L.A. Hart, *Punishment and Responsibility* (1968) (Oxford: Clarendon Press) p. 183.

the case. Three of the four theories involve some recognition of the concept of 'free will', or 'moral agency', incorporated through the idea that the individual was able to make a choice in his actions. A genetics argument, with its claims of determinism, might threaten this. The concept of 'free will' will be discussed in the next part.

6.4 THE CONCEPT OF FREE WILL

6.4.1 Introduction

Throughout the discussion in this chapter, the idea of 'free will' has been mentioned. The popular understanding of criminal responsibility is that it is based on free will, and several of the theories of punishment see this as being either a required or a relevant factor. The difficulty in using a term like 'free will' lies in the fact that the concept has a different meaning or focus depending on the discipline of the person using it, and this meaning can even differ internally in each discipline. This section will discuss some of these different perspectives on free will before considering how a genetics argument fits with some version of this concept.

6.4.2 Free Will from a Philosophical Perspective

6.4.2.1 Compatibilism v incompatibilism

Philosophical approaches to free will begin with a consideration of determinism. Determinism is the concept that every action is determined by conditions which cause that action to occur, and it is therefore impossible for any other action to have occurred. As Hoefer describes it in the *Stanford Encyclopedia of Philosophy*, determinism is 'the idea that every event is necessitated by antecedent events and conditions together with the laws of nature'. These external factors which determine conduct may include social, religious or biological factors.

For some philosophers, the concept of determinism does not preclude the existence of free will. This group are referred to as 'compatibilists', on the basis that they see determinism and free will as being compatible concepts. For others, known as 'incompatibilists', determinism leaves no room for free will. There are three main groups of incompatibilists, categorized by how they respond to this incompatibility: libertarians, who deny that the universe is determined; hard determinists, who deny that free will exists; and hard incompatibilists, who deny both free will and determinism. These will be discussed further below.

6.4.2.2 Incompatibilist positions

For incompatibilists, free will requires that man be the ultimate or originating cause of a given action. If determinism is accepted then an external cause becomes the first cause, and therefore free will cannot exist. Determinism and free will are inconsistent positions, and therefore, whether free will exists depends on an acceptance or rejection of determinism. The three different schools of thought discussed below take differing positions on this.

6.4.2.2.1 Libertarians The basic libertarian position is that determinism is false and free will is possible. For this group, 'free will' means that in a given situation an individual has more than one course of action available to him, and he can therefore choose which to take. The imposition of responsibility for this action (Robert Kane refers to this as the 'Ultimate Responsibility'[48]) derives from the fact that the individual could have chosen the alternative (i.e. non-criminal) course of action, but instead chose the criminal action.

6.4.2.2.2 Hard determinists[49] Hard determinists accept determinism as true, and consequently therefore reject the idea of free will. For this group, scientific explanations of determinism must be accepted. This group would say that society can't resist science based on purely intuitive grounds about one's own sense of freedom. Since science suggests that determinism is the most likely theory, this relegates free will to an illusory or false concept.

6.4.2.2.3 Hard incompatibilists Hard incompatibilists deny both determinism and free will. A leading proponent of this approach is John Locke. In his opinion, determinism is irrelevant, and the concept of free will makes little sense. Voluntary behavior exists when a person can postpone acting long enough to reflect or deliberate on consequences. This is not, however, free will: 'the will in truth signifies nothing but a power or ability to prefer or choose'.[50]

---

[48] Robert Kane, *Oxford Handbook of Free Will* (2002) (Oxford: Clarendon Press).

[49] This group can also be described as hard incompatibilists, free will sceptics, illusionists or impossibilists.

[50] John Locke, *An Essay Concerning Human Understanding* (1836) (London; New York: Penguin Books 1997).

6.4.2.3 Compatibilism

Compatibilists consider free will and determinism to be consistent. Their justification for this position comes in large part from their definition of free will. Unlike incompatibilists, who require man to be the ultimate or originating cause of the action, compatibilists utilize a different definition of free will. For compatibilists, free will is the freedom to act according to one's determined motives without hindrance from other individuals. Where the incompatibilist concept of free will is metaphysical, the compatibilist concept is non-metaphysical, somewhat resembling autonomy.

Thomas Aquinas[51] described the compatibilist approach in this way:

> Free-will is the cause of its own movement, because by his free-will man moves himself to act. But it does not of necessity belong to liberty that what is free should be the first cause of itself, as neither for one thing to be the cause of another need it be the first cause.

For Aquinas, God was the first cause of any action, but this did not prevent the presence of free will in man.

6.4.3 Free Will from a Scientific Perspective

The purpose of scientific inquiry can be understood as seeking to explain why things happen. This can be contrasted with the purpose of philosophy, which is the study of ideas about knowledge, reality and existence. Because of the differing focuses of the two disciplines, differing understandings of free will can result, but the fact that scientific focus is on causation will mean that a different approach to understanding free will is likely to be adopted. This part will discuss the concept of free will from three different scientific perspectives: mechanism, neuroscience and behavioral genetics.

6.4.3.1 Mechanism

Mechanism is a school of thought that sees living beings as complex machines, the operation of which enables behavior to be explained. As an example of this approach, Descartes,[52] in *Treatise on Man*, wrote:

---

[51] Thomas Aquinas, *Summa Theologica* (1917) (New York: McGraw Hill 1964).

[52] Descartes, *Treatise of Man* (1972) (Cambridge: Harvard University Press 1972).

> I should like you to consider that these functions (including passion, memory and imagination) follow from the mere arrangement of the machine's organs every bit as naturally as the movements of a clock or other automaton follow from the arrangement of its counter-weights and wheels.

While philosophical determinism suggests that actions are caused by external causes, mechanism seeks to take causation a step further, by seeing living things as complicated machines and seeking to provide a more detailed explanation for the action. According to Elster,[53] determinism usually 'takes the form of citing an earlier event as the cause of the event we want to explain … [but] to cite the cause is not enough: the causal mechanism must also be provided, or at least suggested'.

6.4.3.2 Neuroscience

Recent advances in neuroscience have challenged the concept of free will, supporting instead a more mechanistic approach. Some of these advances have been discussed in previous chapters, for example the use of brain scans to identify increased serotonin in the brain, which affects behavior.

One common example of a neuroscience experiment suggesting mechanism rather than free will is Libet's experiment of measuring brain activity in individuals carrying out the action of raising their hand.[54] The results showed that there was brain activity at a nonconscious level approximately 550 milliseconds before the hand lifted, but that the subject only became aware of the intention to lift the hand 200 milliseconds before the act. This suggests that the action was initiated before the individual was aware of this, negating the idea of the individual making a conscious choice to lift the hand. As Quek[55] described it, 'the consciousness is informed of the decision, but does not make it'.

How to interpret such a result has been the subject of debate. For some, this suggests that a person's will is mechanistic, rather than free. Others argue that the distinction between initiating and implementing actions is too vague, or that the fact that the task involved random finger

---

[53] Jon Elster, *Nuts and Bolts for the Social Sciences* (1989) (Cambridge: CUP) p. 3.

[54] Benjamin Libet, 'Do we have free will?' in Libet, Freeman and Sutherland (eds) *The Volitional Brain: Towards a Neuroscience of Free Will* (1999) 47 Exeter, UK: Imprint Academic.

[55] Joel Quek, 'Our brain "Kant" tell us? A Kantian perspective of how neuroscience challenges our notions of moral responsibilityand the legal implications' (2012) 1(1) UCL J.L. and J. 2012, 1(1), 22, 25.

movements rather than a deliberate, motivated act means that the claimed challenge to free will as it applies in the criminal justice context is not justified. Libet himself favors a middle ground, retaining belief in the concept of free will on the basis that even if the conscious mind did not initiate the act, it still has the ability to veto it.

6.4.3.3 Behavioral genetics

Behavioral geneticists unsurprisingly suggest a different approach. The studies on the MAOA and serotonin genes and their interaction with childhood environment suggests that certain individuals are predisposed to impulsive or aggressive acts. This is not a mechanistic argument, however, as the addition of the environmental factor makes the causation between genes/environment and the behavior more difficult to explain. It might still support a determinist argument, which doesn't require the same level of causative explanation. Alternatively, the fact that this research indicates only a predisposition to impulsivity or aggression allows for the idea of some level of free will. This may not be the understanding of free will favoured by incompatibilists, but it will likely meet the compatibilist definition.

6.4.4 Free Will from a Folk-psychology Perspective

It is important to consider not just theoretical or scientific understandings of free will, but to also consider the common societal understanding of the term. This will be important in considering the criminal law's approach to free will, due to the role of non-scientific or non-philosopher members of society (for example those writing the legislation, judges and jurors) in determining liability and punishment. These people will often approach notions of free will from a 'commonsense' perspective, also known as a 'folk-psychological' perspective. Folk psychology is simply a term used to describe the inbuilt human capacity to explain and predict the behavior and mental states of others.

What is clear from empirical studies since the 1950s is that this folk psychological understanding of free will has tended to minimize or ignore the causative effect of genetics or the environment on conduct. As an example, in a study by Sundby[56] less than half of the 165 jurors interviewed reported taking situational factors into account in sentencing.

---

[56] Scott Sundby, *A Life and Death Decision: A Jury Weighs the Death Penalty* (2005) (New York: Palgrave Macmillan) p. 208.

Atiq[57] concludes that studies show that individuals 'have a tendency to ignore the situational causes of crime, and an emphasis on free will to the exclusion of situational factors is correlated with punitive harshness'. This appears to indicate a strong preference among jurors for some concept of free will.

In a study by Nicholls and Knobe,[58] it was concluded that in relation to behavior 'people's ordinary understanding appears to involve something more [than determined mental states and principles], a separate self that stands outside all these states and processes and can choose to ignore their promptings'. In other words, free will is a standard part of the reasoning process. In another study of 800 jurors,[59] 32 per cent thought that the relevant criminal acts 'were entirely the result of free will' as opposed to situational factors. The mean response attributed 76 per cent of the causal responsibility to free will. In a third study by Nahmias,[60] participants were introduced to an alternative universe where 'thoughts, desires and plans are completely caused by earlier events that trace back to their particular genetic make-up and upbringing'. Even given these parameters, 72 per cent of participants thought free will existed, and 77 per cent thought people were deserving of credit or blame for their actions.

The folk psychological understanding of free will, therefore, arguably envisages a person as being generally capable of practical reason, who has the ability to decide to act and should therefore be liable for the consequences of those actions. This is most in line with the compatibilist or libertarian approach.

6.4.5 Free Will from a Criminal Law Perspective

The criminal law starts from the premise that all adults are sane and therefore legally responsible for their conduct. It imposes liability if

---

[57] Emad Atiq, 'How folk beliefs about free will influence sentencing: A new target for the neuro-determinist critics of criminal law' (2013) 64 Hastings L.J. 1619, 1631.

[58] Shaun Nichols and Joshua Knobe, 'Moral responsibility and determinism: The cognitive science of folk intuitions', 41 No s 663 (2007)

[59] C.E. Tygart, 'Respondents' "free will" view of criminal behavior and support for capital punishment', (1994) 6 Int'l J Pub Opinion Res 371, 373.

[60] Eddy Nahmias, Stephen Morris, Thomas Nadelhoffer and Jason Turner, 'Surveying freedom: Folk intuitions about free will and moral responsibility', (2005)18 Phil. Psychol. 561.

prohibited actions occur and an appropriate mental element is established. In some cases the law makes allowances (through the establishment of narrowly defined defences) for the impact of external forces which might impact on either the capacity of the individual, the voluntariness of the conduct, or the establishment of mens rea.

It is arguable therefore that the term 'free will' in the criminal law is effectively a shorthand expression, used to refer to someone who has met the relevant criteria for a particular crime. Hart,[61] for example, describes the role of a mens rea element in a manner that suggests he sees it as excusing those people who might not have 'free will':

> The general requirement of mens rea is an element in criminal responsibility designed to secure that those who offend without carelessness, unwittingly, or in conditions in which they lacked the bodily or mental capacity to conform to the law, should be excused. A legal system would be open to serious moral condemnation if this were not so.

The US Supreme Court[62] has commented similarly that 'a belief in freedom of the human will and a consequent ability and duty of the normal individual to choose between good and evil [is] universal and persistent in mature systems of law'.

Beyond comments of this nature, however, the law does not appear to be overly concerned with justifying its approach, or explaining how free will forms part of this. Jones describes the theory of criminal punishment as being of 'peripheral concern'[63] for courts and legislatures, and quotes Weinreb[64] who concludes that it is 'as if we were clear about when it is correct to punish even if we cannot sort out exactly why it is correct'. Packard agrees, explaining that:[65]

---

[61] H.L.A. Hart, *The Concept of Law* (1961) Oxford: Clarendon Press p. 178.

[62] *Morissette v United States*, 342 US 246, 250–51 (1952).

[63] Matthew Jones, *Overcoming the myth of free will in criminal law: The true impact of the genetic revolution* (2003) Duke LJ 1031, 1031.

[64] Lloyd L. Weinreb, 'Desert, punishment, and criminal responsibility', (1986) 49 Law & Contemp. Probs. 47, 50–51.

[65] Herbert Packer, *The Limits of the Criminal Sanction* (1968) Stanford, CA: Stanford University Press pp. 74–75. See also *Blocker v US* 288 F2d 853 (1961): 'while philosophers, theologians, scientists and lawyers have debated for centuries whether such a thing as "free will" really exists, society and the law have no choice in the matter. We must proceed … on the scientifically unprovable assumption that human beings make choices in the regulation of their conduct and that they are uninfluenced by society's standards as well as by personal standards.'

> The idea of free will in relation to conduct is not, in the legal system, a statement of fact, but rather a value preference having very little to do with the metaphysics of determinism or free will … very simply, the law treats man's conduct as autonomous and willed, not because it is, but because it is desirable to proceed as if it were.

The legal system therefore arguably adopts a concept of free will which is not clearly defined, and may not be consistent with scientific understanding or philosophical thought. This inconsistency can be considered acceptable, however, given the underlying objectives of the criminal justice system. While science and philosophy both seek to understand why people act the way they do, the law is more of a social construct. It is a system of rules intended to set standards for conduct in a particular society, and to therefore guide or influence the behavior of its members through operating as part of their reasoning process. It assumes that people generally act rationally, and will therefore take a particular law (and the consequences of breaching it) into account when deciding whether to act. As a consequence of this approach, its determination of moral responsibility does not need to be consistent with science's developing understanding of free will or philosophical debates on determinism. Each of these disciplines are serving a different purpose: explanation, understanding, or responsibility.

As Searle[66] wrote:

> Once we have the possibility of explaining particular forms of human behavior as following rules, we have a very rich explanatory apparatus that differs dramatically from the explanatory apparatus of the natural sciences. When we say we are following rules, we are accepting the notion of mental causation and the attendant notions of rationality and existence of norms … the content of the rule does not just describe what is happening, but plays a part in making it happen.

The commentary to the US Model Penal Code similarly makes it clear that the law and science are addressing different matters: 'the term "voluntary" as used in this section does not inject into the criminal law questions about [theoretical] determinism and free will … there is sufficient difference between ordinary human activity and a reflex or a convulsion to make it desirable that they be distinguished for purposes of criminal responsibility by a term like "voluntary".'

---

[66] John R. Searle, 'End of the Revolution', *New York Review of Books*, Feb. 28, 2002, at 33.

6.4.6 Conclusion

This section has discussed the concept of free will from a scientific, philosophical, folk perspective, and finally a legal perspective. What is clear from this discussion is that the underlying objectives of each discipline have impacted the approaches taken in understanding the concept of free will. The term has developed differing, and perhaps divergent, meanings between, and even among, each discipline. The next section will consider whether this is a sustainable reality, or whether the increasing philosophical debates and changing scientific understanding also requires a reconsideration of the legal system.

6.5 DOES THE LEGAL SYSTEM NEED TO CHANGE?

6.5.1 Introduction

As discussed above, recent advances in scientific understanding, particularly in neuroscience and in behavioural genetics, have led to new discussions on the concept of free will. This has resulted in an increasing debate among scientists, philosophers and legal academics as to whether the criminal justice system needs to rethink its justifications for imposing liability and for punishing individuals. There are three possible options resulting from this debate. First, the criminal law can be completely redesigned on the basis that its foundational concept of free will has been challenged by developing scientific understanding of causes of behavior. Second, the criminal law can retain its current position on the basis that legal free will is sufficiently different from scientific or philosophical free will that amendments are not required. Third, it can alter its understanding of why we punish to incorporate this new understanding. These options will be discussed in turn.

6.5.2 Option One: The Legal System Must Change in Response to This New Evidence

A reconsideration of the criminal justice system would be in line with an incompatibilist position. For hard determinists, the emerging scientific understanding from neuroscience and behavioral genetics provides additional support for their denial of the existence of free will. A similar approach would exist for hard incompatibilists, who similarly reject free will. Some of this group, for example Locke, accept a concept of voluntary behavior as justification for punishment, however Libet's experiment can be seen as challenging this position. If the subconscious mind merely informs the conscious mind that an action is to take place, there is no opportunity to postpone the action or to refrain from acting. Hard determinists and hard incompatibilists would likely claim, therefore, that the argument for the law to reflect science has been strengthened. The third group of incompatibilists, Libertarians, accept the existence of free will and impose liability on the basis that a person has the ability to choose not to act and should be punished if he does not exercise this appropriately. As with Locke's concept of voluntary behavior, Libet's experiment might provide a challenge to this.

A reconsideration of the criminal justice system is not necessarily required by compatibilists, on the basis that they understand the scientific and legal uses of the term 'free will' as being aimed at achieving different goals and therefore having different meanings. Their idea of free will resembling autonomy, however, might also be challenged by recent research, particularly Libet's experiment.

There are four key arguments for reconsidering the criminal justice system:

1. To maintain credibility, the justifications for criminal responsibility and punishment must be defensible.
2. To be effective, the criminal law must understand the reasons underpinning criminal acts.
3. To maintain credibility, the law must reflect developing scientific understanding of causes of crime.
4. A failure to revisit theoretical underpinnings means that an important justification for punishment – rehabilitation – is not being given appropriate consideration.

6.5.2.1 To maintain credibility, the justifications for criminal responsibility and punishment must be defensible

The argument here is that the concept of free will is inherent in the underlying justifications for criminal responsibility (including defences) and punishment. If recent research suggests that a more mechanistic approach to behavior is more accurate, then the overall primary presumption of the criminal justice system is faulty. Society's moral justification for imposing punishment is therefore not present.

Morse[67] describes it in this way:[68] '[I]f this particular materialist and determinist view of humans were right, that is, if we are really not acting agents at all, the present foundations of law and morality rooted in agentic personhood would collapse.'

In basic terms, the argument is that while someone from a non-scientific or philosophical background might struggle with accepting a mechanistic approach, it is not appropriate to completely set aside scientific evidence because it is incomplete, problematic or raises ethical concerns.

6.5.2.2 To be effective, the criminal law must understand the reasons underpinning criminal acts

A criminal justice system that focuses primarily on retribution responds after the fact to criminal acts rather than working to prevent actions before they occur, an approach which is the primary goal of rehabilitation, deterrence and incapacitation. Beccaria[69] recognized the importance of operating before the fact when he said simply that 'it is better to prevent crimes than to punish them'. Roscoe Pound[70] agreed, commenting that 'in order to deal with crime in an intelligent and practical manner, we must give up the retributive theory'.

The argument here is that in order to prevent crime in the most intelligent and effective manner, its causes must be understood.[71] If science is providing new insight into causes of crime, through either neuroscience or behavioral genetics studies, then it is only logical that these are taken into account.

---

[67] Stephen Morse, 'Criminal responsibility and the disappearing person' (2007) 28 Cardozo L Rev 2545, 2569.

[68] See also Green and Cohen: 'as people become more vividly acquainted with the mechanistic nature of human decision making, they will find retributivist punishment increasingly unpalatable and adopt consequentialist punishment practices instead.' Joshua Greene and Jonathan Cohen, 'For the law, neuroscience changes nothing and everything', (2004) 359 Phil Transactions Royal Soc'y London B Biol Sci 1775, 1776.

[69] Beccaria, *On Crimes And Punishment* (1764) (reprint) (London: Empire Books 2012).

[70] Roscoe Pound, *Inherent and Acquired Difficulties in the Administration of Punitive Justice* (1908) (Cambridge: Harvard University Press 2008).

[71] Judge Bazelon commented that 'society can never hope to achieve a just and lasting solution to crime without first facing the facts that underlie it'. David L. Bazelon, *Questioning Authority: Justice and Criminal Law* (New York: Knopf Publishing 1988) p. 23.

6.5.2.3 To maintain credibility, the law must reflect developing scientific understanding of causes of crime

It was suggested above that the law is designed as a system of rules intended to set standards for conduct in a society, and therefore to guide or influence the behavior of its members. If this is accurate, then the law relies on society as a whole to accept its rules as valid in order to function most effectively. A law that fails to keep pace with the current state of knowledge risks being seen by the society it is intended to guide as being outdated, and therefore not valid. Roscoe Pound,[72] for example, wrote that the criminal law 'is so rooted in theological ideas of free will and moral responsibility and juridical ideas of retribution … that we by no means make what we should of our discoveries', and another scholar[73] commented that 'available scientific evidence about insanity is ignored by a legal system that embraces 'medieval concepts of sin and punishment'.

6.5.2.4 A failure to revisit theoretical underpinnings means that an important justification for punishment – rehabilitation – is not being given appropriate consideration

Of the four justifications for punishment, rehabilitation is the one which appears to be carrying the least weight in current times.[74] If the law was to be reconsidered in light of recent scientific developments this might provide an opportunity to re-consider a focus on rehabilitation, and therefore on reinforcing rehabilitation as an important goal, leading to more research into understanding and treating causes of crime.

6.5.3 Option Two: The Legal System Does Not Need to Change

The argument here is that there is an important difference between philosophical (or scientific) free will and legal free will. This would be in line with a compatibilist position. Since compatibilists understand 'free will' in the legal sense to take a different meaning to scientific 'free will', recent developments in science do not necessarily require changes in law. As long as the science does not render the legal concept of free will completely unsustainable, there is no reason to alter the legal system.

There are six key arguments for this position:

---

72 Roscoe Pound, 'Book Review', (1909) 3 Am. Pol. Sci. Rev. 281, 283–84.

73 Michael L. Perlin, 'Unpacking the myths: The symbolism mythology of insanity defense jurisprudence' (1989/1990) 40 Case W. Res. L. Rev. 599, 730.

74 There are some exceptions, notably in the development of drug courts and the treatment of sex offenders. These will be discussed in more detail later.

1. Science and the law have two different goals.
2. The law has historically adopted a unique approach to free will.
3. Determinism continues to be a matter for debate.
4. Folk psychology will adapt.
5. Changing the criminal justice system is practically unworkable and societally unacceptable.
6. Reliance on free will is a necessary evil.

6.5.3.1 Science and the law have two different goals

Science is generally concerned with identifying causation. In the medical sciences, this aids the ultimate goal of diagnosis and treatment. Finding a causative relationship between genetics or biology and an individual's conduct aids this goal. The law, on the other hand, is concerned with creating standards for a functioning society. Setting minimal standards for behavior (with limited exceptions for those unable to meet these) aids this goal. As science and the law have different goals, they are justified in taking different approaches. This is frequently commented on by judges in insanity cases, who point out that even though medical experts might have an opinion as to whether an individual has a disease of the mind, this is a different criterion to whether the legal definition is met, and therefore, whether a person should be considered to be morally responsible for his actions.

Legal responsibility is a normative judgment, a decision by society as to which conduct is acceptable and which should be prohibited. Society also decides on the minimum state of mind required for liability. While 'neuroscience can inform as to whether a person has these minimum capabilities', this should be considered to be a guide only.

6.5.3.2 The law has historically adopted a unique approach to free will

The idea that science, philosophy and law might have differing approaches to the concept of free will is not new. Farahany and Coleman[75] put it simply: 'the legal system did not rely upon a theoretical understanding of free will to begin with, and need not do so now'.

---

[75] Nita A. Farahany and James E. Coleman Jr, 'Genetics and responsibility: To know the criminal from the crime' (2006) 69-SPG Law & Contemp. Probs. 115, 138.

The original idea that moral responsibility lay in the ability to act voluntarily came from 17th–18th century Britain, and was in part developed by John Locke, who was a compatibilist. Morse concludes that:[76]

> Causation is not compulsion, and predictability is not an excuse. Just because an offender is caused to do something or is predictable does not mean the offender is compelled to do the crime charged or is otherwise not responsible. Brain causation – or any other kind of causation – does not mean we are automatons, not really acting agents at all, or otherwise excused.

6.5.3.3 Determinism continues to be a matter for debate

As shown above, arguments relating to determinism have existed for centuries, with scientists and philosophers disagreeing over whether determinism is a valid theory and if it is, what impact it should have on the justice system. The emerging neuroscience and behavioral genetics scholarship is simply another contributor to this debate. Without any evidence that the current arguments are significantly enhancing the debate, or are advancing one position over the other, there is no justification for reconsidering the criminal justice system at this time.

In fact, the history of genetic arguments in the courts calls for caution before making any fundamental changes to the criminal justice system. The eugenics movement in the 1930s and the XYY arguments in the 1970s both argued for a reconsideration of the specific role that genetics evidence should play in imposing criminal liability and punishment, and therefore for a reconsideration of the criminal justice system as a whole. As has been seen in both of these examples, subsequent scientific studies found the science to be problematic at best, or incorrect at worst. If the criminal justice system had been altered in each of those cases, it would have needed to be altered back in response to these subsequent studies. Such alterations would have been appropriate in light of contemporary scientific understanding, but the changing approaches would have resulted in the law becoming unfair, inconsistent and unpredictable.

The law as it currently stands has sufficient flexibilities to allow for genetic arguments to be taken into account, particularly during sentencing. This should be regarded as sufficient, until the science reaches a more acceptable stage of certainty. In *Landrigan*, it was commented that 'the science is not yet at this stage'. While scientific understanding might perhaps have reached a sufficient stage of certainty to allow for its

---

[76] Stephen Morse, 'Avoiding irrational neurolaw exuberance: A plea for neuromodesty' (2011) 62 Mercer L. Rev. 837, 848.

consideration as part of a specific trial, it is arguably not at such a stage as to justify a redesign of the criminal justice system as a whole.

6.5.3.4 Folk psychology will adapt

Although it might appear that the law is inconsistent with, and ignoring, recent scientific developments, this is not entirely accurate. Genetic evidence is being admitted into court, and this will affect the folk psychology understanding of free will. As neuroscience and behavioral genetics research develops, lawyers and expert witnesses will continue to introduce judges and jurors to relevant findings and these will, as appropriate, become part of the folk psychological understanding of free will.

Green and Cohen,[77] for example, argue that: '[N]euroscience will probably have a transformative effect on the law ... New neuroscience will change the law, not by undermining its current assumptions, but by transforming people's moral intuitions about free will and responsibility.'

This adaption might occur in one of two ways. First, if people adopt a compatibilist approach there is a risk that the criminal justice system will end up not punishing criminals enough. This has been seen in the recent cases of *Waldroup*, where he was charged with first degree murder and first degree attempted murder, but was convicted of significantly lesser charges, and in *Bayout* and *Albertani*, where the evidence led to a reduction in sentence. Second, people will 'become more trusting of the deterministic explanation without giving up on the possibility of free will entirely' and will take into account other factors. This is supported by studies which indicate that although determinists punish less harshly, they nevertheless continue to hold criminals morally responsible. This has occurred in some cases discussed above, where the genetic evidence has been taken into account, but has been only one factor in an overall consideration, and has not outweighed the aggravating factors in each case.

6.5.3.5 Changing the criminal justice system is practically unworkable and societally unacceptable

The argument here is simple: retaining free will as a default position allows the criminal justice system to function. If every individual charged with a crime was assessed separately for environmental risks and genetic

---

[77] Joshua Greene and Jonathan Cohen, 'For the law, neuroscience changes nothing and everything', (2004) 359 Phil Transactions Royal Soc'y London B Biol Sci 1775, 1775.

propensities, this might result in a more just outcome on a case by case basis, but might also lead to some unjust consequences for the system as a whole. The individual would be required to sacrifice some rights, including the right to be tried without undue delay, the right not to be compelled to testify against himself (by having to provide a DNA sample) and the right to privacy.[78]

The criminal justice system has shown its ability to adapt, when considered appropriate, to incorporate new scientific understanding. This has been seen in the genetic propensity cases, where judges have addressed the issue of when, and for what purpose, to allow testimony relating to this. It will likely continue to develop, or react, to science where appropriate. Major changes are not therefore required. As Justice Marshall commented:

> We cannot cast aside the centuries long evolution of the collection of interlocking and overlapping concepts which the common law has utilized to assess the moral accountability of an individual for his antisocial deeds. The doctrines of actus reus, mens rea, insanity, mistake, justification and duress have historically provided the tools for a constantly shifting adjustment of a tension between the medical views of the nature of man.[79]

6.5.3.6 Reliance on free will is a necessary evil

The final argument might be the most important. Even if 'free will' is not strictly accurate from a scientific perspective, a belief in free will plays an important role in society in general as well as in the criminal law specifically. Kant commented that 'life becomes meaningful for us as human beings when we can believe that what we do is the result of free choice and has, thereby, a moral meaning'.

The fact that there is a societal benefit to retaining a belief in free will is sufficient justification for its continuing presence in the criminal justice system. As Fodor describes it:[80]

> if a belief in free will were really to collapse, that would be, beyond comparison, the greatest intellectual catastrophe in the history of our species. If we're that wrong about the mind, then that's the wrongest we've ever been about anything … Nothing except, perhaps, our common sense physics … comes as near to our cognitive core as intentional explanation does. We'll be in deep, deep trouble if we have to give it up.

---

[78] These will be discussed in the next chapter.

[79] Mr Justice Marshall, *Powell v Texas* USSC 392 US 514, 516 (1968).

[80] Jerry Fodor, *Psychosemantics: The Problem of Meaning in the Philosophy of Mind* Cambridge, MA: MIT Press xii (1987).

This is supported by a study by Baumeister,[81] in which participants were induced to disbelieve in free will. The study showed, as a consequence, individuals began demonstrating antisocial tendencies like increased aggression and a reduction in willingness to help.

The criminal law operates to guide behavior in order to enable people to live together in a society. It is necessary to foster 'better social arrangements' and 'greater individual liberty', and on the basis that 'social systems are strengthened by holding people responsible for their conduct'.[82] It is undermined by shifting responsibility to other factors such as genetics or environment, and therefore belief in the illusion of free will is necessary.

6.5.4 Option Three: Alter Understanding to Incorporate New Evidence

The third option is more of a middle ground. It accepts the compatibilist position of the second option but also recognizes that justifications for criminal responsibility and punishment have been challenged in some cases by developing science, and makes incremental changes to reflect this.

An application of this option might result in some changes occurring to the current system while maintaining the concept of moral responsibility and the justifications for punishment. As an example, while genetics evidence is being admitted as a mitigating factor in death penalty cases in the United States, it could be more widely accepted as mitigating in all cases. For countries that include lists of mitigating factors, for example New Zealand's Sentencing Act, this list could be amended to include any genetic or biosocial factors. While this evidence would possibly be considered admissible anyway, an express inclusion might give these factors more credibility before the courts.

Another example might be the promotion of rehabilitation as an important aim, to the extent that this is possible. Many jurisdictions have drug courts or mental health courts, which recognize the link between these issues and recidivism rates. New Zealand additionally has a secure unit for sex offenders, known as Te Marama. If we accept that MAOA increases a person's likelihood of impulsive aggression, teaching anger

[81] Roy Baumeister, 'Prosocial benefits of feeling free: Disbelief in free will increases aggression and reduces helpfulness', (2009) 35 Personality & Soc. Psychol. Bull. 260.

[82] Seymour Halleck, 'Responsibility and excuse in medicine and law: A Utilitarian perspective' (1986) 49(3) Law and Contemp Problems 127, 127.

management or impulse control techniques might be beneficial. This might be coupled with medication to increase the amount of MAOA or serotonin, if possible. This will be discussed further in the next chapter.

As Kirchmeier[83] concludes, 'the immediate changes to the criminal justice system do not have to be drastic, but society should seek knowledge and understanding over maintaining ignorance'. One potential issue with making some incremental changes, however, is the possibility of going too far. While it may be appropriate in some cases to take genetic evidence into account either at trial or at sentencing, if this became the default position it may result in a distinction being drawn between 'genetic' and 'non-genetic' defendants. The consequences of this will be discussed further in the next chapter.

6.6 RECONSIDERING THE CASE OF CHILD B

In the scenario, the aftermath of the trial and sentencing of Child A and Child B raise issues of punishment theory. Comments are made in the media that society needs to be protected from genetically programmed killers and that Child B should never be released. Little is said about Child A.

These comments raise issues about whether it was appropriate to punish Child B. The justification for punishing Child B is that he is morally blameworthy. Setting aside the issue of his age (which will be discussed in the next chapter) can this really be the case? Moral blameworthiness requires a rational, self-determined action and some level of self-control. Where these do not exist, society arguably loses its moral justification for punishment. Three of the four theories of punishment rely to some extent on the idea of free will determining actions. Could Child B satisfy this standard? Does he really have free will? Who is more morally blameworthy: Child B, whose Low MAOA status and childhood maltreatment in the words of the police 'genetically predisposed [him] to murder', or Child A, who had Low MAOA but suffered no maltreatment and was therefore morally responsible for his actions, and more able to decide whether to commit the crime? If it is considered that Child B had free will as a result of the combination of genes and childhood environment, is it even fair and just to judge him in a court

---

[83] Jeffrey Kirchmeier, 'A tear in the eye of the law: Mitigating factors and the progression toward a disease theory of criminal justice' (2004) 83 ORLR 631, 656.

system that appears to require free will as a prerequisite in three of the four justifications for punishment?

6.7 CONCLUSION

This chapter began by raising the issue of whether an increased knowledge of genetics should require a reconsideration of the criminal justice system. An examination of the requirement of moral responsibility suggested that this might be necessary, however a consideration of the theories behind punishment and even the understanding of free will suggests that any major reform of the criminal justice system is unnecessary, unworkable and undesirable. While perhaps not consistent with some schools of philosophical and scientific understanding, it is not so inconsistent with all schools so as to warrant an urgent reconsideration. Its flexible approach to punishment, allowing judges to consider the goals of retribution, deterrence, incapacitation and rehabilitation, for the most part without regarding one theory as dominant, suggests it can also adapt to consider genetic arguments.

Possibly the strongest argument for not altering the criminal justice system results from the role of the people involved. If and when philosophical theories and scientific understandings become more consistent and mainstream, these will begin to be adopted into the reasoning of judges, jurors and legislators in relevant cases. Such incremental change is likely to produce more societally acceptable results than a complete reconsideration could provide. Caution and moderation will also allow any unintended consequences to rethinking moral responsibility to be identified and considered. The next chapter will consider some of these consequences.

7. Introduction to ethical issues

7.1 INTRODUCTION

The previous chapters have discussed the current state of the science and the law in relation to genetic arguments, and whether the theoretical justifications for the criminal justice system need to be reexamined in light of this understanding. This chapter will move to the future, considering where this increasing scientific understanding and application in the courts might lead. Although some of the discussed scenarios might seem unrealistic (and indeed in some places, quotes from dystopian films and literature will be used to make a point), there is a grounding in reality in all of them.

This chapter will consist of two parts. The first part will discuss the concept of compulsory genetic testing for Low MAOA. This is a concept that was raised in relation to XYY syndrome in the 1970s, and has recently begun to occur in discussions on genetic links to crime in relation to Low MAOA. The second part will discuss potential consequences of judges or juries continuing to accept a genetics argument, and of mandatory genetic testing for Low MAOA (or another gene with a potential link to antisocial behavior). This part will be written in the style of a legal Issues Paper. An Issues Paper is a document often provided by a Law Commission to highlight issues in a particular area of law that may be required to be addressed as part of any consideration of law reform. Utilizing this style of writing for this chapter has been chosen for two reasons. First, it emphasizes the lack of complete, detailed, discussion of the matters to be discussed. Most of the issues raised deserve much fuller consideration than can be accomplished in this book, and so are merely being raised and explained briefly here. Second, this style helps to emphasize that these are potential issues only. They may not be realistic in terms of current understanding of science or may not be acceptable to society. For both of these reasons, and for other reasons, some of these issues might be seen as unlikely or unable to occur. They will still be raised for discussion, even if they are best seen not as a potential reality but as warnings of where a slippery slope, which may have begun with the cases discussed in previous chapters, might take us. The fictional nature of this part of the chapter should make these points clear.

The Issues Paper is set in current society, but assumes that the events in the Case Study of Child A and Child B in Chapter 1 have occurred.

7.2 MANDATORY GENETIC TESTING

7.2.1 Introduction

It has been suggested on occasion that mandatory DNA testing should be introduced. In 2006, then UK Prime Minister Tony Blair called for a universal DNA database, commenting that it would 'help[] us track down murderers, rapists'. He did not see 'any problem' with the public being required to provide DNA samples because people who committed serious crimes 'should be convicted'.[1] In 2012, UK Prime Minister David Cameron called for a universal genetic health database to help fight cancer.[2] This has been described by some as introducing a universal Criminal DNA database by stealth. In 2013, a Belgian justice official argued for a universal database, stating 'we must dare to think how to protect the citizen. In return for protection, you have to make a sacrifice. Our privacy legislation goes too far'.[3] These are just a few examples, used to illustrate the discussions already occurring. The language used in these examples suggests further calls for the introduction of a universal database will likely occur.

Once society becomes more familiar with the idea of the link between MAOA, serotonin and dopamine genes, and behavior it is not unrealistic to imagine that the topic of compulsory genetic testing will arise. Ravinesh Kumar,[4] for example, has commented that 'although likely to be highly controversial, we may decide to identify "at-risk" individuals prone to developing antisocial tendencies by screening for the MAOA

---

1 'DNA databases should include all' *Daily Telegraph*, 24 October 2006.

2 'DNA tests to revolutionise fight against cancer' *Press Release*, 20 December 2012.

3 'Belgian justice official demands universal DNA database' *Daily Telegraph* 17 November 2013.

4 Ravinesh Kumar, *Violence begets violence; or does it? A brain enzyme protects victims of childhood abuse from becoming antisocial and criminal* (2003) 63 *Clinical Genetics* 180–3.

functional polymorphism and recognizing those who harbor the "low-activity" variant'. As another example, Appelbaum considered that 'the pressure to identify [at-risk] individuals through screening at birth may be irresistible'.[5]

Chapter Two highlighted some problems with the scientific understanding of MAOA and the other relevant genes. In summary, the main problem with the MAOA studies is the lack of consistent replication. This might indicate differences in design (for example how maltreatment is measured) or might indicate that the connection between MAOA, childhood maltreatment and future antisocial behavior is less clear than some of the studies suggest. A further problem is that the differing results appear to be partially due to racial or gender factors. In *Mobley*, the court commented that the science had yet to reach a level of certainty. This is probably still the case, although it is arguably becoming more convincing. In relation to MAOA, multiple studies have failed to replicate earlier studies, suggesting that there may be additional, but as yet unidentified, factors playing a role. In relation to serotonin and dopamine, there are currently too few studies to establish a sufficient level of certainty of understanding the link between the genes, environment and behavior. For the purposes of this discussion, however, it is necessary to assume a sufficient level of acceptability either currently exists or will exist in the near future. Scientific knowledge has the ability to change quickly, and it is therefore best to consider these issues before they arise.

This discussion will consider genetic testing of newborns, first by looking at past or existing practice in newborn screening and then by considering the possibility of introducing a new test in addition to those already undertaken. It will then consider, as an alternative, the possibility of screening children who display antisocial behavior to determine whether a genetic link exists.

7.2.2 Compulsory Newborn Genetic Testing

7.2.2.1 Newborn screening for XYY syndrome

In 1974 an article published in *Science*[6] described a study of XYY children undertaken by Harvard researchers Stanley Walzer and Park Gerald. The study used information taken from a chromosomal screening

---

[5] Paul Appelbaum, 'Behavioral genetics and the punishment of crime', (2005) *Psychiatric Services* 56: 25–7.

[6] Barbara Culliton, 'Patients' rights: Harvard is site of battle over x and y chromosomes' (1974) 186 *Science* 715 and 'XYY: Harvard researcher under fire stops newborn screening' (1975) 188 *Science* 1284.

study carried out on all children born at the Boston Hospital for Women (a Harvard teaching hospital) since 1968. The study came to light when fellow Harvard researchers challenged its continuation, arguing that XYY syndrome was a 'dangerous myth' and 'the stigma of being … XYY is so great that behavioral problems arise as part of a self-fulfilling prophecy'. A further issue with the study was that there had been no informed consent from the parents: 'parents have been anything but fully informed of the consequences of agreeing to have their babies screened'. A reviewer of the study agreed, concluding that 'elements of "fraud, deceit" and even "duress and overreaching" proscribed by the Nuremberg Code, are clearly present' in the consent form. The study was referred to the Medical School's Standing Committee on Medical Research and also the Medical School's Human Studies Committee, and both concluded that the research could continue. In mid-1975, however, Walzer and Gerald decided to cease the testing due to continuing opposition.

The controversy surrounding this screening programme focused less on the issues of informed consent and more on whether genetic screening itself was acceptable. Opponents argued that it would lead to stigma, and that there was no medical benefit to the child as no treatment would be available. Proponents argued that there was a benefit to the research in developing a better understanding of XYY syndrome. Stetten,[7] as an example, phrased his defence of the study in terms of a 'freedom to enquire' based on the First Amendment. He argued that 'the right to inquire into the clinical consequences of the XYY karyotype seems to me of real importance, and should be protected' and that scientists should 'yield the right to enquire only when the danger is real and present', although steps should be taken to safeguard the privacy of the subjects.

This example provides an interesting comparison with MAOA testing. While one would hope that the issues with informed consent would not arise, the arguments over whether the screening should take place apply equally today. Opponents argued that testing would lead to stigmatization and that there was a lack of a medical benefit to the individual, while proponents argued that the study increased understanding of the condition for the benefit of society in general. These same arguments could apply to MAOA.

---

[7] Dewitt Stetten, 'Freedom of enquiry' (1975) 81 *Genetics* 415.

7.2.2.2 Current newborn screening

The current practice of newborn screening has existed since 1963 when a test for phenylketonuria (PKU) was developed. The next major development occurred in the 1990s, when Tandem Mass Spectrometry was developed. This enables testing for more than 30 disorders at once, using blood from 1–2 heel pricks.

In the United Kingdom, Australia and New Zealand, newborn screening is optional and requires the informed consent of the parents.[8] In all three countries, a 99 per cent screening rate of newborns is reported.[9] In New Zealand, 28 conditions are screened for. In Australia, approximately 30 conditions are screened for, but this number varies between states. The United Kingdom is currently more restrictive, testing for only five conditions.

In the United States, each state tests for between four and 36 different metabolic or genetic disorders. The notable difference with other countries is that screening in the United States is generally compulsory. Only 15 states require parents to be informed, and of these only two require written consent. Most states allow the parents to refuse the screening, but some limit refusal of consent to certain, specific, justifications. The mandatory nature of the screening has been considered problematic, and there have been some challenges, generally on discrimination or religious grounds. As an example of a challenge based on discrimination, in the 1960s there was a requirement that African American children be screened for Sickle Cell Anaemia before attending school. This was argued to be discriminatory due to its focus on a particular racial group. The matter was resolved through legislation being enacted to fund sickle cell programmes in states with voluntary testing which successfully incentivized voluntary, but not mandatory, testing. Today, sickle cell testing is part of the screening programme, but is given to all racial groups.

More recently there have been challenges to compulsory screening on religious grounds. In *Douglas County v Anaya*,[10] for example, parents argued against the screening on the basis of their belief that their child's lifespan would be shortened if blood was drawn for testing. In *Spiering v*

---

[8] The Australian policy specifically refers to the fact that informed consent can be by means of oral consent, recorded in writing on the patients' records.

[9] Office of the Minister of Health, Cabinet Social Policy Committee, *The new policy and governance arrangements for newborn metabolic screening programme blood spot cards* (2011).

[10] 694 NW 2d 601 (Neb 2005).

Heineman,[11] the parents argued that their religious beliefs required 'that parents should insulate their newly born infants from pain during the birth process and for a period of seven days after birth'. They believed that 'subjecting a child to the pain and trauma of a blood draw within seven days of birth violates the religious precept of "Silent Birth" and could cause the child to later suffer physical or mental injury'.

In both cases, the relevant screening laws were examined on 'rational basis' grounds. According to this, if a law is neutral, of general applicability, and is rationally related to a legitimate governmental purpose, the law is valid even though it might incidentally burden a religious practice. In both *Anaya* and *Spiering* this standard for validity was met. Unlike the Sickle Cell screening of African American children, the screening was 'generally applicable to all babies born in the state … [and did] not discriminate as to which babies must be tested'.[12] Nor was it directed specifically at a religious practice. Further, Nebraska (the relevant state in both cases) had a legitimate interest in the 'health and welfare of all children born in [that state]'.[13] In *Spiering*, this was a 'dollars and sense issue' and in *Anaya*, this was described as the need to protect the state from the 'potential social burdens created by children … not identified and tested'. Elsewhere, the legitimate interest has been described more in terms of promotion of health, to 'limit the morbidity and mortality attributable to selected inherited diseases' or to 'promote child welfare through early detection and treatment of selected conditions'.

7.2.2.3 Adding a condition to the screening list

The World Health Organization has published principles for determining whether newborn genetic screening is appropriate. These are:

1. The condition sought should be an important health problem.
2. There should be an accepted treatment for patients with recognized disease.
3. Facilities for diagnosis and treatment should be available.
4. There should be a recognized latent or early symptomatic stage.
5. There should be a suitable test or examination.
6. The test should be acceptable to the population to be tested.
7. The natural history of the condition, including development from latent to declared disease, should be adequately understood.
8. There should be an agreed policy on whom to treat as patients.

---

11 448 F Supp 2d 1129 (D Neb 2006).

12 *Anaya*, 694 NW 2d 601 (Neb 2005).

13 *Anaya*, 694 NW 2d 601 (Neb 2005).

9. The costs of case-finding (including diagnosis and treatment of patients diagnosed) should be economically balanced in relation to possible expenditure on medical care as a whole.
10. Case-finding should be a continuous process and not 'a once and for all' project.

While other professional bodies have published slightly different versions,[14] the common considerations tended to focus on the condition (its frequency, and whether it is an important 'health' problem), the ability to test for and treat the condition, and whether there is a clear benefit to the child in the screening.

7.2.2.4 Predictive testing

Predictive testing is the term given to testing for conditions that have two characteristics. The first characteristic is that there is no evidence (or symptoms) of the condition at the time of testing, and the second is that the result of the test indicates a high chance that the condition will occur in the individual (or his/her children) in the future. Predictive testing, by its nature, is ethically problematic. Where it is currently offered for adults, guidelines emphasize the importance of consent and autonomy in decision making. Where it is offered for children, separate guidelines generally exist which focus on the best interests of the child and the preservation of autonomy and future choice. As an example, both the Clinical Genetics Society in the United Kingdom and the American Society of Human Genetics guidelines advise against testing for disease that begins in adulthood if there is no pre-emptive or definitive treatment available in childhood. The best interests of the child test in this case will generally favor delaying testing until the child can decide for himself. Where the disease will begin later in childhood but there is no effective treatment before the condition develops,[15] the focus is on finding a balance between the psychosocial benefits and harms of testing. The Clinical Genetics Society suggests that not testing should be the general rule in these cases.

In determining the best interests of the child, both the potential benefits and harms should be considered. Potential benefits of predictive testing would include decreasing anxiety and uncertainty about the future, and allowing the child and parents to be able to make more realistic life

---

[14] See, for example, the American Medical Association, 'Testing Children For Genetic Status' and Ethical Guidelines 'E-2.138 Genetic Testing of Children'.

[15] Common examples of such conditions are Charcot-Marie-Tooth disease and Familial Adenomatous Polyposis.

choices. It would also increase the child's autonomy, by providing him with more relevant facts to make his or her decision, or to contribute to discussions on how to proceed. Potential harms would include the perception that the child is ill even though currently asymptomatic, psychological concerns, parental guilt if the condition is hereditary, and societal discrimination.

7.2.2.5 Adding an MAOA test to newborn screening

As has been seen above, while there are some conditions like PKU and Cystic Fibrosis that are commonly screened for, other conditions vary between states and countries. It would therefore be possible for one state or country to include a MAOA test in its newborn screening list but for others to consider this inappropriate.

7.2.2.5.1 Satisfaction of the guidelines In deciding whether to add a condition to the screening list, considerations like those listed in the WHO and Professional Guidelines should, but do not have to, be considered. A test for MAOA might satisfy the considerations surrounding the specific condition. In terms of frequency, Low MAOA occurs potentially in between one-third and two-thirds of males depending on racial classification. This would be sufficient to justify testing if the 'condition' was described as simply Low MAOA. If the 'condition' is described as Low MAOA and childhood maltreatment, determining the frequency becomes more problematic. While the genetic test obviously is unable to identify those who will suffer maltreatment, the Caspi longitudinal study found that 65 of the 1037 participants (12 per cent of males, six per cent of total) had both Low MAOA and childhood maltreatment. This is far more frequent than the 0.007 per cent of the population who are born with PKU, and therefore despite the fact that the test only gives part of the information, it may be justified in terms of frequency of occurrence. Low MAOA could be also considered to be an important health problem on the basis that Low MAOA individuals are more susceptible to the negative impacts of maltreatment.

The second consideration surrounding testing and whether treatment is available is more problematic. While there is an ability to test for Low MAOA, there is no test for likelihood of maltreatment. There is also no recognized treatment available at this stage, but the possibility of medical treatment in the future will be discussed below.

Third, the benefits and detriments of the screening must be considered. Again, this is problematic. The AMA Guidelines on Genetic Testing of Children consider the most serious disadvantage to the child as being the abrogation of the child's future choice in knowing his genetic status, and point out that many adults in fact choose not to know this information. The Guidelines recommend that testing is refused by doctors where no effective treatment or prevention regime is available. The benefits to the child in MAOA testing are not significant, with the real benefit being that Low MAOA children can be identified and monitored for childhood maltreatment. This idea will be discussed further below. The detriments relate to discrimination. A child with Low MAOA may be treated differently, either by his parents or by society. Any behavioral issues will be viewed through an MAOA lens, rather than seen as typical childhood behavior. In addition, knowledge of their MAOA status, and any subsequent monitoring could easily lead to the test results becoming a self-fulfilling prophecy.

Under this analysis, screening for MAOA should not be considered as it is not in the best interests of the child. The problem with applying the criteria above, however, is that the WHO principles were designed for conditions with a genetic main effect. The criteria naturally become difficult to apply and to satisfy when one attempts to factor in uncertain environmental factors. Further, the criteria are designed for medical conditions, not behavioral conditions. It may be that these criteria are simply not appropriate in this situation. In support of this argument is the fact that the criteria do not take into account the two factors raised in defence of the XYY screening. First, screening, and therefore identifying individuals, is an important way of finding out more about the condition. Identifying and subsequently observing XYY individuals enabled the condition to be better understood. The same would apply for MAOA individuals. Second, and more compelling, is the fact that the WHO criteria do not contemplate that the state has an interest (in protecting society) that does not directly relate to the health of the child. Protection of society and reduction of crime may justify early identification of individuals with a propensity for criminal conduct. For these reasons, it is arguable that the Guidelines carry less weight in determining whether screening for MAOA should occur than they do with other conditions.

7.2.2.5.2 Interests of the state In the two United States religious cases discussed above, it was seen that the religious interests of the parents in not having the child screened were outweighed by the interests of the State in relation to the health of the child. Under a best interests analysis, testing of the child was considered to be the appropriate step.

In considering whether to test a newborn for MAOA, additional state interests arise. For the Low MAOA child who suffers maltreatment, the future consequences are not the development of a disease or medical condition but the possible development of antisocial behavior. In this situation the state still retains an interest in the wellbeing of the child, however the focus of the wellbeing shifts from concern over a physical or mental health issue to the prevention of unacceptable social conduct. In addition, the state's interests in protecting society and reducing crime also become relevant.

The language of *Anaya*, referring to the 'potential social burden' is relevant here. The cost of antisocial behavior is one that the state has a legitimate interest in avoiding. The US Supreme Court has commented that 'a democratic society rests, for its continuance, upon the healthy, well-rounded growth of young people into full maturity as citizens, with all that implies. It may secure against impeding restraints and dangers within a broad range of selection'.[16] The Supreme Court has also commented that the right of parents to control the upbringing of the child may not be interfered with by legislation that is without reasonable relation to some legitimate public purpose.[17]

This reasoning, however, shows how the scope of the interest can become blurred. In the *Anaya* and *Spiering* cases, the interest was focused on the child and his or her health and wellbeing. In an MAOA test, the interest moves closer to being focused on society as a whole, than on the individual child. While the child could benefit (in terms of monitoring Low MAOA for maltreatment) the overall goal of the testing would be societal protection. Mandatory testing may not be in the best interests of the child.

7.2.2.5.3 Voluntary or mandatory The examples of the 99 per cent success rates for voluntary screening in New Zealand, Australia and the UK suggest that screening would not need to be compulsory to be effective. Further, a study[18] on informed consent in Maryland, United States showed that a majority of women preferred to be asked to give consent for genetic screening to be carried out on their newborns. When asked and given a five minute explanation of what the test was, the refusal rate was only five in 1000. The results of this study might suggest that simply adding the test for MAOA to the voluntary screening already carried out on newborns, and providing information to parents, would result in a high acceptance rate.

---

16 *Prince v Massachusetts* 312 US 158 (1944).

17 *Pierce v Society of Sisters* 268 US 510 (1925).

18 Referred to in Lana Wilding, *Newborn Genetic Screening: A Proposal Of New Ethical Guidelines* http://www.ethicapublishing.com/confronting/5CH17.pdf (accessed 25 March 2015).

The potential societal interest in identifying Low MAOA individuals, however, might require that testing, for this gene at least, be made compulsory. If this is the case, the United States' cases can provide some guidance on how religious/privacy arguments may be addressed.

7.2.2.5.4 The relevance of the gene/environment interaction One potential issue with screening for Low MAOA is the relevance of environmental factors. The majority of the studies (with the exception of the Christchurch study) found that it is the MAOA gene coupled with childhood maltreatment that makes an individual more likely to engage in antisocial behavior than an individual without one or both of these factors. The presence of the Low MAOA allele by itself is not helpful in determining the likelihood of the antisocial behavior developing (in fact, in the absence of childhood maltreatment, the Low allele makes the individual less likely to engage in antisocial behavior than a High allele individual).

The conditions currently screened for have a gene main effect. The additional factor of the interaction of the environment with the gene reduces the usefulness of the genetic testing in terms of identifying those likely to engage in antisocial behavior until any environmental influence has occurred.

7.2.2.5.5 Predictive testing Whether screening a newborn for Low MAOA would meet the two part definition for predictive testing is unclear. The first part of the test, that there is no evidence of the condition at the time of testing, would likely be met. A newborn would not be capable of displaying any symptoms of antisocial behavior. The issue is with the second part of the test, that the result would indicate a high chance that the condition would occur. The presence of the Low allele itself, absent knowledge of relevant environmental factors, does not give any useful information as to the chance of the condition (antisocial behavior) occurring in the future. In the Caspi study, for example, two thirds of the Low MAOA cohort (being the ones with minimal maltreatment), did not develop antisocial behavior as defined in the study. The genetic result does not by itself indicate the chance of this behavior occurring to any satisfactory degree of certainty.

This would suggest that screening for Low MAOA would not be considered predictive testing. One consequence of this is that the guidelines put in place for the protection of children in relation to predictive testing would not apply. This might make it easier to permit an MAOA test to be added to the screening.

7.2.2.5.6 Conclusion It would appear that there is no obvious reason not to add an MAOA test to a newborn screening programme. It is clear from a consideration of the conditions currently screened for in Australia, New Zealand, the United Kingdom and the US states, that there is no exhaustive list of conditions. The WHO guidelines might be of assistance, and appear to suggest that MAOA screening would not be in the best interests of the child, but part of this conclusion is the result of applying guidelines designed for conditions with a genetic main effect to MAOA, a condition based on the interaction between genes and environment. Since Low MAOA does not appear to be predictive testing (but we could note again that the definition relates to conditions with a gene main effect) the guidelines of predictive testing of children do not apply. Provided the screening is universal, and not targeted at a particular group in society, it would seem to be available to a government to add MAOA testing to the newborn screening list.

7.2.3 Consequences of Newborn Screening

This part will assume that a decision has been made by the relevant government to test newborns for MAOA levels, and will consider the consequences of a positive result for Low MAOA. It would appear that a government would have two options in this situation. First, it could advise the parents of the result, but otherwise take no action. Second, it could decide to take action, in order to address one of the two elements that increase the likelihood of engaging in antisocial behavior.

7.2.3.1 Take no interventionist action

Under this option, parents would be provided information as to what Low MAOA might mean for their child. This could involve the provision of informational brochures or referrals for counseling sessions or to support groups. Apart from this, the State would not intervene with the raising of the child. While this might seem an attractive option, its effectiveness could be questioned. It is reasonable to think that parents who would take advantage of these opportunities are also the ones less likely to maltreat their children. While knowing the MAOA status might help some parents better understand their child and make them more aware of his or her sensitivity to situations or actions that might not be traditionally seen as maltreatment (i.e. not eating dinner together as a family, or holding a child back in school) the benefits to the child might not be sufficient to justify the loss of his or her future autonomy.

In addition, taking no action might result in issues in the future, should the child engage in antisocial behavior. It is likely that society would react negatively to being informed that the state had information suggesting that this child was likely to engage in antisocial behavior but did nothing to prevent this.

7.2.3.2 Take interventionist action

If the state decided that intervention was appropriate, this could take two forms. First, the state could act to address the issue of Low MAOA. This might involve forced treatment to raise MAOA levels, should such an option be available. Second, the state could act to address the environment factor, taking steps to minimize the likelihood of childhood maltreatment occurring. This might involve monitoring of the child and family, or the more extreme approach of immediate removal of the child from the custody of the parents.

7.2.3.3 Forced treatment

This option will be discussed in detail below, under a separate heading.

7.2.3.4 Monitoring of the child and family

The idea behind monitoring of the child and family is that it would allow for early intervention should the child begin to suffer maltreatment. Conversely, if there is no evidence of maltreatment, there would be no need for any additional steps to be taken. While monitoring may sound like a reasonable option, given the increased potential consequences to the child due to his MAOA status, it is still necessary to consider the potential negative effects of this monitoring.

Depending on how monitoring is to be carried out, there is clear potential for it to result in stress for those involved. For parents, particularly those who would generally be considered 'good' parents, it is easy to imagine the frustration and even anger resulting from monitoring and questioning of parental techniques. This would particularly be the case where there are other children in the family who appear to be 'good' kids, and whose raising is not subject to monitoring. For the Low MAOA child, there would be the potential for confusion in seeing his parents monitored, especially if their parenting of his siblings is not being similarly monitored, or if the parents of the child's friends are not being monitored in the same way. Being treated differently from other children (or as a 'bad' child) might result in feelings of negative self-worth, or even become a self-fulfilling prophecy. The stress caused by this monitoring might itself create issues. While this wouldn't be classified as maltreatment as per Caspi's study, it may be equivalent to some of the environmental factors mentioned in the other studies.

One could also imagine that parental authority would be diminished through this monitoring. The US Supreme Court has commented that 'the history and culture of Western Civilisation reflect a strong tradition of parental concern for the nurturing and upbringing of their children. This primary role of parents in the upbringing of their children is now established beyond debate as an enduring American tradition'.[19] Going against this tradition through monitoring, with the implication of the potential for further interference if necessary, is therefore likely to be viewed as problematic and unacceptable, particularly when there has been no evidence of maltreatment of the child to justify it. Lois Weithorn, a United States academic, has commented that 'out of respect for family privacy and parental autonomy, the state avoids involvement in the family affairs until or unless parents are viewed as having failed their children in some extreme manner, thereby creating a serious danger to that child's wellbeing'.[20] While the state can intervene in raising a child, this is most likely justified on parens patriae grounds of protection of the child's wellbeing, triggered by events that have already occurred at the time in question, and not for events that might occur in the future, or for the benefit of society as a whole.

As another example of state interference being viewed negatively, New Zealand introduced what is colloquially known as the 'anti-smacking' legislation in 2007.[21] This was a controversial law, with many parents commenting in the media that the government was interfering with their parenting decisions. While these parents were strongly against children being maltreated, they argued that there is a grey area where something may look like maltreatment but in the specific context is not. A common example given of this was the grabbing of a young child about to run out into oncoming traffic and giving him a light smack to quickly reinforce the idea that what he was doing was dangerous. Reports also emerged of parental authority being diminished as a result of this legislation, with

---

[19] And in fact in *Troxel v Granville* 530 US 57 (2000), the Supreme Court commented that 'it cannot now be doubted that the Due Process clause of the fourteenth amendment protects the fundamental right of parents to make decisions concerning the care, custody, and control of their children'.

[20] Lois Weithorn, 'Developmental Neuroscience, Children's Relationships With Primary Caregivers, And Child Protection Policy Reform' (2012) 63 Hastings LJ 1487.

[21] Under its official name, the Crimes (Substituted Section 59) Amendment Act 2007, inserted a new s59 into the Crimes Act 1961. The law prevents a parent smacking a child for the purpose of 'correction'.

children responding to any form of discipline by saying to their parents 'you can't punish me. I'll report you'.

It should further be considered that monitoring itself might not achieve its goals. If some form of maltreatment was identified, one could imagine the next step would involve counseling, with removal of the child being a last resort. This would be similar to the current practice. By the stage where removal is being seriously considered, the environmental maltreatment might have already been triggered. The key time for the childhood maltreatment factor is thought to be in the first few years of the child's life, when some levels of maltreatment might not be obvious to those monitoring the parents. In addition, the standard for removal of a child from his family is so high (due to evidence that the trauma of removal and/or the experience of a foster home might be worse than the maltreatment[22]) that this standard might not be met even where actions identified by the MAOA studies as maltreatment have occurred. For this reason, one academic has argued that the bar for removal might need to be set lower for a Low MAOA individual.[23]

Finally, the shifting of limited resources to the specific monitoring of Low MAOA children might mean that serious maltreatment cases amongst High MAOA children are overlooked. Wasserman describes how this might be regarded as 'the unseemly spectacle of a government displaying greater solicitude for potentially violent children, allowing equally maltreated High MAOA children to languish in dysfunctional families because their maltreatment posed little danger to society'.[24]

Brooks-Crozier[25] provides an interesting and detailed analysis of how monitoring might work in practice. She suggests that following MAOA testing, early intervention services can be 'target[ed at] a population of children at risk of criminal behavior'. These children could be monitored through psychological and social work services and home visits, and counselling and support could be provided to the parents and the child to prevent maltreatment occurring.

---

22 It can be argued that the potential for psychological harm that results in removal from the primary caregiver is high. Children form attachments to parental figures, even those who are neglected. In addition, rates of abuse and neglect in foster homes in the US are higher than in the general population.

23 David Wasserman, 'Is There Value in Identifying Individual Genetic Predispositions to Violence?' (2004) 32 JL Med. & Ethics 24, 28.

24 Ibid, 28.

25 Jennifer Brooks-Crozier, 'The nature and nurture of violence: Early intervention services for the families of MAOA-Low children as a means to reduce violent crime and the costs of violent crime' (2011) 44 Conn. L. Rev. 531.

Under her suggestion, all children would need to be tested within 48 hours of birth. This would include females, even though it is very unlikely that a female would be Low MAOA. She provides two reasons for this: 'States … have an interest in identifying female carriers who would benefit from genetic counselling and other supportive services', and in addition testing all newborns would also pick up the 0.2 per cent of the population who have the rare MAOA variant which doesn't require maltreatment as a triggering factor, and is present in both males and females. Testing would be mandatory, and if a parent refused, the state could bring an action against them compelling them to comply. She suggests that the test could be carried out by buccal smear, which might address any religious issues about the taking of blood from a newborn.

Once the results had been determined, 'those who administered the screening test would directly notify the child's health-care provider and the state's department of health of an abnormal result'. The health care provider would then notify the parent or guardian. She suggests that confidentiality measures be put in place to prevent the public from finding out this information. Early intervention services would then monitor the child, and if there was evidence of maltreatment, remove the child from the environment.

Most interesting is her analysis of the cost of such a program. The testing for MAOA currently costs $250. While this is substantial (the cost for current newborn screening is $39.20), she suggests that if MAOA testing became compulsory the increased use of the test would result in the cost decreasing by as much as 80 per cent, to approx $40.[26] Clearly, however, it is the cost of the monitoring which would be the most substantial. While she accepts this, it is her argument that the cost of monitoring and early intervention would in fact be less than the costs incurred due to violent crimes potentially carried out by these individuals if maltreatment occurred. Using the US state of Connecticut as an example, she states that in 2009 there were 5760 aggravated assaults, 651 rapes and 107 murders, and places a cost of $3 billion on this. In the same year, 40,000 children were born. Using the Caspi percentages, approximately 6600 will be MAOA Low and 2400 will suffer maltreatment. If all 6600 were monitored, she estimates a cost of $86.1 million, or $8700 per child.

On paper, her argument that the costs incurred through monitoring would be less than the costs resulting from crimes seems reasonable.

---

[26] This figure is based on idea that demand for paternity tests in recent years has decreased cost from $450 to approx. $80.

Where the analysis is lacking, however, is in its (understandable) inability to go any further. How much did these 6600 Low MAOA individuals contribute to that crime cost of $3 billion? Caspi suggests that approximately 84 per cent of crime was committed by the Low MAOA cohort in his study. This doesn't mean, however, that a monitoring programme will reduce crime by 84 per cent. Lowering the likelihood of childhood maltreatment lowers a Low MAOA individual's likelihood of engaging in antisocial behavior when compared to others. It doesn't completely negate it, as is demonstrated by the fact that Caspi's graph showed that some Low MAOA individuals with no childhood maltreatment had committed crimes.

Overall, from a purely mathematical perspective, Brooks-Crozier's proposal is deserving of further consideration. It does however raise some human rights and privacy implications which must also form part of this consideration.

7.2.3.5 Immediate removal

The most extreme option for intervention is through the immediate removal of Low MAOA children from their parents in order to ensure that no maltreatment occurs. It is suggested that this is unlikely to be acceptable to society, for several reasons.

First, the sheer numbers involved would make removal impossible. Utilizing Brooks-Crozier's statistics, of the 40,000 children born in Connecticut in 2009, 6600 were statistically likely to be Low MAOA. Finding alternative living arrangements for this many babies in one state in each year would be impossible. One only needs to imagine Asian communities, where Low MAOA might be found in 66 per cent of males, to understand how infeasible such an idea might be. The picture that comes to mind is the creation of colonies like the one Carrie Buck was sent to for being considered genetically feebleminded.[27]

Second, the stigma associated with being removed from home at birth due to being 'born bad' or with being raised in a colony (perhaps described as a group home, or even a boarding school) would be significant, and would probably result in the self-fulfilling prophecy emerging.

Finally, immediate removal would deny the two-thirds of Low MAOA children who did not suffer maltreatment in Caspi's study the opportunity of growing up in a family environment, with loving parents and all the benefits (particularly for Low MAOA children) that result from this.

---

[27] See Chapter 2.

7.2.3.6 Conclusion

While adding an MAOA test to conditions already screened for might possibly be considered acceptable for reasons discussed above, this step should not occur unless there is a clear plan in place to address the consequences of the testing. It is difficult to determine what this might be. Doing nothing with this information negates the benefit of testing for the child. Removing the child from his parents based solely on the result of the test cannot be seen as beneficial to the child. Monitoring of the parents may result in some benefit to this child, through early intervention, but the efficacy of this in relation to preventing the environmental trigger of maltreatment arising is unclear. Further, this option is likely to be cost prohibitive. Unless a clear plan of action is in place to respond to the results of the screening, it should be considered that the detriments to the child of the screening would outweigh any benefits to the child or to society.

7.3 TRIGGERED CHILDHOOD GENETIC TESTING

7.3.1 Introduction

An alternative to compulsory newborn testing might be to permit testing during childhood following the occurrence of some form of triggering event. One example of a triggering event might be the opening of an investigation into possible maltreatment. Stone[28] argues that the risks involved in genetic testing are only outweighed when specific environmental factors have been verified. He proposes that the testing should not be used to predict the child's future behavior, but only to understand past events in the child's life. This would allow a better decision to be made as to whether to leave the child in the family home, or to remove him. The obvious problem with such an argument is that once there is an active abuse investigation, severe enough maltreatment is already likely to have occurred to have triggered the environmental factor.

A second triggering event might be the display of specific forms of antisocial behavior. If a child acts in a manner that is considered impulsive or aggressive, understanding whether he has the Low MAOA gene might help understand the underlying reasons for his behavior. There are two obvious problems with this. The first is that this either ignores the impact of environment (the child is acting aggressively

---

[28] Robert Stone, 'The Cloudy Crystal Ball: Genetics, Child Abuse, And The Perils Of Predicting Behavior' (2003) 56(5) Vanderbilt L Rev 1557, 1586.

therefore he must have Low MAOA) or over-emphasizes it (the child is acting aggressively therefore we need to assume childhood maltreatment). The second problem is in defining the standard of antisocial behavior to be met before testing can be requested. If, for example, a school considers it advantageous to have this genetic information about its students, it might over-report behavioral incidents as triggering events when they might in fact be otherwise described as normal childhood behavior.

7.3.2 Stigmatism Involved in Childhood Testing

The discussion of compulsory newborn screening above, raised the issue of stigmatizing those children who had Low MAOA and also their parents, through monitoring of parental actions even where there was no sign of maltreatment present.

Childhood testing following a triggering event might minimize some of these concerns. Requiring a triggering event would reduce the number of Low MAOA children being monitored from 100 per cent to a lower percentage, but more importantly it would remove those who according to the graph in the Caspi study are less likely to engage in antisocial behavior. It would also address concerns in relation to the lack of a benefit to the child in testing. If the child is displaying signs of antisocial behavior, then an MAOA test could be considered to be diagnostic testing, and therefore in the interests of the child to be carried out (assuming there is some form of treatment able to be identified).

While triggered testing might reduce some forms of stigmatization, it may be equally likely to result in new forms arising. If testing is seen as beneficial in understanding the child's situation it might be requested at an earlier stage than the evidence suggests is necessary, either at the first sign of abuse or the first sign of antisocial behavior. One issue with this is the potentially unfair message that it sends to society about the family or the child. In terms of childhood maltreatment, seeking a genetic test might indicate a real concern that the child is being maltreated, and requiring the parents to take the child to be tested might label them as 'bad parents'. In terms of antisocial behavior, seeking a genetic test might indicate a real concern that the child is not just acting in a boisterous manner but is in fact a 'bad kid'. These labels can be severely damaging to the child and his family.

One can also imagine that the standard required to classify something as a triggering event might be judged by different standards depending on the social or racial factors. To avoid stigmatization of some classes,

Wasserman[29] argues that compulsory testing should be introduced. The idea of all of society being required to provide DNA samples to avoid discrimination against particular groups in society has also been discussed above, in relation to DNA databases, and it was argued there that this is not sufficient reason to disregard the rights of other members of society.[30]

7.3.3 Consequences of Triggered Childhood Testing

7.3.3.1 Introduction

In an earlier section, several options were identified as possible responses to a newborn being screened and found to have Low MAOA. A key factor in evaluating those options was the fact that neither childhood maltreatment nor antisocial behavior could have occurred at newborn stage. With triggered childhood testing one of these factors has occurred, meaning the appropriate response to a childhood test will therefore potentially be different. Again, however, the same three options should be considered.

7.3.3.2 Take no interventionist action

While this might have been seen as an acceptable response to a newborn test, it is doubtful it would be appropriate as a response to a childhood test. If the triggering event was serious enough to lead to a genetic test, then this indicates that some form of intervention should be required. Due to the concerns of stigmatism, if the state was not prepared to intervene, the test should not occur.

7.3.3.3 Take interventionist action through forced treatment

This is a legitimate option, which will be discussed below.

7.3.3.4 Immediate removal from the home

The benefit of this approach will depend on the triggering event. If it was childhood maltreatment, then there is a potential benefit to the child in being removed. It is not clear, however, that this potential benefit is any greater or different for a Low MAOA child than it is for a High MAOA child. It is thought that the greatest effect on a child of maltreatment occurs in the first five years of life. After this, it may be that the impact

---

[29] David Wasserman, 'Is There Value in Identifying Individual Genetic Predispositions to Violence?' (2004) 32 JL Med. & Ethics 24, 28.

[30] See back.

of childhood maltreatment on a Low or High MAOA child will be similar, and Low MAOA children should not be treated differently.

If the triggering factor is antisocial behavior, then removal from the home will likely result in the child being moved to a group home or to some kind of facility for young offenders. One would imagine that finding a foster family would not be easy. Placing the child in a young offenders' facility will be regarded as punishment, and will clearly be problematic if the child's relevant antisocial behavior did not reach the standard required for any other individual to be placed in such a facility. The effect of this would be to create a separate standard for punishment for Low MAOA individuals.

7.4 GENETIC TESTING AND THE RIGHT NOT TO KNOW

Any discussion of genetic testing of a child has one particularly serious consequence, the child will be informed of, or will otherwise come to realize, his or her genetic status. The right of individuals (and particularly children) not to know genetic information has received some discussion in relation to predictive testing (which occurs when the individual is asymptomatic), and susceptibility testing (which occurs when testing is to identify whether an individual is at risk of developing a medical condition). Concerns raised in these discussions include that testing children fails to respect their future autonomy to decide whether to be tested for themselves, breaches their confidentiality as test results are disclosed to parents and possibly also to others, and causes psychosocial harm to the child by revealing their results.

In relation to the genetic testing of adults, the idea of autonomy is paramount. The US Committee on Assessing Genetic Risks has stated that there is no justification for mandatory genetic testing, and that it is the decision of the adult as to whether or not he or she wishes to know this information. In Europe, the Committee of Ministers of the Council of Europe Recommendations On Genetic Testing For Health Care Purposes in 1992 listed self-determination and the non-compulsory nature of testing as critical elements of genetic testing. These elements are reflected in the Biomedicine Convention of the Council of Europe, which states in Article 10:

1. Everyone has the right to respect for private life in relation to information about his or her health.

2. Everyone is entitled to know any information collected about his or her health. However, the wishes of individuals not to be so informed shall be observed.

Article 16.3 is more specific: 'the wish of a person not to be informed shall be respected'. In the UNESCO Declaration on the Human Genome and Human Rights it is stated in Article 5 that when genetic material is collected for research purposes, the individual has the right to decide whether or not to be informed of the results.[31]

In relation to the genetic testing of children, the decision will normally be made by the parents, who must consider whether it is in the best interests of the child to be tested. The generally accepted approach is that if it is not in the child's best interests to be tested at that time (in other words, if treatment is not available at the time), the child should not be tested until he or she can participate in the decision making process, or decide for himself.

It is clear that any forced or mandatory genetic testing would constitute a substantial interference with the rights discussed above, and therefore is unlikely to be justified without evidence of a substantial benefit to the testing. Due to the serious nature of the risks raised above, this benefit should arguably be a benefit to the child and not to society generally.

7.5 COMPULSORY GENETIC TESTING AND FUNCTION CREEP

It was mentioned at the beginning of this chapter that UK Prime Minister David Cameron had called for a universal genetic database to assist in research for a cure for cancer.

A previous chapter raised the issue of the creation of a universal DNA database. That chapter also introduced the concept of function creep, which is where technology introduced for one function is then utilized for another.

Once there is a universal genetic database, whether originally designed for health research or crime prevention purposes, it will be an easy step (or creep) to analyzing the DNA information for MAOA status.[32] This is a potential example of function creep which needs to be kept in mind when considering the creation of any form of genetic database.

---

[31] See earlier discussion in relation to DNA databases.

[32] This would not be possible in those jurisdictions which destroy the DNA sample after creating the profile.

7.6 GENETIC TESTING AND A RIGHT TO KNOW?

7.6.1 Introduction

If the decision is made to test a child one issue that may be likely to arise is whether other people have the right to know the results of the test. The groups of people that might be interested in this information include:

1. The direct family;
2. Others likely to be in direct, frequent, contact with the child (for example schools, sports coaches, parents of classmates or friends);
3. The government (particularly the law enforcement and child services branches);
4. Society as a whole.

7.6.2 The Direct Family

The parents of a child who has been tested will have a strong argument that they should be told the results, in order to better understand their child and if possible to more effectively influence his (positive) upbringing. While it would likely be considered reasonable to reveal this information to the parents, it is less likely to be reasonable for other family members to be informed. Obviously, some family members might gain hints as to the results due to observation of familial relations with the child, particularly if the parents begin to treat this child differently or there is some form of parental monitoring. This is, however, different from being directly told, or from having a right to know, this information.

Bell and Bennett[33] argue that genetic information has a shared or familial character, since others are affected by the results. This suggests that genetic information belongs not to an individual, but to his entire family. If this is true, then the family would have a right to this information.

7.6.3 Beyond the Family

Is there any justification for extending a 'right to know' beyond the family group? There are clearly other people who could anticipate close contact with the child who might wish to be informed. The government could claim a public interest in child protection and crime prevention as

[33] 'Genetic Secrets and the Family' (2001) 9 Med L Rev 130.

a basis for access to the information. Schools and others in close proximity to the child (for example sports coaches or music teachers or parents of friends) could claim that due to the level of their interaction with the child, this knowledge would be important to minimize the risk of harm. Finally, society in general could claim an overarching interest in crime prevention and in feeling safe in their communities as a basis for a right to know. The justifications claimed for extending a right to know to these groups are more difficult to evaluate. There are several different perspectives that might be used in this evaluation:

7.6.4 From a Harm Perspective

Wilkinson[34] attempts to answer the question of who has a right to know by applying John Stuart Mill's Harm Principle. According to this, the only reason for restraining the actions of individuals should be to avoid harming others. She extends this to suggest that a decision would be inappropriate if others are harmed as a result. This potentially harmed person should therefore be considered. He then considers that people should be evaluated by the nature of the relationship of the individual to this potentially harmed person (which might be biological, emotional or financial) and the proximity of their relationship. Those that are sufficiently close in both relationship and proximity should be considered when making a decision about sharing genetic information.

An application of this would likely result in the first two categories being permitted to access this information due to likelihood of harm. It would not, however, allow the police to access this information unless they had a proximate relationship to the child. This might be established through repeated investigation of the child, but is unlikely if the child is yet to come into contact with them in relation to criminal activities. The Harm Principle would also prevent society in general accessing this information.

7.6.5 From a Tort Perspective

In tort, the Neighbour Principle in relation to negligence suggests that a person owes a duty of care to his neighbours, those who are so closely connected to a person that he or she ought reasonably to have them in contemplation when he or she considers committing a particular action. Applying a neighbor-type test might extend the categories of those

---

[34] Ruth Wilkinson, 'When Is My Genetic Information Your Business?' (2010) 19(1) *Cambridge Quarterly of Healthcare Ethics* 110.

entitled to know to include those who may be affected by the child's future conduct, for example, people in society living in close proximity. It would not extend to society at large, as tort law denies that a person can owe a duty to everyone on the planet. It might also not apply to police unless an argument could be made that everyone who commits an antisocial act should be aware that the police will be involved in its investigation.

7.6.6 From a Societal Knowledge Perspective

There has been some debate over whether there are any privacy rights in genetic information. One approach is that this should be considered societal knowledge that should be collected and used for the benefit of society (for example, to research causes and treatment of diseases). This absence of privacy rights in genetic information is not currently, however, widely accepted. This point was discussed in Chapter 3.8 in relation to a universal DNA database. It can also be seen in the fact that there are laws relating to genetic privacy in employment and insurance issues. Further, the Universal Declaration on the Human Genome and Human Rights focuses on the principles of consent and confidentiality. Article 9 states that any limitations on this may only be prescribed by law for compelling reasons. Informing society of the MAOA status of an individual, particularly if he has not committed any crime, would likely not meet this standard.

7.6.7 From a Utilitarian Perspective

From a utilitarian perspective, moral goodness is judged by consequences. The act that provides the greatest happiness for the greatest number of people is thus the right act. The individual would therefore have to accept a limitation on his privacy rights for the social good. This would suggest that society's wish to know would take priority over the individual's right to privacy, assuming society could demonstrate a benefit to knowing.

7.6.8 The Counter-argument: From an Individual Welfare Perspective

One perspective that argues against accepting a right to know is the individual welfare perspective. As seen in Article 3.2 of the UNESCO Universal Declaration on Bioethics and Human Rights 2005, 'The interests and welfare of the individual should have priority over the sole interest of science or society'. This suggests that where there is no benefit to the individual (for example, where no treatment is available) society cannot claim a right to know.

Other relevant provisions include Article 8:

> In applying and advancing scientific knowledge, medical practice and associated technologies, human vulnerability should be taken into account. Individuals and groups of special vulnerability should be protected and the personal integrity of such individuals respected.

And Article 14:

> Taking into account that the enjoyment of the highest attainable standard of health is one of the fundamental rights of every human being without distinction of race, religion, political belief, economic or social condition, progress in science and technology should advance:
>
> ...
>
> (d) elimination of the marginalization and the exclusion of persons on the basis of any grounds;

Extending a right to know to society would be more likely to marginalize than to eliminate marginalisation, and therefore should not be permitted.

Article 27, however, allows limitations:

> by law, ... in the interests of public safety, for the investigation, detection and prosecution of criminal offences, for the protection of public health or for the protection of the rights and freedoms of others.

This might allow for a societal right to know, but it would need to be expressly stated in legislation due to the requirement of the limitations being 'by law'.

7.6.9 Conclusion on Genetic Testing

The concept of other people having a right to know genetic information is a problematic one. While one can see some benefits in terms of health treatments and crime prevention, the impact on the individual is significant. It is arguable that the harm principle is the appropriate test: people wishing to access another person's genetic information must demonstrate a substantial risk of harm to themselves that could be avoided by being aware of this information. Otherwise, the privacy rights of the individual should take precedence.

7.7 CONCLUSION TO PART ONE OF CHAPTER

This part has considered the possibility of genetic testing for Low MAOA, either immediately after birth as part of standard newborn screening or during childhood following a trigger event. It then considered the consequences of a finding of Low MAOA following such screening. It is suggested that the consequences for the child in terms of how he is raised and in terms of potential stigmatization may be severe in both cases, and therefore a clear benefit to the testing must first be identified. In addition, there should be a clear, identifiable plan in place in relation to how the state will respond to the test results. Absent these factors, the benefits of requiring testing do not outweigh the detriments and should not therefore be permitted.

7.8 CONSEQUENCES OF THE ACCEPTANCE OF GENETIC ARGUMENTS IN COURT: AN ISSUES PAPER

7.8.1 Foreword

As was explained in the introduction, the second part of this chapter will be written in the style of an Issues Paper, providing an overview and discussion of some of the potential consequences of genetic testing for society. This Issues Paper considers these issues from a position where the events in the Case Study of Child B in Chapter 1 have occurred.

7.8.2 Background

The Rule of Law can be defined as:

> A principle of governance in which all persons, institutions and entities, public and private, including the state itself, are accountable to laws that are publicly promulgated, equally enforced and independently adjudicated, and which are consistent with international human rights norms and standards.[35]

1. To satisfy the rule of law requires, inter alia, equality before the law, fairness in the application of the law, legal certainty and the avoidance of arbitrariness.

---

[35] Report of the Secretary General of the United Nations, 'The Rule Of Law And Transitional Justice In Conflict And Post-Conflict Societies' (2004).

2. The criminal law is based on the idea that individuals are morally responsible for their actions and must be accountable for these actions. This requires an implicit acceptance of the concept of free will. Defences, both statutory and common law, have developed to recognize specific instances in which this moral responsibility is not present. As examples, these include instances where an individual lacks capacity to appreciate the blameworthiness of his actions, or where the individual can appreciate this, but society nevertheless considers that his actions in a particular situation are justified.
3. Increasingly over the past two decades, courts have been asked to consider an argument that due to a specific gene and its interaction with environmental factors, a person's ability to decide to act has been negated. This has a potential impact on that person's moral responsibility for that act. In several recent cases, judges and juries have accepted this argument and as a result have either reduced an offender's sentence or have found him not guilty of an offence requiring a particular level of mens rea. The arguments raised in these cases have been supported by scientific evidence and expert opinion.
4. The implications of both the science and the decisions in these cases requires consideration. If it is scientifically accurate that a significant proportion of society is not able to reach the standard of moral responsibility for their actions then these members of society ought not, rationally, to be held responsible for these actions. Judging these individuals by the same standards as are applied to those who are able to reach the standard of moral responsibility may be considered unfair and therefore problematic under the rule of law. Judging these individuals by a different standard might also be a considered breach of the rule of law through being contrary to equality before the law, legal certainty and the avoidance of arbitrariness.

7.8.3 Scope of the Review

6. This review focuses on potential consequences of the continued acceptance of a 'genetic argument'. For clarity, this argument is that an individual, who has a particular allele of a specific gene and who has additionally suffered some form of childhood maltreatment, and who subsequently engages in antisocial behavior is either not morally responsible for his actions, or is less morally responsible than other individuals and therefore deserving of a reduction in sentence.

7. The review addresses two factors:
   - What are the possible consequences of judges or juries continuing to accept genetic arguments in court?
   - Should the government implement universal, mandatory testing for Low MAOA?
8. The review will identify potential consequences for:
   a) The individual himself/herself;
   b) The family of the individual;
   c) Society as a whole.

7.8.4 Context of the Review

This review has been motivated by the circumstances surrounding, and occurring subsequent to, the murder of Andy Scott, by Child A and Child B. A full report on this can be read in the accompanying materials, but relevant information will be provided throughout the course of this report.

7.9 IMPLICATIONS FOR THE INDIVIDUAL

7.9.1 Background

The case of Child A and Child B highlighted some potential implications for individuals as a result of the continued acceptance of a genetic argument. The first is the issue of forced treatment. The sentence of Child B included an order that he take medication for the rest of his life even after release from jail, to address his Low MAOA. This has resulted in discussions as to the permissibility of forced treatment. It also raised the issue of whether genetic interventions might be more appropriate. The second was the issue of future dangerousness, and how far this should be taken into account in sentencing, particularly in light of the judge's comments that Child B was 'genetically programmed to be a killer'.

Third, the case reignited the debate over juvenile justice. Although both Child A and Child B were 10 years of age and therefore able to be held criminally liable, the genetic argument has raised issues relating to juvenile justice. The most important of these is whether a separate juvenile justice system, justified on the basis that juveniles' brains take longer to develop, can survive the genetics argument. Finally, issues of stigmatization of the individual by society warrant addressing.

7.9.2 Forced Treatment through Medication

7.9.2.1 Introduction

If a person is identified as having Low MAOA or Low Serotonin through either newborn or childhood testing, one option might be to address this through medication. There are currently medications that can increase the amount of MAOA and serotonin in the brain, and further research would likely be developed if this became seen as an appropriate option.

7.9.2.2 Benefits of treatment for Low MAOA

The obvious benefit of treatment is to increase the amounts of MAOA in the brain to levels which are consistent with those found in a High MAOA individual. This would arguably lower the likelihood of antisocial behavior where childhood maltreatment is present.[36]

In terms of Caspi's graph,[37] it is unclear what the implications of such treatment would be. This graph showed that High MAOA individuals are less likely to engage in antisocial behavior than Low MAOA individuals, where there is childhood maltreatment. Removing the Low MAOA data (through medically converting these people into High MAOA individuals) negates the use of his comparison. In other studies High MAOA individuals were found to have lower levels of aggression, measured in terms of responses to provocation, suggesting that converting Low MAOA individuals into High MAOA would have a positive outcome.

A further benefit of treatment is that this is a private solution. While a Low MAOA individual would be required to take medicine, this could be done in the privacy of his home and could therefore be kept confidential. Any stigma associated with being Low MAOA (for example as a result of other people noticing the monitoring of the family environment) would not arise.

7.9.2.3 Detriments of treatment for Low MAOA

Discussion of 'treatment' of Low MAOA involves an assumption that Low MAOA is always undesirable. Again, reference to Caspi's graph suggests that this is not the case. As has been described above, Low MAOA in a positive childhood environment reduces the risk of antisocial behavior. In other words, in a positive environment an individual is better

---

[36] Caspi's graph showed High MAOA individuals are less likely than Low MAOA individuals to engage in antisocial behaviour when childhood maltreatment is present. This comparison isn't helpful if we remove the Low individuals, but some of the other studies simply considered Low MAOA to be the risk allele.

[37] Refer back.

to be Low MAOA than High. Requiring medication might simply result in a change in defence from 'my genes made me do it' to 'my medication made me do it'.

7.9.2.4 Should we also consider treatment for High MAOA in some cases?

If society is considering altering the MAOA levels of some Low MAOA individuals for the benefit of society, should it not also consider the same for the High MAOA individuals with no childhood maltreatment? For these individuals, lowering the amount of MAOA makes them less likely to commit crime.

Further, there are some negative traits associated with High MAOA. While Low MAOA individuals tend to exhibit externalizing behaviors, High MAOA individuals tend to exhibit internalizing behaviors. The most notable examples are the increased risk of depression and mental illness among High MAOA individuals.

7.9.2.5 Voluntary or involuntary treatment

In most countries there is a recognized right for adults to consent to, or to refuse, medical treatment. Specific instances exist where legislation has overridden this, but they are generally very restrictive. In the United States, for example, involuntary treatment for mental illness through hospitalization can only occur if it can be shown that the individual is a danger to himself or others, and will generally only be permitted for a short period of time.[38] Outside of these reasonable limitations, involuntary treatment is an impermissible infringement on rights. It would be difficult for a person with Low MAOA to satisfy these criteria. While this person might be a danger to others at some point in the future, the test would appear to require a more immediate threat. Further, the medication would not be required for a short time, but would be indefinite. Requiring adults to undergo involuntary treatment to increase MAOA levels would require a re-evaluation of the current law.

The situation in relation to children is different. Medical decisions are made by a child's guardian.[39] The court also generally retains the discretion to intervene in the best interests of the child. This discretion is usually exercised in religious objection cases, where parents refuse medical treatment for their child due to religious beliefs but the court

---

[38] *O'Connor v Donaldson* 422 US 563 (1975).

[39] Unless the child is deemed competent to make these decisions for himself, for example, under a *Gillick* competency test.

feels that it is in the child's best interests to undergo the treatment. It is important to note that the courts have generally only intervened when death or serious physical injury is the likely result of the refusal of treatment, and are hesitant to intervene with the private life of the family in cases where the treatment is ongoing. Again, these factors would suggest that a re-evaluation of the law would be required before a court could order a minor to undergo compulsory medical treatment for Low MAOA.

An additional potential hurdle for involuntary treatment would be the untested nature of this treatment. While some individuals currently take medication for Low Serotonin, they will have been individually assessed and will possibly not be intended to take it indefinitely. Until (and even if) studies are done on side effects from long term treatment, and also on its effects on newborns and children, this would not just be considered as involuntary treatment, but as involuntary experimental treatment.[40] An interesting comparison can be drawn with the chemical castration cases from the United States. In these cases, legislation either allowed or required an order be made that a sex offender take chemical castration drugs as a prerequisite for parole. Challenges to this resulted in debates in relation to the untested nature of the drugs used for the specific dosage regime and duration planned,[41] and whether this resulted in it being considered an experimental treatment. Concerns were raised over the mandatory nature of an order for experimental treatment, although this was not seen as significant in this specific context as the legislation required the prisoners to consent to the treatment.[42]

The MAOA or serotonin drugs currently available cannot be taken alongside certain other drugs due to potential side effects. One can imagine a potential issue if taking a required medication for Low MAOA (particularly if the individual had a positive childhood environment and was therefore of low risk of antisocial behavior) meant that the individual was limited in the medication he could take to address a medical

---

[40] See for example, Article 7 ICCPR: 'No one shall be subjected to torture or to cruel, inhuman or degrading treatment or punishment. In particular, no one shall be subjected without his free consent to medical or scientific experimentation'.

[41] The initial drug used, MPA was the female contraceptive pill, taken at between 10 and 1000 times the recommended dosage. Further, while the female pill recommended short term use only, its use on sex offenders was intended to be indefinite.

[42] As it was a parole condition, they could consent and be released on parole, or decline and serve out their sentence in jail.

condition for which he was symptomatic. Would his immediate (or even long term) personal health needs take precedence over a potential behavioral issue that might affect society?

Although it was argued above that medicalization as a treatment could take place privately, the individuals would still need to be monitored to ensure that their MAOA levels remained in the High category (in other words, to ensure they were taking their medication and that it was working appropriately). This would require testing on some kind of regular basis.

7.9.3 Forced Treatment through Genetic Interventions

7.9.3.1 Introduction

One option for the future might be genetic interventions, where the genotype of an individual is changed by altering his or her DNA. Interventions can be either somatic (changing the non-sex cells so that the intervention affects the individual only) or germline (changing the cells that will be transmitted to children).

7.9.3.2 Somatic cell interventions

One study of United States and European researchers[43] showed that over half of the US researchers and 44 per cent of the European researchers thought that somatic cell gene therapy would become 'as routine and pervasive as immunisations or antibiotics'.

The study showed that 51 per cent of US researchers would support somatic interventions for 'reducing tendencies towards aggression', compared to 35 per cent European researchers.

7.9.3.3 Germline interventions

Germline interventions are seen as more problematic, raising safety issues. It has been recognized that if a mistake were made in the process, the child would be the one to suffer.[44] The Clothier Report on the Ethics Of Gene Therapy concluded that in considering germline therapy 'considerable caution should be exercised before contemplating its application to traits that do not have serious implications for health'.

The Council of Europe Convention on Human Rights and Biomedicine would not allow germline interventions for behavioural modifications.

---

43 John Sterling, 'Survey of European Scientists On Ethics Of Scientific Advances' (2005) 25(12) *Genetic Engineering and Biotech News* 6.

44 Cecil Clothier, *Report of the Committee on the Ethics of Gene Therapy* (London: Stationery Office Books 1992)

Under Article 13, modifications would only be permitted for 'preventative, diagnostic or therapeutic purposes, and only if its aim was not to introduce any modifications in the genome of any descendants'.

7.9.4 Future Dangerousness

7.9.4.1 Introduction

> Anderton: 'You're acquainted with the theory of precrime, of course.'
>
> Witwer: 'You've boldly and successfully abolished the post-crime punitive system of jails and fines. As we all realize, punishment was never much of a deterrent …'
>
> Anderton: 'You've probably already grasped the basic legalistic drawback to precrime methodology. We're taking in individuals who have broken no law.'
>
> Witwer: 'But surely they will.'
>
> Anderton: 'Happily, they *don't* – because we get to them first, before they can commit an act of violence. So the commission of the crime itself is absolute metaphysics. We can claim they're culpable. They, on the other hand, can eternally claim they're innocent. And, in a sense, they *are* innocent … In our society we have no major crimes … but we do have a detention camp full of would-be criminals'.[45]

The Minority Report is a futuristic novel set in a society which has been able to abolish violent crime. It achieved this through the creation of the Precrime Unit, which is able to identify criminals before they commit a crime, allowing police to make pre-emptive arrests. In the quoted text above, Anderton (the creator of the Precrime Unit) points out the ethical concerns in relation to this system to Witwer (a new recruit). Instead of prisons housing people who have been convicted of crimes, the new system utilizes detention camps for people who are technically innocent but identified as likely to commit a crime in the future.

Although current technology is not as advanced as that depicted in this science fiction story, the majority of jurisdictions do have sentencing guidelines which allow a sentencer to take into account predictions of future dangerousness when determining the appropriate sentence for a crime. Described in one way, taking future dangerousness into account can be seen as protecting society from a habitual reoffender. Described in another way, this can be seen as punishing someone for a crime they have not committed.

---

[45] Philip K. Dick, 'The Minority Report' (1956) reprinted in Philip K. Dick, *The Collected Stories of Philip K. Dick, Vol 4: The Minority Report* (1988) New York: Citadel, p. 1

7.9.4.2 Early predictions of future dangerousness: XYY syndrome and segregation

When the potential link between XYY Syndrome and criminality was being considered in the 1970s it was argued that mandatory testing for XYY should be introduced, with those found to be XYY segregated to prevent harm to society. This was to occur regardless of whether an XYY individual had done anything to suggest that he was currently, or would in the future be, a danger to society. Even with the relatively low percentage of people in society that were XYY, segregation was seen as unacceptable. It is unlikely that a similar idea would be acceptable in relation to Low MAOA or serotonin.

7.9.4.3 The double-edged sword argument

It is worth noting that some judges considering MAOA arguments in court have raised concerns that while this evidence had been introduced by the defence as a mitigating factor, it might also be used by the prosecution as an aggravating factor. To provide one example, in *Gilson v Sirmons*[46] it was argued that the accused had a genetic link to psychopathy. The court accepted that 'his inability to control his "explosive behavior" may have [some] mitigating effect' but commented that it also had the 'potential of proving [he] was a threat to society, including prison society, and could indicate a propensity for future violence'. There may be an indication in judges' comments in these cases that the use of this evidence as an aggravating factor should not be considered appropriate, or that perhaps the defence would be wise not to introduce this evidence.

In the situation where genetic evidence is not placed before the court by the defence, but sought to be introduced by the prosecution, it will need to be considered whether the defendant can be compelled to provide a DNA sample. If such an order were made, there would be serious implications for the defendant's civil and political rights, notably those rights that relate to self-incrimination or to not be compelled to be a witness.

7.9.4.4 Accuracy of predictions of future dangerousness

While predictions of future dangerousness are often used in sentencing decisions, it has long been recognized that their accuracy is limited. In the US case of *Barefoot v Estelle*[47] the American Psychiatric Association informed the Supreme Court that predictions as to future dangerousness

---

[46] 520 F.3d 1196 (10th Cir. 2008).

[47] 463 US 880 (1983).

were 'extreme[ly] unreliable'. Despite this, the Supreme Court allowed this evidence, on the basis that these predictions were not always wrong, and that disallowing such testimony would be like 'disinvent[ing] the wheel.'

Beecher-Monas and Garcia-Rill[48] have commented that utilizing these predictions despite being aware of their limitations 'is a far cry from the truth-generating methodologies supposedly fundamental to due process, and the movement away from requiring a modicum of credibility is counter to what goes on in civil trials, in which experts must demonstrate the reliability of their testimony'.

The introduction of evidence from scientific studies might increase the accuracy of these predictions. In a recent neuroscience study[49] 40 of 41 participants identified as criminal psychopaths exhibited a specific brain electrical response following exposure to particular stimuli, whereas none of the 29 non-psychopathic participants exhibited this response. Kostiuk[50] argues that this, and other studies, have reached the point of being 'nearly diagnostic' of psychopathy.

The alternate possibility is that the introduction of scientific evidence might result in an incorrect perception that resulting predictions are accurate, through the Christmas Tree or CSI effect.[51] As an example of a concern in relation to this, Barbara Koenig[52] commented that 'the brain offers a seductive promise of prediction. Whether or not these predictions prove to be scientifically accurate may be less important than our belief in their power.'

7.9.4.5 The 'Minority Report' and precrime confinement

If a person has committed a crime then it may be legitimate to consider predictions of future dangerousness as part of the sentencing process. Could it ever be legitimate to do so before a crime has been committed? To punish or segregate a person because his genetic make-up and childhood environment result in a Prediction Report that considers there

---

[48] Erica Beecher-Monas and Edgar Garcia-Rill, 'Genetic predictions of future dangerousness: Is there a blueprint for violence?' (2006) 69 *Law and Contemporary Problems* 301.

[49] Sage Ctr. for the Study of the Mind, Univ. of Cal. Santa Barbara, 'A judge's guide to neuroscience: a concise introduction' 49 (2010), discussed in Stephanie Kostiuk, *After Gina, Nina? Neuroscience-based discrimination in the workplace* (2012) 65 *Vanderbilt Law Review* 933, 943.

[50] Ibid.

[51] See back.

[52] Quoted in Kostiuk, p. 930.

to be a high probability that he will commit a violent crime? In 'The Minority Report', Anderton shows his discomfort for the system he helped create by his choice of words to describe those held in detention camps: these people are 'in a sense … innocent'.

With the right to be presumed innocent being central to criminal justice, the answer would surely be that this would never be legitimate. While the reduction of crime and the protection of society are important goals, they are not important enough to justify the impact on an individual's civil liberties of confinement without having committed a crime. Further, to borrow the language of a previous chapter, if society punishes people before they commit crimes, it will lose the moral right to punish people.

But what if the argument for precrime predictions was phrased not as being for the protection of society, but as being in the best interests of the individual involved? That the identified individual would not be imprisoned, but sent to a residential unit to be raised outside the negative childhood environment? This would likely be seen as more acceptable to society. There is perhaps a logical inconsistency with this approach. On the one hand society must be seen as accepting a high level of genetic determinism to justify restricting the civil liberties of someone who has not committed a crime. On the other hand society must then accept a low level of genetic determinism through justifying placement in a residential unit on the grounds of rehabilitation. Put simply, if the individual's genes and environment give him so little choice but to commit a crime that society should segregate him in advance of any wrongdoing, then no rehabilitation is possible. If the real goal is protection of society, however, this inconsistency might not be looked at too closely.

7.9.5 Juvenile Justice

7.9.5.1 Introduction

> In my view, his history is such that, consistently with the expert opinions placed before the Court, he must be judged as posing a significant level of future dangerousness and to be at a substantial risk of reoffending in both violent and sexual ways. There are also very strong indications from his history of elevating aggression and disruptive behavior, and from the killing itself, that he will develop a significant antisocial or borderline personality disorder, of some magnitude. Whether that can be addressed … and precisely how [he] would behave once freed … are problematic in the extreme.
>
> To sentence a person of his age for the offence of murder, is a formidable challenge.

The quote above comes from *Re SLD*.[53] SLD was a 13-year-old boy with a history of abuse and violent behavior. He also had XYY Syndrome. On the night in question, he broke into a house and abducted and murdered a 3-year-old. In sentencing, the judge struggled with reconciling future dangerousness, SLD's history of abuse, and his juvenile status.

7.9.5.2 The development of the juvenile brain

Neuroscientists consider that the human brain is not fully developed until a person is in his or her early 20s. At the age of 12 children generally begin to develop the ability to reason through logic and the use of abstract propositions, however during the teen years hormonal changes mean that a teenager reacts more from emotion than from logic. As a teenager matures the grey matter in the brain develops, enabling the parts of the brain responsible for impulse control and future planning to develop.[54]

7.9.5.3 The age of criminal responsibility

If a child or teenager does not have the ability to make reasoned decisions on whether to commit a criminal act, then he or she should not be considered to be morally responsible for his or her actions. The focus of juvenile justice is appropriately therefore on educating a youth offender in order to divert them from later encounters with the criminal justice system.

The UN Convention on the Rights of the Child requires under Article 40 that signatory states 'establish a minimum age below which children shall be presumed not to have the capacity to infringe the penal law'. For most countries, a person is considered to be an adult (for the purposes of criminal responsibility) at the age of 17 or 18. Under the age of 10–12 a child is generally considered to be *doli incapax* and therefore not able to be charged or arrested.[55] Between the ages of 10–17, rules vary between states, but often these rules involve the child being brought before a specialist youth court, being given different sentences, and held in secure centres rather than prisons.

---

[53] [2005] QGAAT 51.

[54] National Institutes of Mental Health, *The Teen Brain: Still Under Construction* http://www.nimh.nih.gov/health/publications/the-teen-brain-still-under-construction/index.shtml.

[55] In the United Kingdom the age is 10. In Australia, the age is also 10 but there is additionally a rebuttable presumption of doli capax for juveniles between the ages of 10 to 14. In New Zealand, the age is 10 for murder or manslaughter, but 14 for other crimes. In the United States the age varies, with some states placing criminal responsibility on children as young as six. The United Nations suggests 12 years.

The reason for treating children differently to adults has been explained in the United Nations' *Standard Minimum Rules for the Administration of Juvenile Justice*:

> The modern approach [to criminal responsibility] is to consider whether a child can live up to the moral and psychological components of criminal responsibility; that is, whether a child, by virtue of her or his individual discernment and understanding, can be held responsible for essentially antisocial behavior.

7.9.5.4 Does a genetics argument require a reconsideration of juvenile justice?

The juvenile justice system, like the adult system, is based on the idea of moral responsibility. The issues raised by the acceptance of a genetics argument in relation to moral responsibility have been discussed in Chapter 6.3.2 and apply equally to juveniles. In addition, the juvenile system relies significantly on the belief that education and rehabilitation will divert a youth offender from becoming an adult offender. Rehabilitation was also discussed in the previous chapter, and seen as inconsistent with the acceptance of a genetic argument. While the areas of the brain associated with logical reasoning might not fully develop until the early 20s, the acceptance of a genetics argument (that the person had no choice but to act, and could not have made any other decision) renders this point moot. As with the adult justice system, the juvenile system, both in terms of its underlying principles and its goals, may face significant challenges.

Principles of imposing sanctions (the youth equivalent of sentencing) tend to focus on keeping the child both in the community and with the family to the greatest extent practicable, imposing the least restrictive sanctions necessary, and addressing the underlying cause of the offending.[56] Again, if a genetics argument is accepted, these principles will need to be reconsidered. Applying a double-edged sword argument, keeping the child in the community will pose a danger to the community. Further, keeping the child in the family will allow any maltreatment to continue.

Imposing the least restrictive penalty possible is inconsistent with predictions of future dangerousness as has been discussed previously.

Addressing the underlying cause of the offending will be complicated. One underlying cause is the Low MAOA gene, which cannot be

---

[56] See, for example, 'The New Zealand Children, Young Persons and Their Families Act' 1989, s208.

addressed unless through medical treatment. The second underlying cause is childhood maltreatment. The effects of any prior maltreatment (in terms of combining with the gene to result in antisocial behavior) cannot be addressed. Preventing any future maltreatment might be ineffective as studies indicate that the first few years of life are the key-risk years. Further, this prevention would likely occur through removal of the child from the family home, which is inconsistent with the principle of keeping the child in the family.

It would appear that the same issues that have been identified with the adult system if a genetics argument is accepted will also occur in the youth system. Indeed, it could be said that additional issues will arise due to the principles related to the imposition of sanctions. The acceptance of a genetics argument will therefore arguably present a fundamental challenge to the youth justice system.

7.9.6 Stigmatization and the Self-fulfilling Prophecy

The concerns about stigmatization and the self-fulfilling prophecy have been mentioned above in various contexts, but are worth repeating here. Requiring genetic testing for a particular gene allele, and considering the implications for those individuals found to have this allele, sends a clear message that this is a 'bad gene'. The fact that the gene is linked to behavior then extends the idea of a 'bad gene' to the person being a 'bad person'. There are two potential concerns with this.

First, anyone who knows this information might begin to treat the person differently, either by avoiding him completely or by focusing more attention on him and treating him differently to others. An example of the latter could be found in a school situation where two boys are engaged in the same level of play-fighting, yet the one known to have Low MAOA is punished more severely, or assumed to be the aggressor.

Second, the individual might believe that he is bad, and that he has no choice but to act in a particular way. He might therefore reason that there is no point in engaging in self-control to restrain himself from acting in an aggressive manner. An example of this can be seen in a study by Nelkin and Tancredi, which comments that: '[a] person who believes she is an alcoholic, when informed a particular drink contains alcohol, will consume more of the drink than the average person, even if there is no alcohol in the drink'.[57]

---

[57]]. Dorothy Nelkin & Laurence Tancredi, 'Classify and control: Genetic information in the schools' (1991) 17 Am.J.L. & Med. 51.

7.10 IMPLICATIONS FOR THE FAMILY

7.10.1 Background

The case of Child A and Child B also highlighted some potential implications for the families of these children. Some of these implications were directed specifically at the parents as a result of the contributing factor of childhood maltreatment. Some argued that the parents of Child B should not be permitted to have further children. Others argued that the parents should in fact also be held liable for the murder of Andy Scott due to the maltreatment being a major contributing factor. Other implications were identified for the wider family unit. His uncle was arrested for assault, and received what some regarded as a higher penalty than was appropriate. His two brothers have also had issues. The older brother, previously a very good student athlete, with no prior contact with the police, has joined a gang and has been arrested, pending charges of property damage and assault. The younger brother has been excluded from school for fighting, and the school has stated that it will only let him return if he takes an MAOA test and shows that he has not inherited the Low MAOA gene from his parents.

7.10.2 Limitations on Being a Parent

7.10.2.1 Background

Following the announcement that the mother of Child B was again pregnant, there were arguments from the public that she should not be allowed to have further children.

7.10.2.2 Is there a right to be a parent?

While the right to be a parent might be considered to be a fundamental right by some, it is not clear that this is an unlimited right. The Universal Declaration of Human Rights (UDHR) in Article 16 states that 'men and women of full age … have the right to marry and found a family'.[58] It should be noted that the wording identifies one obvious limitation on the right, being that it is part of the right to marry. The UDHR also allows for other limitations to be placed on rights, for the purpose of 'respect for the rights and freedoms of others and of meeting the just requirements of morality, public order and the general welfare in a democratic society'.

---

[58] See also Article 23, 'International covenant in civil and political rights' and Article 12, 'European convention on human rights'.

7.10.2.3 Implications for eugenics

Negative eugenics, as discussed in Chapter 2, developed from the idea that it is not in society's best interests to allow certain people to have children. These were generally people with specific traits or conditions thought to be hereditary. Criminal tendencies was one such trait. Any consideration of restricting reproduction in a group of individuals will need to consider eugenics arguments carefully.

7.10.2.4 Indications of support for restricting the parental right

While most people would now consider negative eugenics to be indefensible, situations arise on occasion in relation to specific cases where such an argument appears to attract some level of societal support.

In the United States a series of cases in the 1990s considered it acceptable to order women either to not get pregnant, or to submit to forced contraception, if they were considered to be unfit mothers.[59]

In 2007, a New Zealand Emeritus Professor suggested putting the contraceptive pill in the water supply and providing an antidote to suitable parents. Also in New Zealand, it was suggested in 2012 that welfare recipients be 'offered' free contraception. In 2014, an ex-Australian MP more clearly stated that compulsory contraception should be a prerequisite for welfare payments.

It is further not unusual, when child abuse or juvenile offending cases are reported in the newspapers, to hear members of the general public respond with comments along the lines of 'these people should not be allowed to have children'. While these comments should be treated carefully, this provides an indication that some parts of society feel that the right to have children is not unlimited.

7.10.2.5 Should we consider restricting the reproductive right?

It could be argued that in specific cases where there is a familial history of Low MAOA and a recognized history of child abuse, the right of the parents to have further children could be restricted. This could be justified under the limitations permitted in the UDHR, notably in terms of respecting the rights and freedoms of others to feel safe in their community and in terms of the general welfare of society. Restricting the parental right in specific cases would likely not be considered negative

---

[59] See, for example, *People v Johnson* no 29390 (Cal Super Ct Jan 2 1991). Other cases are discussed in Madeline Henley, 'The creation and perpetuation of the mother/body myth: Judicial and legislative enlistment of Norplant' (1993) 41 *Buffalo Law Review* 703, and Steven Spitz, 'The Norplant debate: Birth control or woman control?' (1993) 25 *Columbia Human Rights Law Review* 131.

eugenics. Eugenics was a governmental policy aimed at specific classes of people, not at individuals. Such an approach, particularly in specific situations like that of the family of Child B, may additionally attract public support.

These factors do not mean, however, that such an approach should be adopted. The UDHR additionally talks about the right to be free from 'arbitrary interference with … privacy' in Article 12, the right to dignity in Article 1, the right to be free from 'cruel, inhuman or degrading treatment or punishment' in Article 5, the right to be presumed innocent until proven guilty in Article 11 and the right to a fair and public hearing in Article 10. Preventing parents from having further children is a substantial interference with their private lives and their right to dignity. It could also be seen as a punishment for either maltreating a child, or for having a child who has acted in an antisocial manner. If it is a punishment for the former, this is effectively finding the parents guilty of child abuse without a trial, and imposing punishment in a harsher form than would be imposed on other parents who have abused their children. If the latter, this is not a crime, and therefore the parents are being punished for something that was not an offence at the time the action occurred. Both raise issues under Article 11.

Limiting the rights of parents to have children (whether this right is the one appearing in the UDHR or is simply a societally accepted right) should not be considered. There are other, less restrictive, options that should be considered first, for example, monitoring the family or removing children from their care.

Since the question has been raised, however, some options for limiting the ability to become a parent for 'at risk' adults will be discussed below.

7.10.2.5.1 Forced contraception of 'at risk' adults 'At risk' adults could be required to undergo forced contraception, in order to prevent pregnancy.

In chemical castration cases, a distinction has been drawn between orders for sterilization and for contraception. Forced sterilization has been considered as cruel and unusual punishment and a breach of the right to bodily integrity due to the surgical nature of the procedure, and also its permanence. Contraception, on the other hand, can be carried out with minimal invasiveness (either through the use of oral contraceptive pills or an injection) and is not permanent. The chemical castration cases pointed out that the ability to have children was also not permanent, but only for the duration of parole. In the forced contraception cases in the United States, the reversible nature of the contraception was also highlighted, with an indication that an order for forced contraception could be revoked once the parents had successfully completed parental classes.

A similar approach could be taken to 'at risk' parents. Forced contraception could be ordered, perhaps with the condition that it continue until appropriate parenting classes (in order to reduce the likelihood of maltreatment of their children) be successfully completed.

7.10.2.5.2 Embryo testing If forced contraception is considered too extreme an option, parental licenses might be an acceptable alternative. Under this option, 'at risk' adults who become pregnant would be required to permit genetic testing of the embryo. If the embryo is subsequently identified as having Low MAOA, the parents could be required to undergo parental counseling before being permitted to raise the child.[60] Should testing be refused, it would be assumed that the child was Low MAOA.

Arguments in favour of this approach are similar to those found in the arguments for mandatory newborn testing and counseling, being that the importance of a Low MAOA child being raised in a positive childhood environment will outweigh the parental right to raise the child.

7.10.2.5.3 Pre-implantation genetic diagnosis (PGD) A third option is that IVF clinics could test for MAOA before selecting embryos, with only High MAOA embryos being selected. It should be noted that this is the one issue that is not specifically targeted at 'at risk' adults, but would apply to all adults undergoing IVF treatment.

In countries like the United Kingdom and New Zealand, the use of PGD is regulated by ethics committees, which must grant approval before fertility clinics can carry out the procedure. Generally, factors such as the best interests and benefits to the embryo and the need to accept children for themselves are the relevant factors. The idea of selecting for behavioral traits has not received a great deal of discussion, mostly because it is accepted that behavioral traits tend to be the result of the interaction between numerous genes and the environment, making testing unlikely to be accurate. As an example of this, in 2002 the Nuffield Council published a report entitled 'Genetics and human behavior: the ethical context' in which it concluded that:

---

60 Another alternative is that the parents be required to abort the embryo, but this should be considered too inappropriate to warrant further discussion

> We accept that, at present, the case for permitting prenatal selection based on the identification of genetic predispositions for enhanced abilities remains to be made. We recommend, therefore, that the technique of preimplantation genetic diagnosis, which is currently restricted to serious diseases and disorders, should not be extended to include behavioral traits in the normal range such as intelligence, sexual orientation and personality traits.

While the scientific understanding has clearly improved in the 13 years since this report was published, the discussion in Chapter 2 suggests that it is still not certain enough to warrant a change from the Nuffield Council's submission.

This option effectively advocates 'selecting in' of desirable embryo traits. For this reason, it would have the support of academics who feel there is a moral duty to select the best embryos. A leading proponent of this is Julian Savulescu,[61] who argues that there is a duty to create the best possible child, which would include behavioral enhancement.

Certain issues have been identified with this option. If the screening for Low MAOA is a voluntary procedure, Wasserman[62] comments that 'parents would appear to be selecting children they could mistreat with relative impunity'. Tabery[63] adds that parents would only wish to do this 'if the parents are already intending to maltreat their children'. If the screening is a compulsory procedure then the parents may receive the message that the resultant child is more genetically protected from the effects of childhood maltreatment, and be influenced in their chosen methods of discipline by this.

If this option is considered for further exploration, it ought also to be considered whether the default position should be selection in favour of High MAOA. If the potential parents are predicted to be good parents, and people who may see risk taking as a positive characteristic, there may be a benefit to selecting the Low MAOA gene. It is this prediction that is problematic. It requires a consideration of environmental conditions that will not be known to the geneticist, and may in fact not be known to the parents. While the parents might not intend to mistreat their child there is always the possibility of others physically or sexually

---

[61] See, for example, Julian Savulescu and Guy Kahane, 'The moral obligation to create children with the best chance of the best life' (2009) 23(5) *Bioethics* 274.

[62] David Wasserman, 'Is There Value in Identifying Individual Genetic Predispositions to Violence?' (2004) 32 JL Med. & Ethics 24, 30.

[63] James Tabery, 'From a genetic predisposition to an *interactive predisposition*: Rethinking the ethical implications of screening for gene-environment interactions' (2009) 34 J Med and Phil 27.

abusing the child, or of one parent dying, requiring the other to work long hours and not be as present for the child as they might wish.

7.10.2.5.4 Genetic engineering In the science fiction movie *Gattaca*, a geneticist informs parents that 'I've taken the liberty of eradicating any potentially prejudicial conditions: premature baldness, myopia, alcoholism, addictive susceptibility, propensity for violence, obesity, etc …'

It is not yet possible to genetically engineer an embryo to alter its allele from Low MAOA to High MAOA, however this is worth mentioning here as the ability may develop in the future.[64] Should this occur, the same issues would arise as were discussed under the heading of 'forced treatment'. The key issue for consideration would be whether Low MAOA should in all cases be regarded as the preferred allele.

7.10.2.5.5 Conclusion While it could be argued that there is no right to be a parent, and that therefore it might be possible to restrict 'at risk' parents from having children, this creates a dangerous precedent. Consideration of this cannot be recommended.

7.10.3 Parental Responsibility for Criminal Actions of the Child

7.10.3.1 Introduction

Evidence was presented at the trial of Child B that he had the Low MAOA gene and had been maltreated as a child. Expert witnesses explained that people with a combination of both factors are more likely to commit violent crimes than people with none or only one of these factors. The newspapers immediately asked whether the parents should take some responsibility for their son's actions, whether in crime or in negligence. The basis for such liability will be discussed below.

7.10.3.2 Responsibility under criminal law

The basis for parental responsibility here is unclear. There is no evidence that the parents were in any way involved in the crime. Liability as a party or accessory generally requires an intention to aid or abet the offence, and there is also no evidence of that in this case. It would not be appropriate to impose criminal liability on the parents in this case.

---

[64] Indeed, as this is being written, the United Kingdom House of Commons has just voted to allow 'three person babies' where a modified version of IVF is permitted that combines the DNA of the two parents with healthy mitochondria of a donor woman. Some have argued that this is genetic modification. Others see it as a medical procedure, allowing for the birth of a healthy child.

7.10.3.3 Responsibility under tort law

The law of negligence has in the past considered liability arising in relation to an omission to act which might provide some guidance here. Parents are not generally liable for the actions of their children, but in certain limited and specific circumstances liability might arise due to a failure to control their children. As Todd[65] describes it, 'a duty to control can arise from the parents' knowledge of the child's propensity to cause harm to himself or herself or to others by reason of youth, inexperience, mischievous or malicious disposition, obliging them to take such precautionary measures as are appropriate to their supervisory position'. This list of reasons could potentially be extended to include genetic propensities, meaning that if the parents had knowledge of their child's 'mischievous or malicious disposition' as a result of his Low MAOA status, they might be subject to a duty to control. This duty would require them to 'take such precautionary measures as are appropriate', which might include not maltreating the child. This is clearly an extension of the current law, and requires a level of knowledge that the parents would be unlikely to have unless testing had occurred. It would be unlikely that a suspicion of Low MAOA due to familial history of antisocial conduct and the child's own specific conduct would be enough to trigger this duty.

One potential issue with applying a duty to control in MAOA cases is that the cases imposing this duty are based on an omission to act, whereas in an MAOA case it would be based on a positive duty to protect the child and find alternative means of parenting. The potential for this kind of claim does, however, exist.

7.10.3.4 Conclusion

It is unlikely that the parents of Child B could face liability under criminal law. A possible action in tort might arise, through a breach of a duty to control, but the implications of such an approach require careful consideration.

7.10.4 Privacy Rights of Family Members

7.10.4.1 Introduction

While the privacy rights of the individual child have been discussed above, there are also privacy implications for other family members.

---

65 Todd, 'Law of Torts in New Zealand', (6th ed 2013) at 5.06.07(2).

7.10.4.2 Potential indirect breach of privacy

If it becomes publicly known that one family member has Low MAOA, this might indirectly breach the privacy rights of other family members. Low MAOA is hereditary, meaning that the child has inherited the gene from one or both of his parents. Revealing his MAOA status also reveals this potential information about his parents.

7.10.4.3 Potential direct breach of privacy

Alternatively, it has been argued that genetic information is not a matter of individual rights, but familial rights.[66] If this is accepted, this would mean that revealing one family member's MAOA status would constitute a direct breach of the other family member's privacy

7.10.5 Stigmatization of Family Members

7.10.5.1 Introduction

Revealing the MAOA status of a child might result in stigmatization of not only that child, but also of his family. Potential instances of stigmatization can be identified in the examples of Child B's two brothers.

7.10.5.2 Stigmatization in society

7.10.5.2.1 Introduction Child B's younger brother was excluded from school as a result of being in a fight, while the other child reportedly received only a one hour detention. The school is demanding an MAOA test before permitting the brother to return. The School argues that this is justified in the interests of the safety of the other students.

7.10.5.2.2 The right to know The right to know was discussed above. While various groups in society might wish to know genetic information, this must be balanced against the implications for both the child and his family. Minimizing any potential stigmatization is a matter that will require careful consideration.

7.10.5.3 Stigmatization in sentencing/predictions of future dangerousness

7.10.5.3.1 Introduction Child B's Uncle was recently sentenced for an assault conviction. The judge awarded him the maximum penalty

---

66 Bell & Bennett, 'Genetic secrets and the family' (2001) 9 Med L Rev 130.

commenting that 'there's just too much of this [violent behaviour] in the family. That's three, the child, his parents and now his uncle. That's enough'. The sentence has been criticized for being disproportionate to the offending. It appears to be punishing the individual for actions of his family members, calling to mind the 'three generations … is enough' approach in Carrie Buck's case.

7.10.5.3.2 Civil and political rights Article 14(1) of the International Covenant on Civil and Political Rights begins by stating that 'all persons shall be equal before the courts and tribunals'. As part of this, everyone is entitled to 'a fair and public hearing'.[67] This would require at a minimum that a person be judged for his own actions, and not for the actions of others. The fact that other family members have committed offences is not relevant to the determination of a fair sentence, and must not be considered.

Articles 14(3)(d) and (e) guarantee that the person charged be entitled to be tried in his presence and permitted to examine witnesses against him. If one of the factors involved in the person's sentencing is the conduct of his family members, then these family members are effectively acting as witnesses against him. This 'evidence' has not occurred in his presence, but in a previous trial. Nor has the person had an opportunity to question this witness in relation to his sentencing. The introduction of any evidence in relation to criminal conduct of other family members should be considered a breach of Article 14 and therefore should not be admissible.

Article 14(3)(g) guarantees that the person not be compelled to testify against himself. As suggested above, requiring the provision of genetic information can in a sense be considered as his genetic make-up testifying against him.

7.10.5.4 Conclusion

The importance of a person being judged in relation to himself and not in relation to any activities undertaken by family members cannot be over-emphasized. Predictions of future dangerousness should only be considered when an individual has been convicted of, and is being sentenced for, a violent crime.

---

[67] See also Article 10 'Universal Declaration of Human Rights', and Article 6 'European Convention on Human Rights'.

7.11 IMPLICATIONS FOR SOCIETY

7.11.1 Background

While the case of Child B highlighted issues relating to the individual and the family, it is also important to acknowledge potential consequences for society as a whole if a genetics argument continues to be accepted. The School which is requiring Child B's brother to be genetically tested has also stated that it is considering requiring all of its students to be tested. Any consideration of universal testing raises issues of stigmatization of Low MAOA individuals to such an extent as to result in what could be described as a 'genetic underclass'. The lawyers for Child B have announced their intent to file an appeal based on the argument that his genetic and environmental background required a specialist hearing to decide his level of moral responsibility.

7.11.2 Universal Testing

In Chapter 3 the arguments for and against the creation of a universal DNA database were considered. Many of the benefits and detriments raised in that discussion would similarly apply here.

One notable difference between the two is that the creation of a universal DNA database has a direct link to crime solving. Assuming that DNA is found at a crime scene, a match should be found in the database (absent issues such as degraded samples, mixed samples or human error). This would create near certainty in solving crime, and reduce the resources associated with criminal investigations. The potential benefit can be clearly defined and then evaluated in relation to the human rights and privacy implications. The benefit of a universal MAOA test, on the other hand, is not as easily quantifiable. Absent information about the individual's childhood environment, a simple test for Low or High MAOA does not indicate where on Caspi's graph an individual falls. The effect of the test would simply be to divide society into one of two groups, one of which would be the 'presumed future criminals' group and the other the 'upstanding members of society' group. The reality is, however, that there will be criminals and non-criminals in each group. This idea of dividing society into two classes will be discussed further below.

7.11.3 Discrimination, Stigmatism and the Potential Creation of a Genetic Underclass

7.11.3.1 Introduction

> A reign of doctors will be inaugurated and in the name of science new classes will be added … in the place of the constitutional government of our fathers we shall have set up Plato's Republic.[68]

Since the Human Genome Project began there has been a strong concern that genetics might be the next ground for discrimination. Senator Thomas Daschle[69] put the issue well when he stated that society 'can't afford to take one step forward in science but two steps back in civil rights'. Issues relating to genetic discrimination in relation to health insurance and employment have already been debated, and in some cases have resulted in specific laws: for example, the Genetic Information Non-Disclosure Act in the United States. When introducing this law, Senator James Jeffords argued that Congress should 'take that rare opportunity to be ahead of the curve and enact legislation to pre-empt discriminatory practices and prevent them from ever happening'.[70] Some of this quick response was likely due to memories of sickle cell screening programmes in the 1970s, in which participants reported discrimination both in the workplace and also in obtaining health insurance.

7.11.3.2 Genetic discrimination

Under Article 11 of the Convention on Human Rights and Biomedicine, any form of discrimination against an individual on the grounds of his or her genetic heritage is prohibited. Discrimination relating to genetic information is also referred to in the UNESCO Declaration on the Human Genome and Human Rights, which requires that human genetic data and human proteomic data is not to be used for purposes that discriminate against an individual or for purposes that lead to the stigmatization of an individual, a family, a group or community.

---

[68] I.P. Whitehead, Counsel for Carrie Buck.

[69] Senator Thomas Daschle, 'Faces of genetic discrimination: How genetic discrimination affects real people' *National Partnership for Women & Families* (2004) 2.

[70] Jessica Roberts, 'Pre-empting discrimination: Lessons from the Genetic Information Nondiscrimination Act', (2010) 63 Vand. L. Rev. 439, 470.

7.11.3.3 Genetic stigmatism

Even if differing treatment of Low MAOA individuals does not reach the level of discrimination, these individuals could still be stigmatized by the test results. If this information was released to various parties, for example to a school, one could imagine that the school would focus on the MAOA status as a predictor of antisocial behavior and overlook the environmental conditions, which may not be known. Nelkin and Tancredi[71] suggest that this would lead to 'labeling and stigmatizing students as having a permanent and immutable disability'.

Studies have shown that people treat individuals with physical or emotional disabilities differently, even if this is unintentional. As an example, parents tend to be more protective of the child, or choose their language more carefully in relation to future matters. One could easily imagine a situation where a teacher, informed of a particular student's MAOA status, reacts more strongly to an aggressive act (for example pushing another student) than he would with a High MAOA student or over-reacts to age-appropriate signs of aggression, Alternatively, a teacher could under-react, by failing to set appropriate limits out of fear of response.

On the other hand, some academics have argued that genetic information should be treated the same as any other piece of medical information. In other words, the fact that concerns over privacy are being raised actually feeds the perception that genetic information is determinative. Treating it like any other piece of information will minimize the potential stigma or discrimination.

Treating MAOA status like any other background issue might help others better understand the children. The benefits to society might therefore outweigh the burdens on the individual. It might also help the individual. If he understands that there is a biological explanation for his actions, rather than that he is simply bad, this might empower him to learn strategies to improve his self-control.

Studies on other genetic conditions have suggested, however, that stigmatization resulting from genetic status being revealed is a myth rather than a reality. A study of 3000 patients screened for Cystic Fibrosis[72] suggested that stigmatization did not occur, even though 89 per

---

[71] Dorothy Nelkin & Laurence Tancredi, 'Classify and control: Genetic information in the schools', (1991) 17 Am J.L. & Med. 51 (1991).

[72] Discussed in the Nuffield Council On Bioethics Report, 'Genetic Screening: Ethical Issues' (1993).

cent shared the information with others. The Fragile X[73] society commented to the authors of the study that they had never been informed of issues with stigmatization and 'on the contrary, many have found that they and others have found their children easier to accept and deal with once they have an explanation for their problem'.

7.11.3.4 Racial stigmatism

The potential for racial stigmatism is a factor that cannot be ignored. Studies have shown that the Low MAOA gene is more common in certain racial groups. It has already been seen how these statistics feed negative assumptions about race. A US television show examined this through a fictitious scenario involving an ethnic group known as the Tracey Islanders, who were stated to have a higher incidence of alcoholism than found in the general population. In this scenario, a Tracy Islander agreed to be part of a study looking for a gene variant for alcoholism. The individual agreed due to a family history of alcoholism and a concern that her 21-year-old son might have that condition. The study found that there is a particular gene that increases the likelihood of Tracey Islanders becoming alcoholics. The son is then involved in an altercation when, while drunk, he pushes an off-duty police officer through a window. The police officer died. The son's lawyer suggests using the genetic predisposition to alcohol as a defence. In the TV programme, academics, scientists and legal experts played the roles of various stakeholders. These included other Tracey Islanders who were concerned that such a defence, while of benefit to the son, would further stigmatize their community as alcoholics.

In New Zealand, a presentation at a conference which suggested that the indigenous Maori people were far more likely to be Low MAOA than Caucasian New Zealanders led to discussions on how this could explain the overrepresentation of Maori in prisons and also the prevalence of child maltreatment in the Maori community. The gene was dubbed the 'warrior gene' and became an issue of major political concern.

7.11.3.5 Could a genetic underclass emerge?

While discrimination and stigmatism are a major concern, it must be considered whether the combined effect of these will be the creation of a genetic underclass. In the 1997 movie, *Gattaca*, genetic engineering resulted in the creation of two classes: the 'valids', and the genetically

---

73 Ibid.

inferior 'invalids'. The potential for Low MAOA individuals to form such a genetic underclass is an issue of real concern.

7.11.4 Development of a New Genetics Court

7.11.4.1 Introduction

In the trial of Child A and Child B, both boys were treated equally in the determination of criminal responsibility for their actions. One of the grounds of appeal for Child B was that this was not appropriate. His lawyers argued that his MAOA status affected his ability to be morally responsible for his actions and that this should have been taken into account during the trial phase. In the media they commented, 'if B is found to be legally responsible for the killing he should of course be sentenced. We are not denying this. But first he must be found to be legally responsible. B's genetic make-up must be a major factor in determining this legal responsibility in the same way that scientists tell us that it is a major factor in determining how he responds to situations. Think of it this way: the criminal justice system does not treat adults and children the same way, because scientists tell us that their brains don't reason in the same way. The system doesn't treat mentally competent and mentally incompetent people in the same way, because again, scientists tell us that their brains don't process information in the same way. If scientists also tell us that the brains of High MAOA and Low MAOA don't respond in the same way in given situations, why are we treating them the same? It is inconsistent to ignore what scientists are clearly telling us, and it is unfair to Child B.'

The lawyers raise two interesting questions: first, should the criminal justice system treat High and Low MAOA individuals differently? and second, if so, how should it do this?

There are three options available:

1. Retain the status quo (allow genetic evidence to be introduced at all levels of the trial);
2. Create specific protections for Low MAOA; or
3. Create a separate court system.

7.11.4.2 Option one: retain the status quo

In a previous chapter, the admissibility of genetics evidence at both the trial and sentencing stages were discussed. It was suggested there that this evidence would be admissible, and its relevance could be determined in each specific case. This might be sufficient to address the issues raised by the lawyers for Child B. As more cases refer to genetics, judges will become more familiar with the science and therefore better able to evaluate the evidence before them.

7.11.4.3 Create specific provisions for MAOA

Under Option One, the admissibility and relevance of MAOA would be considered under general principles, in the same manner as other evidence. It may be that specific provisions might be required to be introduced. With growing scientific and societal recognition of the role of MAOA in contributing to behavior, it can be expected that the use of a MAOA argument in the courts will increase. This is particularly so in light of the significant number of males who are Low MAOA.

Creating specific provisions for MAOA or other genetic information might assist the court in understanding when this information is admissible, how its interaction with the environment should be evaluated, and whether it should be considered as a factor affecting mens rea or as a defence. The comparisons that the lawyers for Boy B drew with juveniles and the mentally incompetent provide examples of how such specific provisions can be drafted and used.

7.11.4.4 Create a separate court system

The comparison with juveniles suggests that a third option might be required. While there are generally provisions relating to juvenile criminal responsibility in crimes legislation, this is not seen as sufficient to address the particular needs and interests of juveniles. Instead, separate youth courts have been set up, with specialist judges and rules. Other examples of separate specialist courts can be identified, each dealing with factors requiring specific consideration. These include drug and alcohol courts, mental health courts and sex offender courts.

It may be logical to consider a 'genetics court'. There are several obvious benefits to this. First is the large potential number of defendants raising a genetics argument. Second is the technical nature of the gene and environment interaction. It might be beneficial for these cases to be heard by judges who have received prior training in this area, in order for the scientific understanding and its limitations to become better understood. This might prevent situations as in the *Bayout* case, where the environment factor was ignored, or as in the *Waldroup* case, where the jury might have been blinded by the Christmas tree effect of the genetics argument. Third, as the lawyers for Child B point out, it might produce a fairer result. If the gene and environment interaction is a significant determinant of behavior, then this is relevant to the trial and should be considered as part of the evidence. Finally, creating a separate court might be more efficient. Having a specialist judge would reduce the need for expert witnesses to provide general genetics evidence in each case, leaving them to focus on the specific factors of a particular case. It would also lead to faster and more appropriate decisions as judges developing an expertise in this area are assigned these cases.

7.11.4.4.1 How might a separate court system work? A person who is charged with a crime could undergo a two stage evaluation process. The first stage would involve genetic evaluation, where the person would be screened for specific biological risk factors. If these are present, the second stage would involve a psychological evaluation to identify any potentially relevant environmental factors. Any person with both risk factors could then be assigned to the genetics court for trial. All others would be assigned to the general court.

7.11.4.4.2 Potential issues with stage one It would need to be carefully considered which genes would be tested for at stage one. MAOA, serotonin and dopamine would be the obvious candidates, but there are many other genes with links to behavior. A screening list would need to be created of relevant genes, and criteria determined for the inclusion of any additional genes.

It should also be noted that scientific testing for levels of a particular gene can provide different results depending on the measurement site.[74] This might result in the initial test result being challenged, particularly in light of the potential importance to the case of which court an individual is assigned.

7.11.4.4.3 Potential problems with stage two The standard for satisfaction of the environmental risk factor evaluation would also require careful consideration. While the test for MAOA would be a binary 'Low/High' test, childhood maltreatment is clearly not so easy to classify. The studies on the interaction of MAOA and environment have shown different results depending on which definition of environmental conditions was used, and the likelihood of antisocial behavior in Low MAOA individuals also increases on a curve depending on the environmental factor. These matters, however, can be addressed at trial. If stage two is seen as investigating potential risk factors, which can then be explored in more depth at trial, the issues raised above might be avoided.

---

[74] See Chapter 2.

7.11.4.4.4 Potential problems with a two stage analysis The two stage test suggested above may unintentionally indicate a primacy to the genetic result which is undesirable and suggestive of genetic determinism. It might also lead to game playing of the system through fabrication of maltreatment, which will be discussed below. From a resource perspective, however, this is likely to be the most cost effective method of determining whether an offender should be tried in the general court or the genetic court. The genetic test is likely to be quicker and cheaper than the environmental screening interview. Reducing the number to be interviewed by removing those at low risk genetically, will enable the court process to move faster.

7.11.4.4.5 Consequences of court assignment Assigning a person to the genetic court, while an attempt to more fairly understand the circumstances of the offending, might also have negative consequences. Firstly, it might result in the individual feeling he has been prejudged. A person who is assigned to the genetic court because of a genetic and environmental increased risk of antisocial behavior might feel like this has displaced their rights to be presumed innocent, and to a fair trial. The two stage evaluation might be considered to be replacing the trial, and the trial might then be viewed as simply a sentencing hearing. Secondly, there will be an increased risk of stigmatization by the community, for similar reasons. Newspapers would likely report that the person has been assigned to the genetics court, and the community might therefore assume that he is guilty.

This assumes, however, that the stigmatism will attach to those assigned to the genetic court on the basis that these are the 'different' people in society. Consider an Asian society, however, where 66 per cent of males are Low MAOA. In this society, Low MAOA would be considered normal, and High MAOA would be the 'different' classification. These people might feel therefore that they are being treated differently to their peers.

7.11.4.4.6 Racial issues The statistics relating to Low MAOA suggest that it occurs with more frequency in some racial groups than in others. It is more likely to be found in Asian, Maori and African American males than it is in Caucasian males. This is likely to result in the courts being seen as racially split, with the general court being for the most part the 'white' court and the genetic court being the 'non-white' court. This factor alone might be sufficient to suggest that the two-court system should not occur.

7.11.4.4.7 Game playing, or over or under reporting of maltreatment The above discussion suggests that there are negative consequences to being assigned to the genetic court. There may also be positive consequences, resulting in game playing during the environmental evaluation in an attempt to influence which court a person is assigned to.

If those assigned to the genetic court are able to introduce evidence or raise arguments that those assigned to the general court are not, it may be in the person's best interests to over-report any childhood maltreatment in order to gain a perceived advantage at trial.

On the other hand, if a person feels that there is a benefit to remaining in the general court, he may under-report any childhood maltreatment. This benefit is likely to relate to the issue of stigmatization resulting from assignment to the genetic court. Due to concerns of stigmatization and the impact on future employment, he considered that pleading guilty to murder was preferable to pleading insanity.

7.11.4.4.8 Issues with sentencing In juvenile courts, and in the other specialist courts discussed above, not only is the trial conducted differently, but there are differences in sentencing. While there may be benefits to a genetic court considering liability, by allowing it to take into account the specific relevant genetic and environmental factors, whether different rules should also apply to sentencing would need to be closely considered. If different sentences were available, or different factors were admissible or given more weight in determining length of sentence, this might also result in game playing.

7.11.4.4.9 Would a separate court satisfy the rule of law? The rule of law requires, inter alia, equality before the law, fairness in the application of the law, legal certainty and the avoidance of arbitrariness. The creation of a separate genetics court might present a challenge to this. While the separate court might promote 'fairness', there will no doubt be challenges to the idea of 'equality' and 'legal certainty' as different results might occur depending on which court a person is assigned to. Two different streams of precedent might emerge, one for the general court and one for the genetic court. This is clearly a matter for concern, and one requiring further, fuller, consideration.

7.12 CONCLUSION

This review has considered some potential issues relating to the acceptance of a genetic argument. It has focussed on specific issues that may be faced by the individual, by his family, and by society in general. Most of the issues raised here were discussed only briefly, and further work will be required to fully understand the implications. Even this brief discussion, however, has highlighted the need for this discussion to address the balance needed between two fundamental concerns: the concern of society to be protected from potentially dangerous individuals, and the concern of the individual and his family that their privacy rights are respected and that they are not stigmatized in their community due to genetic test results. These are public policy issues that require consideration by Parliament, and should not be left to judges to address on a case by case basis.

7.13 OVERALL CONCLUSION

This chapter has discussed some potential consequences of an increased acceptance of a genetics argument in the courts. In some ways what we are seeing is similar to the consequences of genetics arguments raised as part of the eugenics movement in the 1920s–30s, and of the debates on XYY Syndrome in the 1970s. There are calls for genetic testing to identify Low MAOA individuals, arguments in relation to their future dangerousness, and an overall feeling that society needs protection from these 'genetically predisposed' killers. In other ways, however, the situation differs. Science has progressed, making the genetic arguments more scientifically convincing, particularly to judges and juries. An increased recognition of the rights of the child have led to calls for childhood testing, and subsequent interventions. Most importantly, the last couple of decades have shown an increasing debate on privacy rights, particularly in relation to genetic information. It is this privacy right, and a related concern about stigmatization of individuals based on genetics, that must form a central part of any discussion on the application of genetic arguments. The issues discussed in this chapter call for a wider debate on genetic arguments in court, and in particular, the societal and ethical consequences of their increasing acceptance in cases discussed in previous chapters.

8. Concluding thoughts

> The mood and temper of the public in regard to the treatment of crime and criminals is one of the most unfailing tests of the civilization of any country.
>
> A calm, dispassionate recognition of the rights of the accused against the state, and even those of the convicted criminal against the state, a constant heart-searching by all charged with the duty of punishment, a desire and eagerness to rehabilitate into the world of industry all those who have paid their dues in the hard coinage of punishment, tireless effort towards the discovery of curative and regenerating processes, and an unfaltering faith that there is a treasure, if you can only find it, in the heart of every man, these are the symbols which in the treatment of crime and criminals mark and measure the stored-up strength of a nation and are the signs and proof of the living virtue in it.
>
> In 1910 Winston Churchill spoke these words to the House of Commons, as Home Secretary

What would he think of the issues raised and discussed in this book? Have we lived up to his idea of civilization? Perhaps the answer would be 'no'. The move to a universal DNA database, whether by design, function creep, or stealth, has slowly eroded the rights of not only the convicted criminal but even of those merely arrested or in the wrong place at the wrong time. The idea of rehabilitation of the criminal has been replaced by incapacitation for the protection of society, and the idea of testing individuals for MAOA status hints at judging a person by his or her genes, not by the 'treasure in their hearts'.

But, Churchill was living in a different time. In 1910, discussions of eugenics were only just beginning, and the negative effects had yet to be discovered. He spoke of a 'constant heart searching by all charged with the duty of punishment' and 'discovery of curative and regenerating processes'. Satisfying these ideals requires the relevant people to be open to new ideas about why people commit crime, and about how best to punish or rehabilitate. Churchill surely never meant that a civilized society is one which stands still and staves off advancement in fear of taking a wrong step. Society will change as scientific knowledge develops and provides a better understanding as to why people engage in criminal conduct, and it may sometimes get it wrong, as our eugenic history has shown us all too well. Or, as the behavioral genetics studies have shown us, it might make important advances in understanding how genetics and the environment both influence particular forms of conduct.

The behavioral scientists are doing their jobs well, attempting replications of the first study by Brunner, expanding on these studies, and providing society with information in order to make informed decisions. Neuroscientists and psychologists are similarly engaged in providing both information and understanding from their respective disciplines. Philosophers and lawyers are playing their part also, debating the ethical and legal issues. A combination of ideas from all of these disciplines will place society and policymakers in the best position to decide how best to respond to the use of genetic information in the context of criminal investigations and prosecutions.

Churchill begins by using the words 'calm' and 'dispassionate'. In thinking about the future, it is important to understand the issue rationally and to understand the emotive newspaper headlines discussed in Chapter One for what they are: journalists also contributing by raising public awareness and igniting debate. The underlying idea in Churchill's speech might be that civilization exists where people are engaged in reflection or debate with the aim of making society better. If this is the case, then maybe today's society is meeting his standard.

This book has attempted to contribute through discussing the current scientific understanding of behavioral genetics, and its application to criminal justice. It has suggested that while the genetic and environment interaction is a factor that should be considered, it is important to recognize it for what it is: one factor, potentially relevant and important, but not determinative.

Genetic arguments in relation to crime are not new – Chapter 2 has shown us that. They have been seen throughout history as we try as a society to understand why some people commit violent crimes and others do not. The MAOA argument may have scientific support, as was demonstrated in Chapter 4, but it must be remembered that so did eugenics, until we realized that there was a problem with both the science and particularly with the consequences of its application.

Chapter 6 built on the discussion of the application of genetic arguments in court in Chapter 5, asked whether the criminal justice system needed to adapt in response to these arguments, and concluded that it did not. The criminal justice system has shown throughout history that it has the ability to adapt to genetic arguments, particularly in the last 80 years since *Skinner*. While a genetics argument poses issues for the justifications for punishment, so have other factors, like non-genetic alcoholism or sex offending. Again, the courts have adapted. Different punishment theories have been emphasized as more important in different times, and the current mixed approach would appear to allow for a suitable consideration of the issues.

Chapter 7 looked to the future, considering where acceptance of a genetic argument might naturally lead us. It discussed what is probably the overall question raised by this book: as scientific knowledge advances, how do we address the competing interests of society and the individual? Does society's desire to be protected from crime outweigh the individual's right to be protected from unwanted intrusion into his genome, probably the most personal information he has?

As one academic convincingly asked:[1]

> Humans represent a unique species as they are endowed with thought, self-awareness, and free volition. How can we avoid allowing that others, by accessing our brainomes, may change our sense of ourselves, how we fit into the world, how we treat others, and how we decide between right and wrong?

The answer might be this: by embracing new knowledge and new understandings, and the insights these reveal, but by then using them in a positive way, not as a means to condemn groups of people based on reasons that might not be scientifically supportable.

---

1 Sara Mariani, Neuroethics: 'How to leave the cave without going astray: Highlights from the annual meeting of the American Society of Neuroscience; November 8–12, 2003'; New Orleans, Louisiana. (2003) 5(4) Med Gen Med 33.

Index